"*Subversive Sabbath* is incredibly well written, accessible, and deeply encouraging. A. J. Swoboda avoids oversimplification and presents a deep, rich, and energetic argument on what it means to be fully human through an obedient pursuit of rest and well-being. This book gives a theology of Sabbath-keeping that was a much-needed encouragement for me. I'm sure it will be for you as well."

—**Ken Wytsma**, founder, The Justice Conference;
pastor, Antioch Church, Bend, Oregon;
author of *The Myth of Equality*

"If I were permitted to recommend only one book on Sabbath-keeping, A. J. Swoboda's *Subversive Sabbath* would be it. This one volume acquaints the reader with a vast literature on Sabbath from both the Jewish and Christian traditions. Through practical reflection questions at the end of each chapter, it provokes changes in doing as well as thinking. It explores the implications of Sabbath not only for one's personal life but for relationships, for worship, for public life, and for the whole of creation. Best of all, it highlights the lavish gift and the countercultural adventure of Sabbath. No one can read this book and ever again associate Sabbath-keeping with 'blue laws' or legalism or boredom. *Subversive Sabbath* dares one to do life as God intended from the beginning."

—**Shirley A. Mullen**, president, Houghton College

SUBVERSIVE
SABBATH

THE SURPRISING
POWER OF REST
IN A NONSTOP WORLD

A.J. SWOBODA

Brazos Press

a division of Baker Publishing Group
Grand Rapids, Michigan

© 2018 by A. J. Swoboda

Published by Brazos Press
a division of Baker Publishing Group
PO Box 6287, Grand Rapids, MI 49516-6287
www.brazospress.com

Printed in the United States of America

Library of Congress Cataloging-in-Publication Data
Names: Swoboda, A. J., 1981– author.
Title: Subversive Sabbath : the surprising power of rest in a nonstop world / A.J. Swoboda.
Description: Grand Rapids : Brazos Press, 2018. | Includes bibliographical references and index.
Identifiers: LCCN 2017040849 | ISBN 9781587434051 (pbk. : alk. paper)
Subjects: LCSH: Rest—Religious aspects—Christianity. | Sunday. | Sabbath.
Classification: LCC BV111.3 .S96 2018 | DDC 263/.3—dc23
LC record available at https://lccn.loc.gov/2017040849

18   19   20   21   22   23   24   7   6   5   4   3   2   1

Contents

Foreword   vii
Prologue   ix

PART 1: SABBATH FOR US

1. Sabbath and Time   3
2. Sabbath and Work   25
3. Sabbath and Health   43

PART 2: SABBATH FOR OTHERS

4. Sabbath and Relationships   65
5. Sabbath, Economy, and Technology   83
6. Sabbath and the Marginalized   103

PART 3: SABBATH FOR CREATION

7. Sabbath and Creation   121
8. Sabbath and the Land   131
9. Sabbath and Critters   145

PART 4: SABBATH FOR WORSHIP

10. Sabbath and Witness   161
11. Sabbath and Worship   173
12. Sabbath and Discipleship   189

Notes   205
Index   229

Foreword

As a physician, I've listened to thousands of hearts. During prenatal exams, I've heard the rapid swish-swishing of babies still in the womb. Often, moms and dads burst into tears when they hear their child's heart for the first time.

I've smiled at the strange murmur those thumb-sized hearts make when they are born into the great big world, fetal shunts closing of their own accord as the baby breathes independently for the first time. I've listened to the chests of three-year-old children as they inhale deeply—and then wonder whether the man in the white coat can hear their thoughts through those tubes attached to his ears.

I've listened to athletes' strong, slow hearts. I've heard asthmatic hearts pounding away in fear and the muffled sounds of failing hearts. I've listened to the hearts of saints and of murderers. I'm in the first generation of physicians to ever listen to the heart of one person after it has been transplanted into the body of another.

Doctors and nurses listen to patients' hearts using a stethoscope. Although this is convenient, it's not necessary. In fact, the stethoscope wasn't invented until a generation after our country became a nation. For thousands of years, physicians listened to heart sounds without the aid of a stethoscope. They simply laid their ear on the chest of their patients. Now it is only children who lay their heads on the chest of their parents to listen to beating hearts.

My daughter used to love curling up in the big green chair by our fireplace in winter and falling asleep listening to my heartbeat. These days, my children are grown. I'm still close to them and hug them every time I see them, but it is only my little granddaughter who's falling asleep on my chest now . . . or so I thought. Last week, my son dropped by our house after a long shift at the hospital. He flopped on the couch next to me, and within a few minutes he was asleep, his head resting on me. He was no longer a pediatrician at the university hospital; he was just my little boy, resting in his father's arms.

I had just finished reading *Subversive Sabbath*, and I got to thinking about our exhausted world, laying our heads down, and hearing heart sounds. These thoughts led me to the thirteenth chapter of John's Gospel—the story of the Last Supper. The chapter begins with Jesus washing the disciples' feet. Later, Judas dashes off to betray Christ. The chapter ends with Jesus giving a new commandment to love one another.

But midway through, an extraordinary detail is recorded. Here we see the portrait of a commercial fisherman with sunburned skin and calloused hands. His name is John, and he's a man's man. Jesus calls him a "son of thunder." Normally, John conveys an image of courage and strength, but at this moment he appears like a little child: "Now there was leaning on Jesus' bosom one of his disciples, whom Jesus loved" (John 13:23 KJV).

There in the middle of the most extraordinary events in human history is a man listening to the heart of God. Don't you wish you could lay your head down on the Maker of the universe and just listen to his heart? Don't you wish that you could lay all your problems down for just a moment and rest on Jesus?

The heart of A. J. Swoboda's book is that you can: starting next Sabbath, for twenty-four hours, you can lay your head on the chest of someone who loves you enough to die for you. *Subversive Sabbath* is an invitation to rest in the Lord.

The Sabbath commandment begins with an odd word: it tells us to "remember." Don't forget how good it is to rest in the Lord, to be loved by the Lord, to hear his heartbeat. A. J. Swoboda's narrative is both a reminder to those who have forgotten and an instruction for those who have never known the peace of Sabbath rest. "Once you start," Swoboda warns, "you cannot stop. It is profoundly life giving."

Ultimately, however, reading about Sabbath is like looking at a picture of food. It will not fill you. It can only whet your appetite. You must finish the book, put it down, and actually do the Sabbath. You must get your life quiet enough one day out of the week to hear God's heart. Only then will you experience the countercultural joy of *Shabbat shalom*, Sabbath peace.

Matthew Sleeth, MD
author of *24/6* and executive director of Blessed Earth

Prologue

Walking home from school, I found Grandma, Grandpa, and Mom standing in the kitchen. I was ten. Their faces shone with a distinct luminescence that I had not witnessed before. Being an only child, I of course presumed the exuberance directly related to my arriving home. My pride was soon popped. They showed me a little piece of paper gently lying atop the newspapers on the dining-room table. That little paper changed everything.

The story is well known in the family: my grandparents had driven up from California the evening before. Stopping at a gas station along the Oregon border, they purchased some snacks, gas, and, as they often did, a lottery ticket. Thinking little of it, they stuffed the ticket in a pocket and continued journeying north. At their hotel that night, Grandpa stayed up to watch the news. The lottery numbers were to be announced. As the numbers were picked from a whirling globe of balls, the first number matched. And the second number. Then the third number. At this point, he shakes Grandma awake. She wipes her eyes as they watch the fourth, fifth, sixth, and seventh numbers match. *All seven numbers*. Jaws dropped. Their minds could not ascertain what had transpired in just a few short seconds. Unimaginable. Unthinkable. How much did they win? What does this mean? The host announced the winning amount. That night, Grandma and Grandpa won $4.6 million.

After a sleepless night, they drove to our home and placed the lottery ticket on our dining-room table. The winnings helped our family in profound ways. Debts were paid. Vacations were had. Tuitions were covered. But the story has a dark side. A profound gift that created momentary bliss eventually led to bickering, infighting, and anger in the family. After nearly fifty years of marriage, Grandma and Grandpa's marriage ended. Family members stopped talking. And a cold bitterness took over. I don't retell this difficult story to shame a single soul. By the grace of God, healing and reconciliation has begun in our family. Yet the fact remains: no one knew how to steward such a gift.

This cautionary tale illustrates an important lesson: more critical than a gift is how we *handle* the gift. We receive something incredible, even unimaginable, yet have no way of knowing what to do with it. Rather than enjoying the gift, we fight over it. Jesus warns of this problem in the parable of the workers and the vineyard (Matt. 20:1–16). As the story goes, a group of underemployed men are hired for much-needed work during harvest season. After their day of work, the manager compensates an amount far and above the going wage at the time. But rather than celebrate both a good day's work and abundant provision, the employees gripe that other workers received similar generosity. This parable demonstrates what so many followers of Jesus do with the grace of God. Rather than enjoy it, we demand account for God's generosity toward others who we believe deserve it far less.

The Sabbath is a gift we do not know how to receive. In a world of doing, going, and producing, we have no use for a gift that invites us to stop. But that is the original gift: a gift of rest. Of course, at the world's beginning, God finishes the very first week by extending to the whole creation a gift: a day to stop, breathe, cease, enjoy, feast. God named it "Sabbath." That Sabbath day—time honored and approved—has sustained and nourished human communities and all of creation since the origins of the world. Still, like many of God's gifts, we have struggled to receive it. In church life, we bicker over its validity. We argue over what day Sabbath has to be. We get trapped in Sabbath rules and nuanced doctrinal rationale for why we no longer need to seriously consider it. We start whole denominations over Sabbath disagreements. We fall into the same trap time and again—not knowing how to enjoy a gift from God. When all is said and done, the worst thing that has happened to the Sabbath is religion. Religion is hostile to gifts. Religion hates free stuff. Religion squanders the good gifts of God by trying to earn them, which is why we will never really enjoy a sacred day of rest as long as we think our religion is all about earning.

This is nothing new: hostility toward the Sabbath has flowed in the church's and the world's blood for a long time. Many early church fathers, such as Justin Martyr, saw the Sabbath day as punishment for the Jews, who he believed needed a day of obedience to be reminded of their depravity. But is Sabbath a punishment? Others have rejected it lock, stock, and barrel, relegating it to the status of relic—antiquated, arcane, unworthy of contemporary consideration, an idea from our "dusty pawnshop of doctrinal beliefs."[1] Others dismiss it as an idealistic, if not impossible, practice. "Who has time to

Sabbath, anyway?" they ask. "I'll sleep when I die. I mean, if the devil never rests, why should I?" But these hollow notions are based on human reason rather than God's good word. A Sabbath proves an awkward fit in our fast-paced, work-drunk, production-obsessed world. Yet whatever skepticism we harbor toward Sabbath, such disdain is not shared by the Bible, Jesus, or much of church history. God's story has fundamentally been a story about a simple gift of a day of rest.

Marva Dawn writes, "The spiritual resources given to us through faith in the Triune God are the best treasures available."[2] The Sabbath is one such treasure. Our problem? We do not know what to do with Sabbath. That is what this book comes to terms with—understanding the gift of Sabbath, how we can receive it, and what receiving it does for the world.

A few points of concern before continuing. First, a note about the book's title. How is the Sabbath *subversive*? The truth remains that Sabbath will be challenging for anyone to live out in our busy, frenetic world. Sabbath goes against the very structure and system of the world we have constructed. Sabbath, then, becomes a kind of resistance to that world.[3] Such resistance must be characterized as overwhelmingly good. In other words, if the Sabbath is hard, then we are doing it right. It is never a sign of health or godliness to be well adjusted to a sick society. Putting up a fight to enter the Sabbath is as critical as anything. By illustration, I have been told that when a cow is born, she innately senses that her departure from her mother's warm womb to a cold, scary, unknown world outside is upon her. In response, she will resist birth and try to stay in the womb. On the other hand, the absence of such resistance is often a sign of a stillborn calf. Relating to our world of death, "going along" is a sign of death. Living fish swim against the stream. Only the dead go with the flow. The Sabbath *is* subversive, countering so many of the deathly ways we have felt at home in. When we live the Sabbath, we slowly depart the womb of the status quo to a scary, unknown, new world. But that is okay. The world's warm womb *feels* nice. But no one can grow up in there.

Sabbath is an alternative lifestyle that goes against everything our world knows. Flannery O'Connor, that famous Southern Catholic novelist, once reported the words of an admirer she encountered in public who had read a book of hers: "That was a profound book," he said. "You don't look like you wrote it."[4] My goal in authoring this book is that if my readers ever see me in public, they might say I look like I wrote it. The truth is, the alternative lifestyle of Sabbath-keeping that this volume prescribes has revolutionized my life, my relationships, and others around me. True, I almost burned out writing this book. If I were writing about anything else I probably would have. But it was, ironically, writing about the Sabbath that refreshed my spirit every step of the way. Even thinking and writing about Sabbath has the power to heal the soul. I have come to believe that Sabbath cannot save your soul, but it very well may save your life. I am different because of the Sabbath. And I am different for having written this book. I want to look like I wrote this book. And I certainly want my readers to look like they actually read it and took it to heart.

By way of organization, the book is outlined into four parts: the Sabbath for ourselves, for others, for creation, and for worship. The outline itself should reflect a conviction that the Sabbath is not just for us. In fact, as Scripture will show us, it is for everyone and everything—even God.

This book, second, has one main intended audience: anyone interested in living life God's way *and* desiring to be a part of Christ's healing work in the world. This includes but is not limited to pastors, leaders, small-group leaders, seminarians, Bible-college students, thoughtful Christians, thoughtful athe-ists, nonthoughtful Christians, nonthoughtful atheists, academics—basically anyone interested in living the Sabbath and seeing the Sabbath extended to others. To help, I have blended top-shelf academic resources with simple Sab-bath practice. This is intentional. There remain plenty of brilliant academic or practical books on Sabbath-keeping. Too often they overlook each other. I think having two Sabbath wings is the best way to fly.

Third, I feel I need to confess some hesitations about writing a book on Sabbath. These circle around two issues. For one, I am skeptical of any kind of fix-it-all theology purporting to be *the* thing that can repair everything. Theology cannot save anyone. It can only point us to the One who saves. Theology as such is only useful to the degree that it delivers us into formed people who know how to worship God and love people. Too often we theo-logians get it into our heads that our scholarly products are what everyone needs to be fixed—a kind of theological snake oil. Madeleine L'Engle once told of a dinner party where she was invited to become a communist. She refused on the grounds that communism purported to be a perfect, fit-it-all system.[5] Similarly, the theology presented here is not a perfect system. Nor is this a perfect book. This book is a stab at the Sabbath question, not the final answer.

For another, I question whether *I* am the right person to write a book on Sabbath. I am not a Jew. I am a Christian. A gentile one at that. In the early stages, I originally wanted to title this book *Bacon for the Sabbath: A Guide to Gentile, Christian Sabbath-Keeping*. The idea was never taken seriously. The truth remains that I am writing about something far outside my scope of scholarship. Others—particularly Jews and Christians in communities that have been keeping a Sabbath for centuries—know far more about the Sabbath than I. Throughout, I lean strongly on those wise and credible voices. But my newfound venture into Sabbath is why I have chosen to write this book. The Sabbath is new to me—ten years to be exact. But I think fresh eyes can be helpful eyes. I have, in the words of Wendell Berry, willingly endured "the risks of amateurism" for the sake of my readers who probably feel like Sabbath idiots as well.[6] Fear, I am learning, is never a credible excuse to ignore responsibility or truth.

Fourth, and finally, gratitude. This book is dedicated to my dear friends Matthew and Nancy Sleeth. In the course of writing, my editorial assistant commented all too often, "You got that from Matthew and Nancy, didn't you?" Unquestionably, so much of what I know about the Sabbath is drawn from the Sleeths, who have made the Sabbath come to life. To both of them, I acknowledge my debt. "The most brilliant people in the world," Albert Einstein reportedly said, "aren't the most brilliant. They are just best at hiding their sources." Einstein was unwittingly describing me writing this book. The only thing original about me is my sin, and even that I plagiarize most of the time. Throughout this volume, I have tirelessly worked to conceal the fact that most of what I know about Sabbath comes from the Sleeths. Matthew and Nancy: you are humble giants. *Thank you.* We all stand on some giant's shoulders. But they never tell you that the giants have to be humble enough to let you get on their shoulders.

Finally, endless gratitude goes to my wife, Quinn. You are my Sabbath wife. I love you. Elliot, my little man, get the griddle hot. Those Sabbath pancakes will not cook themselves. My faithful and humble administrative, editorial, and research assistant, Madalyn Salz, has been invaluable throughout this book's evolutionary process. Without her, it would still be a bunch of napkin scribbles in some box in my bedroom. Aaron Yenney, as well, offered critical feedback regarding many of the concepts herein. Thank you for your insights and a helping research hand. Finally, Theophilus, that church that calls me pastor: I love you dearly even though I do not really understand you. If you are not a miracle, I do not know what is.

None of the names mentioned are responsible for any errors within. I get credit for those.

PART 1

SABBATH
FOR US

1

Sabbath and Time

> Don't underestimate the value of Doing Nothing, of just going
> along, listening to all the things you can't hear, and not bothering.
>
> Winnie-the-Pooh, in *The Complete Tales of Winnie-the-Pooh*

Remembering Sabbath

In 1991, a yet-to-be-identified flea market enthusiast discovered a simple picture frame to his liking. Securing the purchase, the shopper returned home only to discover an ancient document hiding inconspicuously behind the frame. Thinking little of the discovery, he continued about his life. Two years later, a friend stumbled on the document and investigated its origin. The rest is history. The four-dollar frame had hidden a first-edition copy of the Declaration of Independence reportedly worth north of one million dollars.[1] This accidental discovery is not isolated. There was the contractor who found $182,000 in a bathroom wall he was remodeling.[2] A three-dollar Chinese bowl later sold at Sotheby's for $2.2 million—it was a treasure from the Northern Song Dynasty.[3] Then there was that California family who stumbled on a can of ancient gold coins in their backyard valued at $10 million.[4]

To borrow Calvin's words from Bill Watterson's iconic comic strip, "There's treasure everywhere."[5] Not only do treasures of gold and silver lie hidden everywhere around us, but priceless *ideas* do as well. History is the story of ideas lost and found, disappearing and reappearing time and again to the surface.[6]

This is important, for ideas are a matter of life and death. Take slavery, for example, which deems some peoples as inferior to others and regards people as objects to be used. Eugenics similarly witnesses to a whole set of beliefs that suggest only certain human lives are intrinsically valuable—so long as (in the case of Nazism) they are German, have blond hair and blue eyes, and do not have Down syndrome or a disability. One cannot read Hitler's writings on the concept of *lebensraum* ("final solution") and suggest that ideas, even in seed form, are insignificant or not worth debate. In the end, the ideas of a few led to the murder of millions. For this very reason, Holocaust survivor Victor Frankl commented that the very ideas behind the Holocaust did not arise out of nowhere. Rather, these monstrous ideas were disseminated mostly from the cold lecterns of university classrooms across Europe in the years leading up to World War II. The Holocaust was first conceived as a simple, inconspicuous idea—unchallenged and unquestioned by far too many.

Ideas are not neutral, be they religious, philosophical, or scientific. Cultural critic and historian Howard Zinn once wrote, "We can reasonably conclude that how we think is not just mildly interesting, not just a subject for intellectual debate, but a matter of life and death."[7] Christian philosopher Dallas Willard agrees: "We live at the mercy of our ideas."[8] Christ followers, for this reason, must awaken to their calling to critically examine each and every idea, eschewing any false security within the safe harbor of anti-intellectualism. We must, as Paul admonishes, "take captive" any idea opposed to Christ's work (2 Cor. 10:5) with the "mind of Christ" (1 Cor. 2:16). As John writes, we "test the spirits" (1 John 4:1). Avoidance of critically examining our ideas, in the end, is the worst (and least Christian) idea of them all.

Sometimes humanity lives its worst ideas and forgets its best ideas. In Scripture, God's people often forget the ideas of God. For instance, 2 Kings 22 tells the tale of King Josiah. Rising to power at a time when Israel had all but completely forgotten God's law and ways, Josiah sends his secretary into the temple to do some administrative work. Seemingly by accident, Shaphan discovers a number of dusty, old, unfamiliar scrolls. He discerns their identity: scrolls of Jewish Torah! When they are carried to the king, Josiah's heart is cut to its core. He becomes aware of the tragedy: God's people have literally forgotten God's word. In a profound act of repentance, Josiah publicly calls Israel back to God's law. Remembering is a godly act—time and again retrieving the truth of God in the present.[9] Perhaps this is why St. Paul constantly "reminds" the early churches of the gospel of Jesus—the church is the one that so easily forgets it. God's people are indeed saved from their sins. But apparently not from a bad memory.

Have you ever wondered whether there is something *we* have forgotten?
What has the church overlooked in *our* time?

What might *we* have amnesia over?

"Remember the Sabbath" (Exod. 20:8).

Sabbath is that ancient idea and practice of intentional rest that has long been discarded by much of the church and our world. Sabbath is not new. Sabbath is just new to *us*. Historically, Christians have kept some form or another of the Sabbath for some two thousand years. But it has largely been forgotten by the church, which has uncritically mimicked the rhythms of the industrial and success-obsessed West. The result? Our road-weary, exhausted churches have largely failed to integrate Sabbath into their lives as vital elements of Christian discipleship. It is not as though we do not love God—we love God deeply. We just do not know how to sit with God anymore. We have come to know Jesus only as the Lord of the harvest, forgetting he is the Lord of the Sabbath as well. Sabbath forgetfulness is driven, so often, in the name of doing stuff *for* God rather than *being with* God. We are too busy working for him. This is only made more difficult by the fact that the Western church is increasingly experiencing displacement and marginalization in a post-Christian, secular society. In that, we have all the more bought into the notion that ministering on overdrive will resolve the crisis. Sabbath is assumed to be the culprit of a shrinking church. So time poverty and burnout have become the signs that the minority church remains serious about God in a world that has rejected him. Because we pastors rarely practice Sabbath, we rarely preach the Sabbath. And because we do not preach the Sabbath, our congregations are not challenged to take it seriously themselves. The result of our Sabbath amnesia is that we have become perhaps the most emotionally exhausted, psychologically overworked, spiritually malnourished people in history.

Similarly challenging are the cultural realities we face. Our 24/7 culture conveniently provides every good and service we want, when we want, how we want.[10] Our time-saving devices, technological conveniences, and cheap mobility have seemingly made life much easier and interconnected. As a result, we have more information at our fingertips than anyone in history. Yet with all this progress, we are ominously dissatisfied. In bowing at these sacred altars of hyperactivity, progress, and technological compulsivity, our souls increasingly pant for meaning and value and truth as they wither away, exhausted, frazzled, displeased, ever on edge. The result is a hollow culture that, in Paul's words, is "ever learning but never able to come to a knowledge of the truth" (2 Tim. 3:7)—increasingly so. Our bodies wear ragged. Our spirits thirst. We have an inability to simply sit still and *be*. As we drown ourselves in a 24/7 living, we seem to be able to do anything *but* quench our true thirst for the life of God. We have failed to ask ourselves the question Jesus asks of us: "What good will it be for someone to gain the whole world, yet forfeit their soul?" (Matt. 16:26).

We must begin by remembering. If you journey into a contemporary Jewish home prepared for Sabbath, you will likely encounter two candles lit by (more often than not) the woman of the home.[11] On Friday evening, she waves the flames from the kiddush candles—setting the mood for restful intimacy—toward her face to symbolize the Sabbath entering her home. One tradition holds that these candles symbolize a room set for lovemaking.[12] But why two candles? They represent the two lists of commandments, one commanding us "to remember" (Exod. 20:8) and the second "to observe" (Deut. 5:12) the Sabbath.[13] Those two candles are a reminder, the rabbis insisted, that Sabbath observance depended on Sabbath remembrance. To *do*, one must first *remember*.

As said, contemporary Christianity has an acute case of Sabbath amnesia—we have forgotten to remember. We have become what the rabbis called *tinok shenishba*. Literally translated, this means "the child who was captured." Judith Shulevitz illuminates the image of the one who forgets the Sabbath: "The rabbis [discussed] the legal implications of forgetting the Sabbath. . . . What would the penalty for such amnesia or ignorance be? And what kind of Jew could be so oblivious to the Sabbath? Only, the rabbis thought, a Jew who had suffered extreme cultural dislocation. *Only a Jew who had been kidnapped as a child and raised by non-Jews.*"[14] For Jews, forgetting the Sabbath was akin to forgetting one's entire identity. A Jew forgetting the Sabbath was like an Israelite who was raised by Pharaoh. While Christians are going to enter into the Sabbath in a unique way, to remember the Sabbath is to remember who we are—children born of the grace and mercy of Jesus Christ. To keep a Sabbath is to give time and space on our calendar to the grace of God.

Made to Rest

Humans were made to rest. Literally. When God created the world, he entrusted Adam and Eve with a wondrous world of potential where they could explore, discover, play, eat, and enjoy. A new world spanned brilliantly before them. A cadence can be immediately discerned to that creation story: "Let there be light . . . Let there be a vault . . . Let the water . . . Let the land . . . Let there be lights . . . Let us make . . . By the seventh day God had finished the work he had been doing; so on the seventh day he rested from all his work. Then God blessed the seventh day and made it holy, because on it he rested from all the work of creating that he had done" (Gen. 1:3–2:3). There is a rhythm to the week. God finished six days of work by resting for one.

God's rhythm of work and rest soon became the framework for human work and rest: "Six days you shall labor and do all your work, but the seventh day is a sabbath to the Lord your God. On it you shall not do any work" (Exod. 20:9–10). From the beginning, God's own life becomes the model for human life. Diana Butler Bass draws a connection between God's rhythm and ours: "Our bodies move to a rhythm of work and rest that follows the rhythm originally strummed by God on the waters of creation. As God worked, so shall we; as God rested, so shall we. Working and resting, we who are human are in the image of God."[15] To image God is to work and rest as God worked and rested.

Humanity was made on day six of creation. Day seven was that day in which God, Adam, Eve, and the whole garden ceased from productivity and effort. Striking as it is, Adam and Eve's first full day of existence was a day of rest, not work. What a first impression! Social scientists point out that we make up our minds about people in the first 100 milliseconds of our first meeting.[16] Indeed, first impressions matter. Imagine what Adam and Eve learned about God's generosity from their first impression of him on their first day. Their first knowledge of God and the world God had made was that rest was not an afterthought—rest was of first importance.

Adam and Eve had accomplished nothing to earn this gratuitous day of rest. Sabbath is, in my estimation, the first image of the gospel in the biblical story. God's nature always gives rest first; work comes later. This is reflected in all of our lives. Before our lives in this world began, we got nine months of rest in the womb. Before taking up a vocation, we get a few years to just play as children. And before our six days of labor, we receive the day of rest. Karl Barth famously pointed out that the only thing Adam and Eve had to celebrate on that first Sabbath was God and his creation: "That God rested on the seventh day, and blessed and sanctified it, is the first divine action which man is privileged to witness; and that he himself may keep the Sabbath with God, completely free from work, is the first Word spoken to him, the first obligation laid on him."[17] Humanity had only God's goodness to celebrate, nothing more. Work had not even begun. The Sabbath teaches us that we do not work to please God. Rather, we rest because God is already pleased with the work he has accomplished in us.

A problem quickly ensued—God's word was forgotten. Eden's first residents, Adam and Eve, were given God-established boundaries, such as with food: "You are free to eat from any tree in the garden," God says, "but you must not eat from the tree of the knowledge of good and evil" (Gen. 2:16–17).

Adam and Eve could eat from any tree but one. There were similar boundaries around time. One day a week, as a culminating moment in time, Adam and Eve were to rest, or *menukhah*, from their garden activities.

These boundaries soon fell by the wayside. Amnesia set in. The memory of God's word eroded, as reflected in Eve's attempt to explain God's command to the serpent after being tempted to eat the forbidden fruit: "But God did say, 'You must not eat fruit from the tree that is in the middle of the garden, and you must not *touch* it, or you will die'" (Gen. 3:3). Eve, in that critical moment, reveals humanity's vexing and perennial problem: a keen ability to forget what God actually said. Of course, God never commanded Adam or Eve not to *touch* the tree. Rather, God commanded them not to eat from the tree. Eve added to God's word. A good deal of our own sin, we cannot deny, is largely the result of addition or subtraction to what God has spoken. We forget what God actually said or, worse yet, add or subtract to what God has said. Scripture reminds us, "Do not add . . . and do not subtract from [God's word], but keep the commands of the LORD your God that I give you" (Deut. 4:2). That is the human condition: to forget, to add, to subtract, or even to bend God's good word so that it fits our own selfish liking. Humanity is, in this sense, like Jill in C. S. Lewis's *The Silver Chair*, who was told to repeat Aslan's instructions so as not to forget them. "'Child,' said Aslan . . . 'perhaps you do not see quite as well as you think. But the first step is to remember. Repeat to me, in order, the four signs.'"[18] Jill soon forgets, however, and it alters her and her companions' course.

So even if we do remember the Sabbath, we often add or subtract from it. On one side, moralists and legalists add precept upon precept to the Sabbath, as the Pharisees and Sadducees did during the times of Christ, a tendency that time and again infuriates Jesus in the Gospels. Others have subtracted from the Sabbath commandment or ignored it altogether as though it did not matter to God or the well-being of creation. Both of these extremes grieve our Creator. Addition and subtraction are simply different ways of forgetting what God has said.

Not only did a day of rest orient Adam and Eve's life around God; it also orients our hearts, bodies, and minds toward the Creator. Sabbath reminds us that "our time" was never *our* time in the first place. All time is God's time. And the time we have been given is to be used faithfully in worship of him. *Orientation* is a fascinating word based on the Latin word *oriri*, meaning "to rise," as in where the sun rises. The sun rises in the east. Early Christians gave great thought and intentionality to what they oriented themselves toward. For instance, the altar in the earliest churches was intentionally directed east so that worshipers would face Jerusalem as they received the Lord's Supper together.[19] For this same reason, many of the earliest Christians were buried with their feet facing toward the east. Their rationale was simple: when Christ returned and resurrected their bodies, they wanted to be standing and be facing Jerusalem in their resurrection. To be a Christian was, and is, to reorient one's entire life and death around Jesus Christ. Sabbath is an orientation as well—an all-encompassing turning toward the Creator God that changes everything about our lives. Sabbath is that kind of complete reorientation of our lives toward the hope and redemption of Christ's work.

Sabbath baptizes our week into the grace and mercy of God.

The First "Holy"

The Jews were not the only religious people in the ancient world. There were others, such as the Akkadians, Egyptians, and Phoenicians, and they had their own creation stories. When one compares the biblical creation story with these other creation stories, a number of critical differences rise to the surface. For example, the biblical creation story is the only one that contends that matter—creation, people, the world, everything—is intrinsically good. In other creation stories, the world is essentially bad.[20] Another difference is the role of women in creation. In an ancient context where men, rulers, and kings alone bore God's image, the biblical story depicts a world in which men *and* women are created in God's image.[21] Among patriarchal societies, no other sacred text held such a high view of women as the Hebrew Bible. Third, consider God's invitation to rest on the seventh day. In other ancient Near Eastern creation myths, people were created for the purpose of being worked to the bone to accomplish the fiats of the gods; this was particularly the paradigm of the Egyptians.[22] Unlike those other gods, however, Yahweh commands that humanity is to work hard *and* rest well. In no other creation narrative do the gods provide this kind of rest to creation. No other god gave a break. No other god carries the well-being of creation as close to the heart as this One. Again, imagine what first impression that would have given to the Akkadians, Egyptians, and Phoenicians about the God of the Bible and the people who worshiped him.

We worship the God who invented the weekend. This is why biblical scholar Al Baylis contends that "Genesis 1 is one of the most remarkable put-downs ever administered."[23] The biblical creation account essentially served as a theological rebuttal of all the other "gods" who never allowed anyone to rest. In a restless world, Yahweh *required* rest. Again, imagine what kind of first impression that would have given to an ancient person's understanding of

Yahweh. The God of Scripture not only rests himself but invites the world to rest with him.

The impression would undoubtedly have been that Yahweh was the Lord of time.[24] Time, it turns out, is one of the first components of the created order listed in the Genesis account, coming before any physical object such as light, animals, or humanity. God's entire creative action in making everything signifies not only his sovereignty, lordship, and authority over creation but also his sovereignty over time. For this reason, the Jewish people had many "holy days" that helped them remember the sacredness of time and God's role in creating it. The prominent role that time plays in the Genesis narrative resulted in time being understood as sacred, or of ultimate importance, for Jewish faith.

But what kind of time frame does God create? God creates a seven-day week. Theologian Henri Blocher writes, "Nobody reading the panoramic prologue of Genesis can miss the structural fact which gives the text its most obvious arrangement: the framework of the seven days."[25] That is, the framework of seven days is rich with divine intention. Certainly in biblical numerology, the number seven symbolizes divine perfection. But perhaps it goes deeper than that. Echoing church father Basil of Caesarea, theologian Colin Gunton argues that the ordering of seven days establishes a distinct relation between the present time and eternity. That is, the seven-day week was created by God to serve as a contrast to the realm of eternity in which God dwells.[26] Time serves as a contrast to eternity. Have you ever walked into a perfume store at the mall and encountered an array of overwhelming scents simultaneously? Somewhere, you will also see a small cup of coffee beans sitting nearby. What are the coffee beans for? Coffee beans clear the palate so one can distinguish and fully appreciate the nuanced characteristics of each perfume separately, rather than being bombarded by the many scents at once. In a way, time serves as a cup of coffee beans. Time establishes a contrast to eternity, where God dwells.

As has been said, time is basically God's way of keeping everything from happening at once. This is why Jewish scholar Abraham Heschel beautifully describes Sabbath as "eternity uttering a day."[27] Sabbath is a moment of eternal glory momentarily breaking into our finite, present world. The emphasis in Scripture is not on the time of creation, as some so easily assume, but on the creation of time itself. The seven-day week is God's brilliant creation, what one poet calls "the most brilliant creation of the Hebrew spirit."[28]

This seven-day week is not something that can, or should, be tinkered with, although some have tried to. In 1793, France, in an effort to increase human productivity, de-Christianized the calendar by modifying the seven-day week to a ten-day week. New clocks were even invented to reflect the revised week. The experiment, however, radically failed: suicide rates sky-rocketed, people burned out, and production decreased. Why? It turns out humans were not made to work nine days and rest only one in a week. We were made to work six days and rest one. The seven-day rhythm is sacred. The seven-day week is not the result of human ingenuity; rather, it is a reflection of God's brilliance.

In every week, one day is to be set aside for rest. So central to God is the ethical imperative to rest that it is established in Scripture before commands against murder, adultery, divorce, lying, incest, rape, jealousy, and child sacrifice. In fact, of the Ten Commandments, Sabbath is the only command originally expressed directly to Adam and Eve. Why do we Sabbath? Genesis says we Sabbath, first, because God kept a Sabbath and, second, because God built it into the DNA of creation, and it is therefore something creation needs in order to flourish.

As God invites us to Sabbath, we will be tempted to think that Sabbath cannot "work" for us. "I don't have time to take a whole day to rest," people have expressed to me for years. Biblically, however, this is not the case. The biblical story tells us that to rest one day a week is to be truly human, and to not rest is to be inhuman. Humans were made to rest. When we say we don't have time to rest, we cannot find time for something that has already been found. As Dietrich Bonhoeffer once wrote, with God, an imperative is an indicative.[29] That is, what God commands us to *do* tells us something of who God *is*. God invites us to rest. And God rests. Are we stronger or wiser or better than God? As the creation story reminds us, the need for rest is built into the genetic makeup of the universe, and ignorance of such is like humanity trying to genetically modify the whole universe. We should learn from France—God's rhythms can never be tinkered with. As H. H. Farmer once said, "If you go against the grain of the universe, you get splinters."[30]

Even scientific communities increasingly grasp these realities. In 1974, nearly halfway through the eighty-four-day mission aboard the Skylab space station, Colonel William Pogue requested a day of rest from mission control for his overworked and exhausted space crew: "We have been over-scheduled. We were just hustling the whole day. The work could be tiresome and tedious, though the view is spectacular." How spectacular the view and work must have been, but even a breathtaking view from space cannot relieve the human need for rest. What happened? NASA refused his request. Subsequently, the crew went on strike in space, a first of its kind. Disobeying orders, the crew took a space Sabbath. In response, ground control was forced to change their policy.[31] To this day, NASA now schedules time for rest on all space travel. Even NASA factors in rest.

The Sabbath day is a holy day. Interestingly, the only thing God deems as *qadosh*, or "holy," in the creation story is the Sabbath day. The earth, space, land, stars, animals—even people—are not designated as *qadosh*. The Sabbath day was holy. Heschel speaks of the Sabbath as the "sanctification of time": "This is a radical departure from accustomed religious thinking. The mythical mind would expect that, after heaven and earth have been established, God would create a holy place—a holy mountain or a holy spring—whereupon a sanctuary is to be established. Yet it seems as if to the Bible it is *holiness in time*, the Sabbath, which comes first."[32] This holiness of the Sabbath is one of the distinctive marks of Jewish theology, Heschel contends. Again, it is telling that there is no mention of a specific, sacred *place* in the creation story. There is only a sacred day. While space and location are significant, it is important to note that the exact location of Eden is omitted. Yet we know that the Sabbath day is holy.[33]

Adam and Eve were invited to "keep" that seventh day holy. Do not misread the text: they were not to *make* the Sabbath holy. Humans cannot make anything holy. The day's holiness is assumed. They were to *keep* the Sabbath holy, which was already holy before they came to it.[34] This does not mean that there are days that are *not* holy. Time *itself* is holy. Every day is a holy day. Jacques Ellul once identified our religious and cultural tendency to see some days as holy and some as mundane: "Very quickly some days of the week . . . come to rank as sacred."[35] In contrast to our notions of time, the biblical tradition states that *all* time is sacred (Pss. 31:15; 139:16; Isa. 60:22). It is not only theologically inaccurate but also dangerous to suggest that some days are sacred and others are not—time is in itself the first thing designated as sacred. All time is holy, not just the Sabbath. But the Sabbath is set aside as a unique kind of holiness.

The First "Not Good"

God only creates "good" things.

Long before the techniques of italicizing or emboldening text, repetition was the ancient author's literary tool to highlight an idea. So the authors of Scripture would make their point by repeating something over and over again. For this very reason, the creation narrative repeatedly depicts God declaring the *goodness* of everything he made. "It was good . . . It was good . . . And it was very good" (Gen. 1:4, 10, 12, 18, 21, 25, 31). In what might appear as pompous, self-congratulatory commentary, we are actually blessed by the knowledge of God's own recognition of the brilliance of his creation. He is well aware that what he has made is valuable, right, and good. Repeating this refrain each day, the biblical author makes clear that this world is fundamentally made good. The intrinsic goodness of creation speaks to an important practice of Sabbath living—the need of humanity to reflect on and delight in the goodness of what God has made.

Once, when sharing my faith with an agnostic friend, I was asked to make my greatest argument for God's existence. I uttered one word: *mangoes.* I was not talking about just *any* mangoes. I was talking about fresh, ripe, just-off-the-tree mangoes, about have-to-change-your-shirt-afterward mangoes. Mangoes, I explained, were my greatest argument for God's existence. To this day, I cannot eat a mango and say with a straight face that this is a world that has been invented by a jerk. Or that something so delicious could come from nowhere. Creation is good. Why? Because God is good. And his goodness is reflected in what he makes. A mango, as part of creation, is God's love letter to humanity.

There is an Indian restaurant in my neighborhood called Bollywood Theatre. I once went to lunch with my friend Todd Miles, a theologian at a local seminary. Taking in our first few bites, he blurted out, almost surprised by his own proclamation, "You know, A. J., when you think about it, food didn't have to be *this* good!" One could argue that this is the thesis statement of Genesis's first two chapters—a good God makes a good creation. Creation is not bad. Creation is not "just okay." Creation is good. The words of Martin Luther echo this refrain: "God writes the Gospel not in the Bible alone, but also on trees, and in the flowers and clouds and stars."[36] Were it not for lack of space, I bet Luther meant to include mangoes and Indian food. In his goodness, God delights in giving us food that did not have to be this good. And then, if we did not already grasp his goodness, he decides to give us taste buds.

The good news: mangoes and Indian food are merely a foretaste of the good world to come. Consider the final words of the old English martyr John Bradford, who reportedly declared as he died on the stake: "Look at creation—look at it all! This is the world God has given to his enemies; imagine the world he will give *to his friends.*"[37] Bradford's point: we cannot even begin to imagine heaven's mangoes or Indian food. God's good world is a world of delight, one that offers only a preview of the majestic, unimaginable world to come. A world of goodness and blessing, joy and generosity, and, of course, glorious rest. What is the Sabbath but a day to reflect on God and all the love letters sent our way? The Sabbath is celebration, a day of rejoicing over the goodness of what has been made and who made it.

As part of this good creation, Adam was created to tend the garden and name the animals. Yet Adam found that the animals did not serve his every need. Something seemed missing—Adam needed a "helper" to assist in the work of caring for the garden. The text does not suggest that Adam knew what exactly it was that he needed. Rather, God recognizes Adam's need before he knows he is missing something. Recognizing his need, God puts Adam to sleep, saying, "It is *not good* for the man to be alone" (Gen. 2:18). Thus, we encounter the first "not good" in the Bible. Notice *when* the first "not good" happens in the Bible. It was not a result of Adam and Eve's disobedience. Rather, the first "not good" appears *before* the fall. How is this possible?

This first "not good" reveals to us something about humanity's nature. Namely, God did not create human beings to exist with God alone. Adam needed food, water, rest, and relationship. In fact, God's design for humanity was complete only in relationship with God and others. That is, despite the fact that Adam had *most* of his creaturely needs met—such as food, water, work, and even an unmediated relationship with the living God—Adam still lacked something. One need remained to be filled. Adam needed a helper—he needed human community.

God created human beings with needs. We often read Jesus's words "Man shall not live on bread alone, but on every word that comes from the mouth of God" (Matt. 4:4) as meaning we just need God and can forsake all physical needs. But that is not what Jesus meant. He was saying we live on God's word and his being, but we *also* need bread. Both. Adam needed food. He needed work. He needed God. And he needed a helper.

Needs are not bad. If God is sovereign and the "first good" comes before sin invades the world, then why did God wait to create the woman until later? In my mind, there can be only one rationale: God desired Adam to have a deep recognition of his own needs. It is one thing to have a need. It is another thing to come to *recognize* and *deeply appreciate* that need and be humble enough to have it fulfilled. It is only when we have a need and recognize it that we can confess our dependence on God and be thankful for God's gracious hand. Humility is essentially that: recognizing our own needs and our ultimate inability to fulfill them by ourselves. Imagine the joy and thankfulness of Adam to know his need was fulfilled by God the moment Eve was created.

Jesus asked the blind, hungry, and needy, "What is it that you want?" He was not ignorant of their needs, nor did he want them to be ignorant of their needs. Rather, he wanted them to have a deep awareness of their own needs. We need many things. Humans need relationship. Why was it not enough for Adam to have unfettered access to God? The nature of God—as we can observe from the very beginning of the biblical narrative—is deeply relational and communal. God is a Triune God. "Let *us* make mankind," God says as he creates humanity (Gen. 1:26). Therefore, at the core of the human experience, each human being reflects the image of God, who created humankind after his own being. Humans, made by the Triune God, were created with a need for relationship.[38] Relational needs are not a by-product of the fall. Likewise, the need for rest, or Sabbath, is not an aftertaste of human sinfulness, unlike our chronic inability to receive rest. In fact, as we shall see, Sabbath is a foretaste of heaven.

All of this means that humans' need for rest and sleep was not a result of sin or disobedience. Sleep does not come after, but before, the fall. In fact, we see that the first act of "deep sleep" (Hebrew *tardemah*) is initiated by God, resulting in the creation of the woman. Sleep is a result of God's activity, intended to take place in paradise before it was lost.[39] Likewise, our need for Sabbath rest as well as sleep points not to our sinfulness but to the very way God has created us and thus intended for us to function. Like sleep, the day of rest comes *before* the fall. Rest was not a result of the devil's work. As we were made to eat and breathe and walk, we were made, from the foundations of the world, to rest, or to Sabbath, in God. The need for rest is greatly misunderstood by so many Christians in today's world. I cannot count how many times I have heard a well-intended Christian leader say, "I'll sleep when I get to heaven." What a lamentably nonbiblical cliché. In the end, we will get to heaven much quicker if we opt not to rest. Sabbath rest is no sign of weakness or sinfulness—God himself rested. Is God weak?

If we choose never to rest, as we are built, it will catch up to us. We cannot dodge our needs. Truth is not a set of cold, disembodied rules written in heaven. Rather, as Augustine saw it, truth is reality. Thomas Williams offers a compelling description of this in his introduction to Augustine's book *On Free Choice of the Will*: "Violating the eternal law is not like doing 40 in a 35-mile-per-hour zone when there is no traffic around; it is more like trying to violate the law of gravity. . . . An apple falling from a tree has no choice about whether to obey the law of gravity . . . [but] human beings can voluntarily wreck their lives by running afoul of the laws that govern their nature. This is indeed a sort of freedom, but it can hardly be the best sort."[40] Williams's point? We can violate truth, but by doing so, we will suffer the consequences. God created gravity—not just a law written somewhere, but the actual reality we daily experience. Gravity just *is*. Our belief or disbelief in it cannot invalidate it, change it, or make it disappear. Gravity always wins.

Just like Adam and Eve's need for Sabbath, our need for rest is like gravity. It just *is*. Our feelings and opinions cannot change it. Humans need rest. Animals need rest. Land needs rest. And without rest, things will cease to exist as they should. Still, we may choose to ignore this need for a while, but gravity always wins. When we look honestly at our workaholic, boundaryless, frantic lives, we can hear God say, "Not good." Like he saw Adam's need for a helper, God sees our need for rest. His judgment is his love. Only a malevolent deity could celebrate and enable habits that lead to the death of his creation, calling that which is bad for us "good . . . good . . . good." The truth is, if we do not rest, we will not be well. We might be fine for a while. But over the course of time, our bodies, minds, and souls will pay a hefty price for ignoring gravity.

But when we do rest, we experience incredible healing. Like Adam's intrinsic need for relationship, rest is a need that God built into us. The New Testament calls Jesus the "Lord of the Sabbath" (Matt. 12:8 and parallels). Jesus's rest restores *us*. On one Sabbath, Jesus heals a man with a shriveled hand—"his hand was completely restored" (Mark 3:5). Sabbath and restoration are quite synonymous in God's vocabulary. To Sabbath is to live as God intended. When we enter into that rest, it is like entering back into Eden.

The First "Rest"

Following a close reading of the Genesis account, one notices an unexpected lack of any mention of the word *Sabbath*. Rather, there remains a repetition of the word *rest* (*menukhah*). In fact, the first usage of the actual word *Sabbath* is not until Exodus 16:23. Other notable words are missing in the creation narrative as well. For example, Genesis 1 and 2 lack language concerning "marriage" between Adam and Eve. The exact language of "marriage" is not used until later in Scripture. Now while marriage is not initially discussed, covenant relationship is. Sabbath is not initially discussed, but rest is an integral part of creation. The inspired language of Genesis is that God instituted *menukhah*-rest into creation from the very beginning.

Sabbath and *marriage* are similar in that they are legal terms utilized later to establish what humanity needed to do after its created purpose was usurped. Let me illustrate. I remember the first time I drove by myself. I had the ability to drive wherever I wanted, with whomever I wanted, however fast I wanted. With the steering wheel in my hands, I had freedom and power. However, to ensure that I did not abuse my newly found freedom and power, there were laws in place. The government had established a speed limit and required drivers and passengers to wear seat belts. The laws clarify what safe driving looks like, for my benefit and everyone else's. But the point of the laws is not to keep the laws. Rather, the point of those laws is to remind us what driving safely is all about. In the end, I think God hates law giving. Why? Because law giving implies intent breaking. Sadly, we love living in ways that God never created us to. God gave us a world of delight to work and play in, but over time we continued to ignore his way. God had to institute Sabbath law because humanity had failed to live the intent of God's rest.

The seventh day was the final creation act of God, a day of *menukhah*-rest. As days progress in Genesis 1 and 2, the story feels as though it is building toward something particularly special. This structure seems to offer a lesson, in Lesslie Newbigin's words, "claiming to show the shape, the structure, the origin, and the goal not merely of human history, but of cosmic history."[41] As an architect designs particular rooms in a home, each with a special purpose so that they may function together, the creation structure reveals something of God's intents. First, God built the foundation of the light. Then he built the frame of the seas, followed by the walls of the animals and the inhabitants of humans. What is interesting is that humanity is not created on the final workday. What is the culmination of creation? In Genesis 2:2–3, there are three sentences of seven Hebrew words each, and the middle word of each sentence is the word for the seventh day. This textual feature is utilized to state that the seventh day is the goal of creation.[42] The climax of creation is not humanity, as we have so arrogantly assumed. Rather, the day of rest is the climax, when creation all comes together and lives at peace and harmony with one another. Sabbath becomes the culminating roof of the entire house.

The picture is stunning—the first day for Adam and Eve was not a day to work the garden. God established a weekly rhythmic reminder of his love—the Sabbath. Again, the Bible offers a view of God that is so entirely unlike the gods of other religions' creation narratives. No other god gives rest. No other god beckons us to enjoy Eden's mangoes.

Adam and Eve's first impression of God would have been that God was no slave driver. Still today, we are reminded of that truth each week when we take a day to rest in God's presence. Sabbath is a scheduled weekly reminder that we are not what we do; rather, we are who we are loved by. Sabbath and the gospel scream the same thing: we do not work to get to a place where we finally get to breathe and rest—that is slavery. Rather, we rest and breathe and enjoy God *that we might* enter into rest.

We must distinguish a biblical day of rest from the world's way of rest—a biblical Sabbath should be distinguished from vacations and "days off," although even those we are not proficient at. Studies reveal that 37 percent of Americans take fewer than seven days of vacation a year. In fact, only 14 percent take vacations that last longer than two weeks.[43] Americans take the shortest paid vacations of anyone in the world. And 20 percent of those who do, often spend their vacation staying in touch with their jobs through their computers or phones.[44] The point? Even when we do vacation, we do it poorly.

But even if we *did* vacation well and took great amounts of time off for restorative rest, vacations are a poor substitute for a weekly day of Sabbath rest. I think the devil loves taking that which is of God and giving us cheap knockoffs. When God invents sugar, the devil makes Sweet'N Low. When God makes sex, the devil comes up with adultery. The devil always twists the goodness of God. The Bible is silent on vacations. Why? Because if we kept a weekly Sabbath, we would not need vacations. Vacations are what Jürgen Moltmann has called the "Coca-Cola philosophy" of Western life.[45] In the 1990s, Coca-Cola had a well-known campaign depicting people doing hard work, then popping open a cold bottle of Coke and taking a swig. We yearn for the "pause that refreshes." Unfortunately, we try to refresh ourselves with empty calories, or vacations, which are not what we really need. Our souls stir, longing for Sabbath. Not for the frills of a can of saccharine drink, a sugary vacation.

What differentiates a weekly Sabbath from a vacation? Quite a bit, in fact. When my son was four, he learned how to put his head underwater when swimming. Elliot can hold his breath for a good ten seconds, a feat indeed. Still, he cannot believe how long I can hold mine—upward of sixty seconds. When we both emerge from the water, we catch our breaths. It would be fascinating to watch someone go about their life holding their breath all the time and breathing only when they absolutely had to—a difficult life that would be. A Sabbath is like breathing. Imagine a life where you breath once every sixty seconds. Or, can you think of what life would be like if we opted to breathe for only two weeks out of the year? It is interesting that God's invitation to rest once a week is so hard for us to grapple with, yet we do not blink at the notion of breathing all the time. A rest is not the only thing that matters. What matters even more is the consistency and rhythm of rest that we enter into.

Why do we think we know better than God? Do we think we have a superior understanding of his creation, our bodies? Did we invent ourselves?

While a biblical Sabbath is different from a vacation, it is not just a "day off" either. It is possible for one to not be at work physically but still be at work in one's heart. Culturally, it is assumed that when we are not at work, we are free to do as we please. But in reality, our jobs and bosses do not really allow us to disengage from work even in our off hours. It is presumed in the modern workplace that we will all continue to work at home. This is exacerbated by the fact that, as we will discuss in a later chapter, we often do not Sabbath because technology invades every part of our life. With our computers in our pockets, what should be a Sabbath day turns out to be a day at home where we are thinking about work. This problem has been identified as a cultural crisis in France. Because of the modern rhythms of work that are mediated through personal computers and phones, people, in the words of one cultural commentator, "leave the office, but they do not leave their work. They remain attached by a kind of electronic leash—like a dog."[46] More often than not, our "days off" are days where we are spatially at home, but emotionally and mentally at work. Do these "days off" constitute a Sabbath day?

A biblical Sabbath is a day when we are spatially, and emotionally, not at work. "Days off" are actually, in the words of Eugene Peterson, "bastard Sabbaths."[47] They are days when we are technically at home but really at work. This cultural crisis has led the French government to undertake drastic measures to outlaw employers from sending work emails after hours, barring an emergency.[48] A business now faces stiff penalties if it requires employees to work when they are to rest. A "day off" cannot sustain the human soul. Only a Sabbath can. By contrast, Sabbath is a day when our hearts are at rest from striving, doing, producing, and—most important—responding to emails. A Sabbath day is not merely stopping our work; it is also stopping our thinking and scheming about work.

The Taste of Sabbath

We conclude this chapter with the words of Isaiah 58:13, which instructs us to "call the Sabbath a delight."[49] Sabbath *is* a delight. Not useful. Delightful. Yes, there are innumerable by-products of honoring the Sabbath: we become healthier, happier, and more available to God and others. But we must be cautious—the Sabbath being delightful is different from the Sabbath being useful. Sabbath does not always pay off the way we wish it would. Resting is costly. Nor is Sabbath the day we get to do whatever we want or whatever feels right. Sabbath is to be cherished as a delight in itself, not something we use to get elsewhere. All the things of God are like that—we do not use them as tools to get something. Nor do we use God. Jean-Jacques Suurmond, a Dutch theologian, speaks to our pragmatist tendencies to only love God or follow the life of God if it is useful: "Anyone who tries to prove God's existence by demonstrating the need for God makes the same mistake as those who claim that in our modern secularized society God no longer has any function and has thus become superfluous. Both begin from the usefulness of God. . . . God is not useful. God does not serve any purpose, since God is an end in himself. . . . God has often either been reduced to a useful, predictable idol, or is experienced as absent."[50]

We do not love God because God is useful to us. We love God because God is worthy of being loved. "God is interesting," writes Gunton, "in and of himself."[51] Or to echo Karl Barth: "God *is*."[52] Sabbath, likewise, should not be understood in merely useful or pragmatic terms. A Sabbath is done out of obedience to God, not to get something. While there are endless benefits to keeping a Sabbath, we do not do it *for* the benefits, in the same way that we do not enter a marriage in order to make love. Sex is a benefit of marriage, not the reason for marriage.

Gerald May once lamented how a pragmatic culture often treats the Sabbath: "We know we need to rest, but we can no longer see the value of rest as an end in itself; it is only worthwhile if it helps us to recharge our batteries."[53] Sabbath is something enjoyed for its own sake, inviting us to play. And play is not undertaken to accomplish; it is undertaken for its own sake. Dorothy Sayers once argued that most legalistic Sabbath-keepers had added to "Thou shalt not work" the phrase "Thou shalt not play."[54] God never outlaws Sabbath play. On the contrary, Sabbath is time for creation to play in the world of God once again—as *re*-creation. Sabbath is the celebration of God's life and his work in our lives. But our overproductive lives have no space for play or celebration. Years ago, Harvard theologian Harvey Cox argued that the death of God in our culture was related in some way to the fact that we no longer celebrate, or integrate festivity, in our culture. That is, our celebration deficit is part of our loss of God in culture. And when festivity and play ended, argued Cox, culture and community begin to erode at their very core.[55]

The Sabbath creates space for rest and play in our lives. The prophet Zechariah looks hopefully to a future day in which our cities would have space for play: "This is what the LORD Almighty says: 'Once again men and women of ripe old age will sit in the streets of Jerusalem, each of them with cane in hand because of their age. The city streets will be filled with boys and girls playing there" (Zech. 8:4–5). Such an urban environment has space, places for play, for walking, for talking. Even children play in the street. Can you imagine New York City without Central Park? Whenever God dreams of a city, like a dream for our lives, he dreams of places where we are not so crowded and full that we have no room to play in the streets. The Sabbath makes room for us to play outside once again, like when we were kids.

Rather than rest God's way, we have replaced Sabbath with a kind of therapeutic individualism that seeks to self-entertain, self-please, self-soothe. Christopher Lasch has described this kind of therapeutic culture that is focused on getting the self to sense bliss: "People today hunger not for personal salvation, let alone for the restoration of an earlier golden age, but for the feeling, the momentary illusion, of personal well-being, health, and psychic security."[56] Soong-Chan Rah connects our false desires for blissful happiness with deep individualism and the human creation of a culture that is all about the self and what the individual wants.[57] Sociologist Philip Reiff echoes this point in his prophetic text *The Triumph of the Therapeutic*. Reiff argues that all pleasures (in his example, "sexual") are intended to be subordinated under the reign of God, but they are not a substitute for God. In today's age, when we have ceased celebrating God and have begun celebrating celebration, we have turned the means into the goal. "Religious man was born to be saved," writes Reiff, and "psychological man is born to be pleased."[58] What was intended by God to be a celebration reflecting on his goodness and the goodness of his creation has been, once again, replaced by the devil's false forms of celebration: drunkenness, loss of self-control, and debauchery. We sell ourselves short by celebrating for celebration's sake rather than for God's sake. The authentic call to Sabbath is to enter into celebration as God intended it to be, not what we think it should be.

But the Sabbath is not a form of indulgent individualism dressed in religious piety. Sabbath is about delighting in God for his sake and the sake of the world. Marva Dawn has said that Sabbath is about four things: ceasing, resting, embracing, and feasting.[59] It is in Sabbath that we enjoy, we delight, we relish in the goodness and generativity of God. We play. We feast. We rest. We echo with God, "It is good!" And in our Sabbath play, we discover that to play is to pray.[60] Hear the words of Donna Schaper: "Sabbath keeping is a spiritual strategy: it is a kind of judo. The world's commands are heavy; we respond with light moves. The world says work; we play. The world says go fast; we go slow. These light moves carry Sabbath into our days, and God into our lives."[61]

Once we get a taste of Sabbath, there is no going back. Our family Sabbaths each Wednesday. On Tuesday evenings, after preparing for the Sabbath, we sing a song together. Some families sing the *L'khah Dodi*, a traditional Jewish song sung on Friday nights. It goes, "Come in peace, and come in joy, Thou who art the bridegroom's pride; Come, O Bride, and shed thy grace, O'er the faithful chosen race; Come, O bride! Come, O bride!" Our family sings a song called the *Shabbat Shalom*, or "Sabbath Peace." Each person in the family is named.

Shabbat Shalom to A. J.
Shabbat Shalom to Quinn.
Shabbat Shalom to Elliot.

We have six chickens, and we usually name them in the song too. Then we eat a big meal, read books together, and go to bed. In the morning, we wake up. We have two rules on the morning of the Sabbath. First, nobody makes their bed. Second, pancakes. Pancakes are essential to our Sabbath. As Quinn sleeps in, I often get up early with Elliot, and together we craft the largest pancakes known to man. Sitting on the counter, he helps me stir the batter. Then we cook them up. Elliot will pour syrup on that thing like nobody's business (I sometimes worry he has a problem). Then we eat. It is a pancake feast—slappy cakes, bacon, eggs, coffee with extra honey in it.

The pancakes are essential. I read at one point that some Jewish fathers, on the morning of the Sabbath, would give their children a spoon of honey. What a beautiful tradition! The idea was simple: that they would always remember the sweetness of the Sabbath for the rest of their lives. It is similar to the way the earliest Christians took Communion: with milk and honey. This symbolism was to remind them that in Christ they had come to the promised land. That is my hope—that when I am dead and gone and my boy is all grown up, if anyone even whispers the word *Sabbath* around my son, he will just start drooling. It is a Pavlovian experiment of the highest order.

Nathaniel Hawthorne once wrote that the Sabbath sunshine was unlike any other sunshine during the week—that sunshine is a "shadow of great truths."[62] Pancakes are a shadow of great truths.

All are welcomed in, friends. The Sabbath awaits. Come and delight in it. I can almost see you drooling.

QUESTIONS
for Reflection

- What do you think about a weekly day of rest happening from the outset of creation, not just when the law was given?
- Why do you think God designed Adam and Eve's first day to be one of rest?
- Take a moment to reflect on the fact that this world was made fundamentally good. What does reflecting on the goodness of Sabbath bring about in your heart?
- How might you confess your dependence on God by recognizing your own needs? What are those needs?
- How might entering rest be likened to entering back into Eden?
- What does Sabbath rest indicate to us about God's intent for humanity?
- Imagine what it would have been like to be Adam or Eve. What would have been your first impressions of God?

- Why do we not rest? What might this tendency reveal about our trust, or lack thereof, in God?
- How might you begin to envision Sabbath as the celebration of God's life and his work in your life rather than a tool or something that is merely pragmatic or useful?
- How might Sabbath be an invitation to celebration?

2

Sabbath and Work

Six days a week the spirit is alone, disregarded, forsaken, forgotten.
Working under strain, beset with worries, enmeshed in anxieties,
man has no mind for ethereal beauty. But the spirit is waiting for
man to join in.

Abraham Heschel, *The Sabbath*

The Sanctity of Work

In the previous chapter, we examined the biblical roots of a theology of Sabbath and time. Our journey now moves us toward engaging human work with explicit regard to how the Sabbath renews our vocation in this world. In the beginning, Adam and Eve worked. Their tasks? To care for, and nurture, the garden of Eden. The responsibility of naming the animals was placed on Adam. They were to "be fruitful and multiply." What this teaches us, of course, is that nothing remains as close to human identity as the work God has invited them to partake in. Work was not, and is not, punishment for sin. Work precedes sin.

Have you ever wondered whether you will have a job in heaven?

Will we work for eternity?

Will resurrection offer us all a much-desired career change?

If humans worked in the garden, will humans work in heaven?

In a little examination of the prophet Isaiah, *When the Kings Come Marching In*, Richard Mouw discusses the biblical portrayal of the new

Jerusalem, where "the earth will be filled with the knowledge of the Lord" (Isa. 11:9). This soon-coming new Jerusalem is intricately detailed as a resurrected, renewed *old* Jerusalem. Mouw points to the "flocks of Kedar," "rams of Nebaioth," and the "ships of Tarshish," which freely enter the new Jerusalem carrying silver, gold, and costly woods of cypress, plane, and Lebanese pine. These are welcomed alongside camels from Midian, Ephah, and Sheba carrying gold and frankincense. What is this all about? The prophet Isaiah, Mouw contends, is using extraordinary measures to describe the future Jerusalem in fundamentally physical, real, elemental, *earthy* terms. "Animal, vegetable, mineral," concludes Mouw, "are all brought into the renewed Jerusalem."[1]

By no means is this the only depiction of the new Jerusalem that includes animals, technology, and artistry. Concluding a parallel passage in the New Testament text of Revelation 21, John depicts the new Jerusalem in equally earthy terms. Heaven is depicted as a city. Unlike popular Christian art, heaven is not depicted as that place where the saints reside eternally on billowy white clouds while playing harps and reading hymnals. What *is* found, however, is an actual city where Christ is the ruler; the city includes a river, buildings, food, drink, feasts, and jewels and metals gathered from the nations. There, we will have physical bodies—"He will *wipe* every *tear* from their *eyes*" (Rev. 21:4). The new Jerusalem will be spiritual *and* physical. Mouw even suggests that the "ships of Tarshish" referenced in Isaiah—widely identified as icons of pagan culture—will enter the new Jerusalem as sanctified items that have been cleansed of their former pagan "functions." In heaven, they will still be boats. This time, however, they will be boats for the glory of Yahweh, not the tyranny of the pantheon.[2]

This is the renewal of all things. Isaiah and John both look forward to that time when Christ will rule and reign. In fact, the biblical language regarding the future is noticeably absent of humans "going to heaven." Quite the opposite, in fact: John sees "the new Jerusalem, *coming down* out of heaven from God, prepared as a bride beautifully dressed" (Rev. 21:2). God makes all things new. God does not make all new things. This distinction underscores a theological reality—a great similarity and continuity will exist between this world and the next. Mouw drives this point home: "The Holy City is not wholly discontinuous with the present conditions. The biblical glimpses of this City give us reason to think that its contents will not be completely unfamiliar to people like us. In fact, the contents of the City will be more akin to our present cultural patterns than is usually acknowledged in discussions of the afterlife."[3] The Bible's depiction of the new Jerusalem is surprising: heaven will look a lot like earth.

The new Jerusalem is a renovated, not replaced, city. Indeed, this raises countless theological possibilities and problems. What of our bodies? What of our artistic creations? Will we have tattoos in heaven? I have long surmised that we may retain our tattoos in the world to come. I wonder if our tattoos—like the "ships of Tarshish"—will continue into glory but be sanctified of their old purposes, resurrected into the glorious presence of Christ. Why would this not be the case? Jesus had the marks of his death on his resurrected body. Other possibilities of the eschaton remain to be teased out.

In light of all this, could it be that many of our creations and achievements might actually resurrect into the new world? In a groundbreaking work, theologian Miroslav Volf echoes Mouw by contending that human work and cultural flourishing must be understood not as being destroyed in the coming of God's kingdom but as being purified. In fact, Volf argues that our technological advancements that have changed human culture for the good, such as Gutenberg's press, may actually be *included* in the renewal of all things. "Through their work," contends Volf, "human beings contribute in their modest and broken way to God's new creation."[4] Humanity does not have the power to resurrect our work. Still, God may resurrect the very human city we have built. In short, the new creation, unlike the first, will not be created *ex nihilo* (out of nothing). It will incorporate aspects of this present creation.

What, then, does one do with texts regarding a coming worldly destruction? For example, 2 Peter 3 says the "present heavens and earth are reserved for fire, being kept for the day of judgment and destruction of the ungodly" (2 Pet. 3:7). This does not necessarily mean that the world must be *destroyed* for God's kingdom to fully come. Evangelical biblical scholar Douglas Moo points out that the thrust of 2 Peter 3, among other texts, describes a world being renewed rather than destroyed. Moo points out that throughout Scripture, fire is an image of purification, not of destruction. Fire retains things of value but annihilates the worthless.[5] We must be cautious: this is not to say that we are currently building the new Jerusalem and that heaven only comes down on the earth metaphorically. Rather, this is to suggest that God will take elements of the present creation and resurrect them while purifying the new creation of worthless elements. In the same way that we cannot resurrect Christ from the grave, we cannot "build" the new Jerusalem. The new Jerusalem, we remember, comes down out of heaven from God (Rev. 21:2). Heaven is not from around here. The new city comes down to us and is put on top of our existing one.

I have a hunch: we *will* have jobs in the new Jerusalem. We will work. As Eden was a place of work, so will heaven be. Work was not a result of sin. Why? Because humans are *homo faber* (humans who work), created to "tend and keep" and enjoy the fruits of their work. So close to their human function was work that the biblical author uses the same word for "tend" as "worship." To care for the garden was to worship the Creator. Eden was a divine domain of work and worship, not a world of sedentary laziness or unproductivity. The created world was to be creatively worked and nurtured. Work is not a mistake or a curse. Yet work becomes our curse when it becomes what we worship. "Labor is not," writes Abraham Heschel, "only the destiny of man; it is endowed with divine dignity."[6]

Jewish rabbis have a phrase, *melechet machshevet*, to illustrate this reality, meaning that our work "is done unto the realization of God's plan and vision."[7] When Adam and Eve were placed in the garden, they were placed with a purpose to work and cultivate and nurture the created space. Their task was to bring about God's desires through their vocation. Our task *is* and *will be* no less. Our work is valuable, and it matters to God. Although work is holy, the human tendency as a result of sin is to exalt work as the central part of the human vocation. But work, or activity, is not our core identity. At the heart of the human vocation is to *be* with God, not to *do* anything. It is tempting to think of Sabbath as the intrinsic result of a job well done, but it is not. Sabbath is not a wage for our hard work. Sabbath is not a benefits package. Rather, work is a reflection of Sabbath-keeping. Work is a benefit of our rest.

Worshiping Work

"Achievement," once wrote Mary Bell, "is the alcohol of our time."[8] Work is our drug, our numbing agent, escape hatch, and anesthetizing behavior. Achievement makes us feel the semblance of some glow of heightened, idolized identity where we are what we do. In this modern world, we have become addicts to doing, making, producing, and accomplishing. Our modern dogma is that of Batman: "It's not who you are underneath. It's what you do that defines you."[9] How did it come to this? Why has our work taken center stage in our lives?

We are what we accomplish—or so goes the unquestioned popular dogma. The origins of this devilish approach to life are illustrated in the early pages of Scripture as we observe the destructive effects of sin taking root. Adam and Eve were created to work in the garden, yet their relationship to that work fundamentally changes once sin invades the garden. We see that work—done in service to God and creation—immediately gets twisted into acts of abuse and sinfulness and injustice. When Adam is assigned the responsibility of naming animals, God extends to him freedom and creativity to live in harmony with and have authority among the created realm. In the ancient world, to name something or someone was to have a sense of authority over it. Naming the animals implied Adam's God-ordained authority over God's creatures and his responsibility to them. But he is to name the animals and the animals alone. Thus, the woman is given no name in Genesis 1 and 2 when she is created. She is simply called "woman." The implication is profound: Adam had authority over the animals. But with the woman, who was his helper, he was to walk side by side.

The fundamental relationship between the man and the woman was one of mutuality. As Peter Lombard long ago observed, we must remember that Eve was taken out of Adam's side, not from his head nor his feet. Why? Because Adam was never to rule *over* the woman or be ruled *by* her. Rather, she came out of his side; she was to be his helper.[10] Similarly, Matthew Henry in his *Commentary on the Whole Bible* writes, "The woman was made of a rib out of the side of Adam; not made out of his head to rule over him, nor out of his feet to be trampled upon by him, but out of his side to be equal with him, under his arm to be protected, and near his heart to be beloved."[11]

Sin changes everything, turning the good world upside down. Once Adam and Eve sin, the blame game begins. The first couple hide from God, and their very relationship to the land and the rest of creation is changed. They are banished from the garden of Eden, becoming wanderers on the earth, displaced from place. Now, their work will be toilsome. God was left with a difficult choice—discipline was necessary. He offers strong words of discipline to each guilty party. God curses the serpent, saying he will be at enmity with the woman and her seed. God then speaks to the woman and says child labor will be painful and she will yearn for her husband, but he will "rule" over her. Then, to Adam, he describes how Adam's relationship to work will be greatly marred. Then he speaks over the man and woman the consequences of their decision. Immediately, we see a change in the relationship within humanity's first family. The very next thing Adam does reveals that something is shattered in their relationship.

Adam *names* the woman "Eve."

Her new name meant "mother of the living." In fact, naming the woman becomes the very first thing Adam does after God names their punishment. Immediately. Remember, God never instructed Adam to name Eve. When God created Eve out of the side of Adam, Adam sang a song over her—"this is now bone of my bones and flesh of my flesh." But Adam did not name her at first. She was his partner, his wife, his "suitable helper." Adam had permission to name the animals, but Eve was not an animal. From the beginning, man and woman were to work together, side by side, in the garden, tasked with loving and serving God, each other, and creation. This act of Adam naming Eve initiates, I believe, a perversion of God's desire that Eve would work alongside Adam in loving, mutual harmony to work and care for the garden. In fact, God saw it coming when sin entered the world. When God tells Eve that Adam will "rule over her," he is simply lamenting what is to come. God is not commanding it. His language is descriptive, not prescriptive. Adam naming Eve, putting her in her place, was neither what God ordained nor desired. It is interesting that he names her for what he sees she is good for—having babies.

Sin turns the world upside down. Just as Adam's relationship to the woman is perverted, so is his relationship to his work. God says of Adam's work: "By the sweat of your brow you will eat your food until you return to the ground, since from it you were taken; for dust you are and to dust you will return" (Gen. 3:19). Adam's work—which originally brought life and fruitfulness—now turns to toil. When some Christians read the curse narrative, they wrongly assume that work itself becomes the consequence of sin. As New York University's Daniel Fleming has aptly shown, the phrase "by the sweat of your brow" does not mean that physical labor is cursed. Rather, this was an ancient way of speaking of a new anxiety around work that is the result of fear and accomplishment.[12] Sin, in the words of Sandra Richter, causes work to become about "perspiration-inducing *fear*."[13] Humanity ceases to work as God intended and starts to worry about its work identity.

After the fall, humanity becomes enslaved to work.[14] The very vocation God created to serve the world ceases to be an act of worship to the Creator and becomes about self-fulfillment. Humanity ceases being purpose driven and becomes fear driven. It is interesting that as God judges Adam, he says, "[The ground] will produce thorns and thistles for you, and you will eat the plants of the field" (Gen. 3:18). Notice the word *plants*; the Hebrew word is *eseb*. The word is used for an annual, any plant that must be planted every single year. An annual dies every year. A perennial, however, is any plant that produces year after year without needing to be replanted. I have long theorized that the food God planted in Eden was exclusively food from perennial plants that came back every year—apples, asparagus, oranges, and pomegranates. Notice that Eden had trees. Trees produce food year after year after year. God's provision is visible even in the landscape.

After their exile from Eden, however, humanity relies on annuals for survival. No longer will Adam and Eve reside in the garden that God himself had planted with all of its perennials; they are now forced to raise their own plants that will die each year. Annuals are the landscape of displacement, of a people not at home. The only way one can eat perennials is by being established in a place. The joys of a perennial must be enjoyed in the same place year after year.

Eden was abundant with perennials. This is why Adam and Eve could rest *and eat* on their first day of existence—the work was already done for them. God himself had planted the garden. Can you imagine living in a place free from toil, a garden of perennials, the way Adam and Eve did? In exile from Eden, humanity has been thrust to self-production and subsistence rather than trust and abundance. The annual replanting year after year illustrates a world without rest. Ours has become a world mostly of annuals. Do not be misled: annuals are not bad. But they are not the fullness of God's original design. Perennials and annuals were meant to exist together, but we have an unhealthy reliance on annuals, which is taking a toll. In fact, our heavy reliance on annuals is actually destroying our planet. In his book *Dirt*, David Montgomery describes the reality that we are "skinning our planet."[15] Ecologists would tell us that our methods for cultivating crops, primarily annuals, deplete the earth's soil at a rapid rate. The Levitical commands to let the land rest every seven years were the result of what? Sin. Why? Before exile from Eden, humanity lived off of the perennial foods of the garden and never needed to let the perennials rest. The land only needs to rest when we work it. Again, God gave us a world of delight to work and play in. Only when we ignored his way did he have to give a law to call us back to the original aim.

Have you ever wondered why Jesus wore a crown of thorns at his death? Why thorns? Thorns are *eseb*. At his death, Jesus literally wears on his head the sign of the curse—thorns from annuals. Our curse became his crown. It was as he wore our annual that he brought the perennial grace and love and forgiveness of the Father.

What we learn is that sin changes our relationship with work. In a world of perennials, work was not something that humanity did to falsely find its meaning. Instead, work was done in the context of trust and provision. After sin, work that was originally entered into as an act of worship became the thing we worshiped. I think God knew humanity would sin. And I think God knew we would be prone to worship our work, which is why God initiated rest and Sabbath *before* the fall. In sin, humans are prone to worship the good things of this world over the Ultimate, the Creator. "They exchanged the truth about God for a lie," writes Paul, "and worshiped and served created things rather than the Creator" (Rom. 1:25). We turn *good things* into *ultimate things*. This gives us a helpful theological and biblical framework for understanding *why* we are workaholics. Work is not the problem—it is our replacing God with work that is a problem.

That is why even good work can turn bad. I have a friend who travels the world and speaks on rest and well-being. She is brilliant. Catch the irony: she burned out speaking about rest and well-being. How is it possible for someone to burn out traveling the world teaching on rest? By putting a good thing in the wrong place in our lives.

Nearly ten years ago, as a college pastor at the University of Oregon, I toiled nearly eighty hours a week doing the "work of the Lord." No boundaries. No rhythms. No intention. No rest. Every crisis was *my* crisis. Every complaint was *my* problem. Everything and everyone came to *me*. Anxiety was the norm; fear was my god. The long and short of it: I began to burn out. And I knew there was a problem when I started hoping I would burn out.[16] Burnout offered a way out of all the insanity. Though I had never thought it possible, I was, in Paul's words, beginning to "weary in doing good" (Gal. 6:9). The cost was high. I constantly got sick, my marriage was struggling, and my ministry became misery as I went frantically from crisis to crisis.

Flannery O'Connor has this little throwaway line where she speaks of a priest who is "unimaginative and overworked."[17] That was me. There was only one problem: the ministry was thriving. People were getting baptized. Students were repenting. The group was growing. It all came to a head one Saturday morning. After an eighty-hour workweek, I scheduled an appointment with a student in our college ministry for 10:00 a.m. that Saturday morning. Having not slept well for over a month, I missed my appointment, not even hearing the sound of my alarm. I woke up to a voicemail on my phone: "How could you miss this appointment? Pastors shouldn't miss appointments. You have failed me."

I had become a "quivering mass of availability."[18] A need-filler. A gofer. A Christian handyman, available to everyone and everything but the Lord my God. Standing there, I nearly broke my flip phone over my knee and threw it against the wall. I had been working tirelessly only to let one more person down. I could not go on like I had been. By the sovereign grace of God, I had been reading a book by pastor and theologian Eugene Peterson. Through reading the book, I discovered something I had completely ignored in ten years of Bible reading—this thing called the Sabbath. Peterson eloquently discussed how one day a week he would say no to ministry demands and go on hikes, eat good food, read poetry, and meet with God. I was intrigued. Was this not a waste of time? Was he not wasting his time on selfish endeavors? Then it clicked.

Up until this time, I had thought Sabbath-keeping was selfish. And I thought that if I did rest, it was a sign of weakness. Then I had the epiphany of a lifetime: I had been trying to be self*less*. In helping everyone else, I had forgotten myself. I had become the preacher of the gospel who needed the gospel himself. Or, worse yet, I subconsciously thought God wanted me to forget about myself so I could serve others. But that is not the gospel. Jesus loves me too. I could love others only to the extent that I could recognize God's love for me. I could see to the needs of my community only to the extent that I admitted my own needs. I could care for God's people only to the extent that I would allow him to care for me. In forgetting all this, I had neglected to care for the body God had given me, the spirit he breathed into me, this soul that he molded with his own hand.

Wisdom prevailed. I admitted my limits and embraced my finitude. It was one of the first "not goods" in my life where I recognized I had a deep, human, God-created need. In living for everyone else, I had been trying to be omnipotent and omnipresent, neither of which God desired for me to be. As I read the Gospels, it became clearer and clearer to me that Jesus himself was not selfless. Jesus went into the mountains and prayed to the point that even his disciples could not find him. Jesus ate. Jesus drank. Jesus slept. He took care of himself. And never once was Jesus hurried from place to place, controlled by a busy schedule. Jesus lived a rhythm completely different from anyone around him. The rhythm of his life was, in itself, a prophetic act against the rhythms of the world.

Sabbath rhythms are not meant for paper; they are meant to be practiced. "Holy days, rituals, liturgies—all are like musical notations which, in themselves," one Jewish scholar writes, "cannot convey the nuances and textures of live performance."[19] We are not to know about the Sabbath. We are to know the Sabbath. In the years since starting to practice the Sabbath, my family and I have become avid, albeit imperfect, amateur Sabbath-keepers. One day a week, my family turns all the screens off, lights some candles, prays, and invites the God of Sabbath to bring us rest. This practice, which, again, we do far from perfectly, has saved my marriage, my ministry, my faith, and, I might even say, my life. However, we have come to find that Sabbath never just happens. In our 24/7 world, I have never once seen someone *accidentally* keep a Sabbath. Sabbath is an action of great purpose, one that demands feisty intentionality. It requires us to live in a rhythm that squarely opposes the dangerous pulse and the habits of our world. Sabbath-keeping is not just a small vignette in the Bible. Page after page, story after story, book after book, Sabbath comes to us. This is not a minor motif in the story of the Bible—it is one of the greatest themes of the Bible. Sabbath is not extra credit. It is a commandment, not a suggestion.

Sabbath is God's eternal way of helping us worship our good God and not worship the good work he has given us to do.

The Sabbath, Jacques Ellul contends, "shows that work is not after all so excellent or desirable a thing as people often tell us."[20] In other words, Sabbath provides work with a healthy framework within which good work can be done. The fourth commandment, we must remember, only prohibits us from work on Sabbath. Nothing else is prohibited. This simple act of not working revolutionizes our lives by re-centering our identity on *being* with God rather than on what we *do* for the world. Workaholism, in the end, is the result of our sense of self not fully coming into the light of Christ. Workaholism is very different from alcoholism—for the alcoholic there is no slowly reintegrating alcohol into their life after getting clean. They must go cold turkey; there can only be a clean break. Workaholism is different. For a workaholic, the issue becomes learning to live rightly in relationship to work. A workaholic will most likely have to get back to work. As for my work, studies continue to reveal that pastoral burnout is connected to the pastor's sense of being and worthiness.[21] I became a workaholic chiefly because I had not allowed the grace of Jesus to reside in the depths of the caverns of my soul. I even used to think the Sabbath was a break from ministry. Now I see Sabbath *as* ministry. It frees people. It helps others in the church. It establishes boundaries. And, above all, it proclaims the good news of Jesus. As I read Peterson, one question came back to me over and over again: How can I preach salvation by grace when my life is built on an altar of workaholism?[22]

In our culture, in place of a meaningful relationship with Jesus where we are defined by the Father's love, we will continue to relish our overstuffed, busy lives. Busyness will be our trophy. More often than not, the only way we can truly feel good about our lives is if we are burning out doing it. We want scars to brag about. We have, as Barbara Brown Taylor writes, "made an idol of exhaustion. The only time we know we have done enough is when we're running on empty and when the ones we love most are the ones we see least."[23] It seems this cultural mantra has been treated like a command from God, but God never asked us to work to the point of burnout.

We were not created just to work.

Work is not our Ultimate.

Defining Work, Defining Rest

In teaching, preaching, and writing on the Sabbath, I have observed some generational differences regarding rest. At one point, a baby-boomer pastor confessed his frustration over the Sabbath principle because he perceived millennials as being lazy. His sentiment was that the older generation worked too much and the younger generation worked too little. Certainly this may be true. Indeed, older generations may very well tend to work seven days a week, while younger ones may work only three or four days a week. Each generation has its own neuroses. One may even wonder whether the younger generation does this as a response to overworking in their parental generation. But this raises a critical point: Sabbath rest assumes work. That is, the Bible has a word for Sabbath minus any work: laziness. Likewise, the Bible has a word for work without a Sabbath: slavery. Rest is not truly possible without work, and work is not done appropriately without rest. A balance is required for them to both be what they were created to be.

The weighty sense of *qodesh*, "holiness," implies uniqueness from the other weekdays. Sabbath was set apart from the other days—it embodied a different purpose. Six days of work, one day of rest. That was the cadence. Consider any piece of music. Music is never merely an endless stream of notes played at the same tempo; rather, there are pauses, intentional breaks, and a variety of notes. Even the Psalms have a *selah*—a pause—to the praise of Yahweh. Work without rest is like music with no rhythm, the Psalms minus *selah*, every song with no refrain.

Mark's Gospel illustrates how Jesus embodied a rhythm of both work and rest. In one account, Jesus's disciples return from healing the sick, raising the dead, and preaching the kingdom. Kingdom activity indeed was happening among them. The ministry success was so remarkable that the disciples "did not even have a chance to eat" (Mark 6:31). Mark's portrayal likely hits close to home for many whose work offers but a few paltry minutes to stop for fast food on the way to the next activity. How does Jesus respond to such an insane workload? Jesus sees, and responds, to the disciples' needs: "Come with me by yourselves to a quiet place and get some rest" (Mark 6:31). Jesus does not condemn their hard work. Rather, he honors their hard work, inviting them to rest within it. The flow of discipleship was engagement, ministry, and work, followed by rest, quiet, and solitude. Work and rest are meant to be bedmates. In Matthew's Gospel, in fact, we find that Jesus calls himself both the "Lord of the harvest" (Matt. 9:38) and the "Lord of the Sabbath" (Matt. 12:8). Personally, that reminds me that Jesus is Lord over my work and Jesus is Lord over my rest. He is not Lord over just one. Both are realms of his lordship and my discipleship. Jesus is Lord of rest *and* work.

Still, the transition between work and rest can be daunting. As anyone begins to Sabbath, they will often report on the difficulty in transitioning from days of work to the day of rest. Certainly, Israel knew precisely how challenging this transition was. In Egypt, Israel was enslaved under Pharaoh's rule. Then, after the Passover, they were led to Mount Sinai, where God gave them the Ten Commandments. One commandment was to Sabbath one day a week. One can only imagine how difficult this commandment was to receive for the simple fact that they had been living in a system of slavery for so many years that they had come to objectify themselves. Israel had maybe even come to see themselves merely as their own slavish work. Henri Blocher describes Israel's relationship of work to rest:

> Now what is the meaning of the Sabbath that was given to Israel? It relativizes the works of mankind, the contents of the six working days. It protects mankind from total absorption by the task of subduing the earth, it anticipates the distortion which makes work the sum and purpose of human life, and it informs mankind that he will not fulfill his humanity in his relation to the world which he is transforming but only when he raises his eyes above, in the blessed, holy hour of communion with the Creator. . . . The essence of mankind is not work![24]

The transition from slavery to rest proved nearly impossible for Israel, as it might for us. Their story is our story. In fact, in any Passover Seder meal, it is read, "In every generation—*bachol dour va dour*"; or, "every Jew must feel as if he himself has come out of Egypt." Israel's journey toward the Sabbath is *our* journey to the Sabbath.

By experience I have learned that I rarely enter the Sabbath day with a finished to-do list. In fact, there is no such thing as a finished to-do list for a pastor. Ministry is never done. Nor is anyone's work ever really done on the Sabbath. We rarely rest because the work is done. In fact, it often feels like there is more work at the end of the day. I normally find that I go into my Sabbath with tasks and conversations intentionally set aside for afterward.

For each of us, the Sabbath is such an important rhythm because it dethrones our workaholic tendencies and reminds us that the ultimate work is not that which can go on a to-do list. Rabbi Heschel ponders this very question: "Is it possible for a human being to do all his work in six days? Does not our work always remain incomplete?"[25] The Sabbath reminds us that nothing that is worth doing can be fully achieved in one day. Indeed, our work is always incomplete. By the grace of God, Sabbath is not the result of all the work being done. Mark Buchanan brilliantly touches on this:

> The rest of God—the rest God gladly gives so that we might discover that part of God we're missing—is not a reward for finishing. It's not a bonus for work well done. It's sheer gift. It is a stop-work order in the midst of work that's never complete, never polished. Sabbath is not the break we're allotted at the tail end of completing all our tasks and chores, the fulfillment of all our obligations. It's the rest we take smack-dab in the middle of them, without apology, without guilt, and for no better reason than God told us we could.[26]

If we wait for the work to be completely finished before we can rest, we will never enter rest. The powerful lesson is that God remains at work on the Sabbath—in *us*. Listen to something interesting from the creation story: "Thus the heavens and the earth were finished. . . . And on the seventh day God finished the work that he had done" (Gen. 2:1–2 NRSV). Note, first, that God "works." When humanity works, we are imitating God. Work is not only a human activity—it is also a divine action. But there is a mystery in this story: God "finished" his work on the sixth day and then "finished" it on the seventh. How can God finish something on two different days? Heschel calls this the "puzzle" of the text.[27] Theologian Nathan Stucky unpacks this seemingly confusing passage: "The text suggests that on the seventh day, creation is both finished and unfinished. . . . Creation remains incomplete or unfinished. God finishes creation on the seventh day, not by way of further creative activity but by way of God's own rest and the implied invitation to all creation to participate in God's rest."[28] God had finished his work on day six, yet it was not complete until day seven, when he provided creation with *menukhah*, the rest of God.

The lesson of this paradox is beautiful: work is never actually complete without rest.

Early on, I experienced something extraordinary and unusual in my Sabbath-keeping. When I skipped a Sabbath, my week would go by in the blink of an eye, and I would be far less productive. It seems counterintuitive: the more days I had to work, the less I accomplished. But when I *did* Sabbath, it was as though God stretched my time. I once heard that some Jewish mystics believed that when we take a day of rest, as a gift, God literally stretches our time on the six days we do not work. I don't know exactly how it works, but I can say from experience that it was almost as though God was finishing my work. He was putting the finishing touches on that which I had been doing all week long. It was as though God were multiplying the fish and the loaves of my work. Not only would there be enough—it was like there were leftovers.[29]

I once encountered a story that illustrated this. There is a legend that says that when the Oregon Trail was brimming with prairie schooners, those who kept a Sabbath arrived in the Oregon territory sooner. The ones who did not keep a Sabbath arrived much later.[30] When we entrust our responsibilities to God and rest, God puts his finishing touches on our work.

Sabbath is not God stepping away from creation or from us.[31] Sabbath is God finishing us, fulfilling us. This teaches us a lesson, does it not? Unreflective creativity and impulsive labor is not the work that God honors—that is merely anxious "sweating from the brow." To work and toil and strive and never take a moment to stop and enjoy it all is living under the curse rather than God's promise. Reflective labor, however, is at the heart of God. The ultimate work is the work of God in our lives. Martin Luther writes of Sabbath, "The spiritual rest which God especially intends in this commandment is that we not only cease from our labor and trade but much more—that we let God alone work in us and that in all our powers we do nothing of our own."[32] Sabbath is the day that we rest in God's presence even when our to-do lists are not even close to done. We choose to enter rest even before the work is complete. Why? Sabbath is not a reward for a job well done. Sabbath is the result of a world that is oriented toward a good and generous and loving God.[33]

What is work, and what is rest? This is a very important question to ask. Jesus, of course, kept a Sabbath. Luckily, alongside practicing Sabbath, Jesus taught a great deal about Sabbath. Every generation has certain issues and questions it wrestles with. Perhaps the most controversial conversations in our time are about sexuality and racial injustice. In Jesus's time, however, cultural conversations were often about the Sabbath. Jesus dealt with the popular issues of the first century, refusing to skirt around them. So it should not be surprising how many conversations about the Sabbath Jesus willingly entered: "What is Sabbath?" "What is work?" "What can one do on the Sabbath?" Among the religious classes of his time—particularly the Pharisees and Sadducees—there was great consternation and disagreement over these questions. "Is it lawful to heal on the Sabbath?" they asked at one point (Matt. 12:10). Is one to save a sheep if it falls into a pit on the Sabbath, as Matthew 12:11 suggests? Is picking heads of grain work, or can it be done on the Sabbath day, as Matthew 12:1–8 and Mark 2:23–28 discuss? Conversations around these particular questions were quite heated largely because Sabbath observance was one of the main ways a Jewish person in the first century demonstrated to the world and their community that they were indeed Jewish.

In those days, great attention was devoted to the question of what was work and what was not work. This question is illustrated in what was called *melachah*, or the thirty-nine categories of work, a list the rabbis wrote to spell out what was forbidden on the Sabbath day. The list included the following:

- kneading
- baking
- slaughtering animals
- hammering

- dyeing wool and weaving
- performing strenuous activity
- traveling
- worrying
- earning money
- tying a knot
- plowing
- planting or harvesting
- lighting or extinguishing fire
- cutting fingernails
- writing more than one letter of the alphabet
- boiling eggs
- putting out a lamp
- getting a haircut up to an hour before afternoon prayers before the Sabbath so that if the scissors broke, they would need to be fixed[34]

Many of these were connected to biblical commands. For example, the prohibition against lighting a candle is derived directly from Exodus 35:3. Others, however, were not biblically rooted. Even today there are many Sabbath prohibitions that surpass the biblical commands. In Jerusalem today there are "Sabbath elevators," in which people do not have to stop at floors other than the desired one. Sabbath elevators are not derived from any biblical mandate. This invention came out of a culture that was formed by these lists. These rules may seem extreme to us, yet they articulate how serious this conversation was in the first century.

The same question presses today: What constitutes Sabbath rest, and what constitutes work? Jesus, again, offers us clear teaching on this particular question. In Mark 3:4, Jesus asks a question that summarizes the purpose of the Sabbath: "Which is lawful on the Sabbath: to do good or to do evil, to save life or to kill?" Sabbath is, for Jesus, about doing good and not evil, saving life, not killing. Our family has summed it up like this: Is the activity in question life *giving*, or is it life *taking*? That is, does it bring us life, rest, hope, wholeness? Or does it drain us, pour us out, stress us, or load us down?

Instead of asking "Is this allowed on the Sabbath?" the question we should ask ourselves is "Is this day full of *menukhah*?" Sabbath is a day we are to be free from work, toil, and productive activity. In short, it is a day we are no longer trying to improve the world. John Murray points out that "Sabbath

. . . is not defined in terms of cessation from activity, but cessation from the kind of activity involved in the labours of the other six days."[35] The question is not always what we are doing but what we are ceasing doing. Tilden Edwards adds, "If its intent signifies human power over nature, if it shows human mastery of the world by the purposeful and constructive exercise of intelligence and skill, then it is *meluchah*, work, that violates the restful intent of Sabbath time to recognize our dependence on God as ultimate Creator and Sustainer."[36] The pressing issue is the *purpose* behind the activity. Why is it being done? Yet God is the only one who can discern the hearts of people. Why does God reprimand Sarah alone when both she and Abraham had laughed at God for the promise of a child in old age (Gen. 17:17; 18:12)? Why is Abel's sacrifice acceptable to God and yet Cain's is not? Because God alone knows the purposes of the human heart.

Does this mean that we should refuse to help others on the Sabbath? By no means. Emergencies happen on the Sabbath. This is a particularly important question in pastoral ministry. Emergencies arise in the life of a church. So what are guiding principles for when to help or when not to help?

First, we must recognize that "Sabbath emergencies" will happen. They do to everyone. They did to Jesus. They will to us. And it is important to recognize that the "Sabbath was made for man, not man for the Sabbath" (Mark 2:27). It was on a Sabbath day that my grandfather passed away. Because our phones were off, my mother-in-law had to drive to our house to inform us that he had died. Emergencies do happen on the Sabbath. And we must remember that the Sabbath exists to serve us, not the other way around.

Sabbath is a benevolent servant but a malevolent master. Through properly understanding our relationship to it, we learn to resist legalistically closing ourselves off from acts of compassionate love toward others needing help. The Jewish tradition, in light of this, speaks of the "necessary works" of the Sabbath—being the Sabbath acts of care and compassion toward others.[37] Crises happen on the Sabbath. We will need to attend to them. Jesus, we find, cast out demons and healed the lame on the Sabbath. This has direct import to our lives today. For example, if a storm hits on the Sabbath, is a farmer expected to ignore the needs of his animals? Or should he not care for a crop in bad weather, though his livelihood depends on it? For a pastor, what if someone loses a family member on the Sabbath? Situations like these create a need for discernment. This much is true: Sabbath is no hall pass from responsibility or compassion. We will learn to care for people, animals, and crops in a discerning and sensitive way. The underlying principle is that we are called to be more faithful to Jesus than we are to the rules of the Sabbath. Jesus is the Lord of the Sabbath. Thus we act in obedience both by resting and caring for others. I have often wondered whether, in the parable of the good Samaritan, the Jewish priest passing by the man robbed on the Jericho road was late to some Sabbath engagement. The Sabbath should never be a disengagement from the love of neighbor.

Second, not every disturbance on the Sabbath is a "Sabbath emergency." Our technological society allows us to be reachable at any and all moments of the day. As a result, we are pressured to be perpetually available. What should we do when our phones are in our pockets all the time? In our family, one of us will leave our phone on during the Sabbath in case of an emergency. More often than not, my wife will leave her phone on. She discerns whether an issue that arises is indeed a legitimate emergency or something to which a response can wait. Discerning the difference between a legitimate Sabbath emergency and something that can wait is an art form acquired over time. In my work, two parishioners in a relational spat is not an emergency. An elder needing to talk through a finer point of theology is not an emergency. A conversation about a roommate who needs to do the dishes better is not an emergency. I learned long ago that if I am needed to help resolve everyone else's "emergency," then I am discipling people to be more dependent on me than on God and even on each other. Thus, if I am compelled to respond to every pressing need, I am creating a context in which my parishioners have an unhealthy relationship of dependence on me. The result: I start developing an overinflated sense of my importance. The longer I have kept a Sabbath, the more I have found that *not* answering nonemergency Sabbath issues actually releases people to grow in their dependence on God and on other people in the community. Again, Sabbath *is* ministry. My Sabbath-keeping helps others learn to minister to one another.

Psalm 92, known as the "Psalm of the Sabbath Day," is deeply edifying in this regard. The psalm was written to be read on the Sabbath day and was used in public worship as God's people gathered to praise the God of Sabbath. While reading it, one is struck by the immediate presence of God. The psalm, writes Norman Wirzba, demonstrates a strong "contrast to our current stressful, exhausting, death-wielding ways."[38] It overflows with thankfulness, praise, a strong declaration of the love and mercy of God, rejoicing with songs and with instruments, looking on God's works with joy, and trusting in God's justice. As we think about what to do and not do on the Sabbath, we should be quick to realize that our question should be less about certain activities and more about how we are posturing our hearts. Psalm 92 invites us to bow low and love the God of Sabbath.

What defines work? And rest? Our hearts. Are we entering into trust and love and peace and goodness? Are we being thankful? Can we be still? Sabbath invites us into the freedom of God's love. Hear the psalmist's invitation: "It is good to praise the Lord, and make music to your name, O Most High" (Ps. 92:1).

QUESTIONS
for Reflection

- How might Sabbath be a way of resisting the instinct to worship work?
- Can you identify areas of your own life where work or achievement have served either as a numbing agent or as what provided your identity?
- How might your work be driven by either fear or purpose?
- Why did God give the law of Sabbath rest?
- What do you think about rest being a way to worship God?
- How might admitting your own needs allow you to care for the needs of your community?
- What needs of yours are currently unmet?
- What are the rhythms of your life saying to the world around you? Do they indicate that you serve a God of grace or that you serve at the altar of workaholism?
- Have you experienced a time when God did the seemingly impossible when you entrusted something to him (like God stretching time)?

3

Sabbath and Health

More than the Jews have kept *Shabbat*, *Shabbat* has kept the Jews.

Jewish saying, in Nina Beth Cardin,
The Tapestry of Jewish Time

No

As I define it, a cult exists anywhere people are not permitted to say no.[1] A cult is that place where a yes is assumed or even forced, where individuals are indoctrinated, lost in the crowd, swept along mindlessly to do what their leaders tell them to do. In cult life, people are pulled along from obligation to obligation without reference to thought or conscience, as though they have no choice in the matter. Religious fanaticism is a cult. Secular fundamentalism is a cult. Consumerism is a cult. And some of our relationships, environments, and commitments have become cults. We say yes to these things with little to no permission or freedom to do otherwise.

Sometimes we say yes because we will lose our job if we do not, or we might lose a friendship, or we may be kicked out of our cherished organization. There are many reasons we choose not to say no. We may have what has been called FOMO, a "fear of missing out." With every new picture on social media of everyone else having fun, we wonder, *Why weren't we invited?* Seeing and hearing of stories from afar, of parties down the street, of relationships being built without us, we come face-to-face with the reality that we are not the center of the world, as we once dreamed. And so jealousy rages. How can the world be okay without me at its center? How can everyone seem to be having so much fun without me? Why is my life not as exciting as everyone else's?

Jesus, however, shows us a different way in contrast to so much of our world that forces false forms of obedience. Jesus actually taught his disciples a vocabulary that included both yes and no.[2] Respecting people's inherent dignity, Jesus gave people incredible freedom to walk away from even him: people were free to abandon him, disciples were permitted to turn their backs on him, and apostles were given room to deny him. Yet Jesus desires that we say yes to following him, and as we do, a primary aspect of discipleship is learning how to say yes *and* no to the things of this world. Disciples have boundaries. We are not to say yes to everything. This critical set of skills is often lacking in our day.

No is one of the hardest words for any person to learn—particularly religious people. Often the restrictive and demanding ethos of our world creates a hostile environment where we feel forced to become "yes-people" in our jobs, our relationships, and even at times our churches. Often we feel free to say only yes to please those around us. The devil is most successful, indeed, when he pushes us to feel obliged to be yes-people who have no choice or little ability to say otherwise; he considers his job done when we feel trapped to say only yes to the masses, our closest friends, or even our religious authorities. The pressure can be overwhelming. As a result, we have become a generation of yes-people who feel unable to stand strong in the Spirit, who has already defeated the world and the devil's schemes. But we *are* able.

The Sabbath is God's stand against the tyranny of always having to say yes. The Sabbath is God's gift of a no to us in our obsessive, compulsive patterns of living. The Sabbath is God's solution to FOMO anxieties. On the Sabbath, we are "in" because we are *with* Jesus Christ. God is with us. And the world does not define us. We were never at its center anyway. The Sabbath, it turns out, is mentioned fifty-eight times in the Bible. God repeatedly invites us to say no to the world that we might say yes to God.

Corrie ten Boom once wrote, "If the devil cannot make us bad, he will make us busy."[3] Be they relational, occupational, or church responsibilities, we are each faced with a thousand daily choices about what we will and will not give our time and energy to. Because we often do not take time to establish boundaries, we constantly catch ourselves defaulting to yes. Think of it this way: every yes takes a little space out of our lives. Soon, after a thousand yeses, we find ourselves exhausted and marginless. This commitment creep has happened to every one of us—an open week quickly becomes a hodgepodge of yeses that we gave ourselves to unthinkingly. Before we know it, our calendars are filled with who-knows-what for the purposes of who-knows. And often there are theological reasons for this: the neurotic yes is secretly given because we see human effort as the only way God's kingdom can be built in this world. But God's kingdom can never be built with human hands. We almost always assume that the more we do, the more God is doing. But this kind of control, this kind of effort, this neurosis becomes, in the words of Carl Jung, "a substitute for legitimate suffering."[4] That is, we prefer to say yes to keep everything going smoothly rather than take a stand on the things closest to our hearts in fear that we will be seen for who we really are.

God's rest is always more effective than human work. God rests, and the world is finished. Jesus rests in the tomb, and the world is being restored. The Spirit rests on us, and the church is empowered.

The root sin of busyness is sloth—that laziness of spirit in which the muscles of intention of discernment and boundary have atrophied. In sloth, we refuse to do "what we are created to do as beings made in the image of God and saved by the Cross of Christ."[5] Sloth of spirit is the inability to say no and have boundaries. The Sabbath straightens up our spirits and awakens us from the lull of the eternal yes. Therefore, a no is the language of intention. No one accidentally says no these days. Except for laziness, a no actually comes from a place of self-knowledge, of self-restraint, of self-awareness. For the Christian, a no should be spoken with the discernment of what God has spoken yes over. We must be sensitive to what God has called us to in order to be free to say no to other prospects. We must have ground in our week that is fallow, free from commitments, free of obligations, a place where life can flourish. A no creates healthy margin in our lives. Have you said no to someone today?

Jesus says no often in the Gospels. To many he was a disappointment: to his family, his disciples, his hometown, religious folks, crowds, rulers. Consider, for example, how in Matthew 19:16–30 Jesus instructs a rich young man that he must sell everything and give to the poor. Downtrodden, the man walks away, unwilling to meet the demands of discipleship as laid out by Jesus. The text never suggests that Jesus ran after him begging that he might reconsider his decision. Jesus does not negotiate with the man, compromising on selling only half the possessions instead. He simply lets the man walk away in disappointment. He would not compromise his kingdom for the rich. Others said they would follow Jesus after settling family businesses and burying their dead. Continuing his pattern, Jesus said they were not ready for his kingdom: "Let the dead bury their own dead" (Luke 9:60). For Jesus, discipleship was not a life choice one took *after* checking off everything on one's to-do list. Jesus was primary. The to-do list was always secondary.

Time and again, we see this same principle fleshed out in the Gospels. In Mark 8:11–13, the Pharisees approach Jesus again to ask him for a sign to prove that he is from heaven. Frustrated by their demands for a miracle, Jesus "sigh[s] deeply" and says, "Why does this generation ask for a sign? Truly I tell you, no sign will be given to it." Stepping into a boat, he sails to the other side, never waving his magic miracle wand. In his death, Jesus could have pulled out a grand finale of the spectacular. Onlookers deride him with wagging fingers in judgment: "So! You who are going to destroy the temple and build it in three days, come down from the cross and save yourself!" Their words are as cold and callous today as they were then: "He saved others . . . but he can't save himself!" (Mark 15:29–31). Jesus heard their words. This was the guy who invented the world. He could have ended the suffering. But he did not. He responded to their mocking words with a no. The decision to drink this cup was his. The decision was his and no one else's.

Nobody ever accused Jesus of being a yes-man. Jesus, Tony Horsfall writes, "would never allow himself to be 'bullied' into doing anything."[6] Likewise, the Spirit of Jesus says no. Acts 16 records the instance of Paul approaching Bithynia, a region in modern-day Turkey where the gospel had yet to be proclaimed. The harvest was plentiful. Yet Paul's missionary venture was soon disrupted: "When they came to the border of Mysia, they tried to enter Bithynia, *but the Spirit of Jesus would not allow them to*" (Acts 16:7). Imagine Paul's consternation, even anger. Souls hung in the balance. The door of ministry was wide open. And as he was about to go in, the Spirit said no. Not this time. Not here. Not now.

Being a Sabbath-keeper is basically the art of letting people down at a rate they can handle. There are times we cannot meet the needs of others. There are times we trust God to help others through others. Not every need represents God's will for our lives. How freeing! Sometimes we cannot do everything we desire, even if those desires are good and wholesome. Jesus is Lord—we are not. Paul had to learn that lesson through his Bithynia experience. If this remains true, we are freed from any kind of messiah complex that maintains that we must do something about everything. If Jesus said no, so can we. If the Spirit said no to Paul, the Spirit will probably say the same to us at some point along the way.

The Sabbath teaches us that we are but humans, not superheroes. Recently, a study by the Duke Global Health Institute examined clergy health.[7] It found that one of the greatest contributing factors to a pastor's well-being is when they are seen by themselves and their congregations not merely as pastors but as actual human beings. In other words, if the organization sees the pastor as a utilitarian cog in a system, curating sermons, building the church, filling needs, the pastor is more likely to crumble under the weight. Yet when pastors are seen as real human beings with real human needs, they are given permission to care for themselves and be human. This hits a sensitive nerve for the twenty-first-century church. For, by and large, pastors and leaders are viewed as mere worker bees or Christian celebrities rather than real people with real needs and limitations. Often those in ministry burn out because they presume that their own presence and giftedness is the reason the church is thriving. For that season of time in college ministry when I was working eighty hours a week, things were hopping. People were coming to faith, baptisms were up, small groups were thriving. The subtle notion that took over my mind was that it was all because of me. And the applause kept me going. When things are going well, it is easy to think that things are going well by my own merit.

But that is ministry done out of our own power, not resurrection power. "Sabbath . . . is a little death," Barbara Brown Taylor once said.[8] The truthfulness of these words should ring true in our hearts, for they help us understand a little bit about what the Sabbath is all about. It is resting from striving. Sabbath wakes us out of solely existing to accomplish and compete. The life of Jesus, it turns out, brings full circle the Sabbath rest of God in creation. God rested on the seventh day when he created the world. Likewise, Jesus, as he re-created the world through his death and resurrection, rested on the seventh day—Holy Saturday. There, in a holy, borrowed grave, Jesus rested as his Father did at creation. Sabbath is, indeed, a little death, a secret station of the cross forgotten by culture and the church. It helps us embrace our finitude, humanness, and vulnerability.

God made the world with rhythms. There is a rhythm to the days of the creation story. There is a rhythm to God's response to creation—God said . . . it was good.[9] There are seasons. There is the coming and going of the ocean's waves. The leaves turn. These are creations of a brilliant God. Obeying God's rhythms of rest for our lives brings life not only to our spirits but also to our minds, bodies, and emotions. We submit to those rhythms of the One who knows us better than we know ourselves. "Only he who obeys a rhythm superior to his own is free," writes Nikos Kazantzakis.[10] The Spirit is, in the words of Jesus, life giving.[11] As the Lord healed on the Sabbath in the Gospels, the gospel frees us to be healed by the Lord of the Sabbath. Sabbath brings about a new rhythm that is largely out of sync with the rhythms all around us. That is a good thing. The life of a Christian is not to be conformed to the patterns and timelines of the world.

Sabbath as Shalom

When we keep a Sabbath, our entire existence begins to experience ripple effects of rest. We sleep better. We are more awake to the people we are with. We have more energy. We pay closer attention to being people of gratitude. In other words, we enter into peace. In a way, the Sabbath has a kind of healing effect within our lives. Imagine what it would be like if the norm of our lives was that we got the rest we needed. Imagine that. But that is rarely the case, as Henri Nouwen once suggested: "We aren't rest-filled people who occasionally become restless. We are restless people who sometimes find rest." The status quo of our lives is that we live in a Sabbath deficit. The result is that we sleep less, we are less interested in what other people have to say, and we have less gratitude. What if there is a direct connection between a Sabbath day and the biblical notion of peace?

Creation was made to be at shalom, "peace." Eden was created in a state of shalom as a world free of war, murder, cancer, and strife. In that place, the land, the critters, the plants, and the humans existed at peace with God and each other. Cornelius Plantinga offers a helpful definition: "The webbing together of God, humans, and all creation in justice, fulfillment, and delight is what the Hebrew prophets call *shalom*. We call it peace, but it means far more than mere peace of mind or a cease-fire between enemies. In the Bible, shalom means *universal flourishing, wholeness and delight*—a rich state of affairs in which natural needs are satisfied and natural gifts fruitfully employed, a state of affairs that inspires joyful wonder as its Creator and Savior opens doors and welcomes the creatures in whom he delights."[12] That shalom, however, was destroyed by human sinfulness and dominance over creation. Estimations are that a species goes extinct every hour.[13] Creation, in Paul's grieving language, is "groaning" under the weight of our disobedience and dominance (Rom. 8:22). A world under the rule of the "prince of the world" is marred by death, destruction, and chaos. Yet a world under God's care is marked by shalom. Part of the shalom of creation was the day of rest that God instigated in the first week. While we must come to see that a weekly Sabbath has a personal benefit to us as individuals, we must also see that the Sabbath helps to usher in that same peace that was shattered by the dark power of sin. In short, Sabbath is a glimmer of Eden's shalom in our world marred by chaos.

Shalom is holistic and is meant for all of God's creation. God desires shalom of the body, of the soul, of the spirit, of the mind, of the land. A holistic view of shalom of this kind, however, is often found more in non-Western contexts, writes Gary Badcock. He contends that African Christianity is more likely to see the peace of God in terms of the wholeness of a person, a community, and a nation rather than dichotomized or individualized peace.[14] Sadly, Western culture often celebrates shalom even if it comes at the expense of others or creation. We must be careful, however, not to view shalom in merely personal, individualistic terms. The implications of shalom are far wider. That is, the peace of God is not just for our bodies, souls, and spirits alone. God desires shalom for everyone and everything. Randy Woodley, a theologian specializing in contextualizing the gospel among First Nations people, reminds us that shalom should be personal *and* systemic.[15] Shalom is for the individual and for the whole world.

But once the world becomes a place with little to no shalom, the Sabbath is no longer one of the central elements of its society. In one of my earlier books, I discuss the ancient Jewish principle called *tikkun olam*—the restoration of the world. This idea is first found in the classic rabbinical teachings known as the Mishnah (ca. 220 CE) referring to legal protection for the disadvantaged, such as women in divorce proceedings or slaves seeking freedom. Later, medieval Jewish mysticism connected *tikkun olam* to a story about earth's origins. In the beginning, there was only darkness. Out of God's love, the world emerged as a great ray of light, which was gathered and held in large vessels created for that very purpose. But the light was so vast that the vessels broke into shards, and the wholeness of the world was scattered into a thousand fragments of light, lodged in people and events. According to the story, we are each born with the capacity to find the hidden light, to lift it up, and in doing so to restore wholeness to the world. And so *tikkun olam* has come to mean "repairing of the world." It is God restoring the brokenness of a design that has been shattered and finds itself without peace—that is, without shalom. *Tikkun olam* is God restoring our shattered bodies, minds, communities, and ecosystems through our letting go of our own mastery over the world and entering into the mystery of God.[16]

Sabbath is part of the "repairing of the world" God is ushering in. This does not mean that if Sabbath were done by everyone, the world would be left sinless. The Sabbath, writes Robert Ellis, "is not a final leap forward to *shalom*." In other words, the Sabbath does not complete the task; it steps and inches toward God's project of shalom in this world.[17] But we so quickly forget the Sabbath's healing power. It is not uncommon in pastoral ministry to talk to people about their exhaustion. When the topic arises, I love using it as an opportunity to discuss the biblical invitation to rest. Often a person will ask for prayer to get rest. Quite frankly, I often feel tempted to refuse to pray for them. The fact that one is exhausted when overworking eighty hours a week and never keeping a Sabbath is not a prayer issue; it is an obedience issue. We should not pray for God to do what *we* are supposed to do. The problem remains that we are not entering into the thing, Sabbath, that very well could begin to repair our lives. Similarly, Joel Salatin, a Christian pig farmer, writes that when people ask for prayer to be made healthy but do not live in a healthy way and eat healthy food, God will not acquiesce to our petitions. In short, "we're ingesting things that are an abomination to our bodies . . . and then requesting prayer for the ailments that result."[18] God is not likely to answer in prayer what you are unwilling to repent of.

Why do we pray for rest when we have the answer to prayer in the practice of the Sabbath? Exhaustion is real. We all get exhausted. Exhaustion is even a common experience for biblical characters. Elijah walks in triumph on Mount Carmel only to be lonely, tired, depressed, and exhausted (1 Kings 19:3–9). Gideon, likewise, pursues his enemies and grows exhausted (Judg. 8:4). David, after Shimei's abusive rancor, arrives at his destination exhausted (2 Sam. 16:13–14). And Daniel gives into exhaustion and gets ill (Dan. 8:27).[19] It is possible to be close to God and yet experience exhaustion. Sometimes the pursuit of God is an exhausting enterprise. Which is why recovery often requires much more than a prayer for rest. We pray for healing rest without being willing to allow God's disruption of our overworked schedules. But can that really work? Who expects to lose weight without changing their diet? Or desires to run a marathon without training? Praying for rest without going through the effort of learning how to Sabbath is as difficult a prayer to answer as any. Could God do it? Yes. But I suspect that we do not need to pray about our exhaustion—we need to learn how to rest. We need to act on taking a Sabbath.

When we do, Sabbath rest begins a process of God repairing our broken bodies. Nearly half of all US adults—117 million people—have one or more chronic health conditions.[20] As a result, countless Americans are looking for resources, drugs, and devices to cope with their conditions. In some cases, our anesthetizing behaviors, as we might call them, put off the pain of the way we are living for a time. But these coping methods often mediate the long-term effects of the ways we live. Again, like gravity, if we choose to never rest, we can expect there will be consequences in our health.

This is why, throughout Jewish and Christian history, the Sabbath has been conceived as a day for miracles and healing. In Exodus 16:17–18, for example, the Israelites experience the manna miracle on the Sabbath day. We see the connection between Sabbath and shalom in the Gospels when Jesus heals a man on the Sabbath. Jesus asks, "Why are you angry with me for healing a man's whole body on the Sabbath?" (John 7:23). Sabbath is about wholeness. Those in the temple courts might have forgotten this, but Jesus certainly had not.

While we need to be cautious of observing the Sabbath in mere pragmatic terms, there remain real practical and pragmatic effects from the Sabbath.

Although our minds and emotions may not discern it at the time, when we take a day of Sabbath rest, changes are beginning to take place deep inside us that may be indiscernible—we *are* being renewed, rejuvenated, remade in the shalom that Christ brings. We must trust that this is taking place even though these changes may not be immediately perceptible. In the same way, when it comes to exercise, a personal trainer tells us what to do, not what physiological processes are taking place in our bodies. We must trust that our personal trainer knows what is happening below the surface.

Jesus seemed to believe the Sabbath to be an ideal day to heal and restore broken people. Jesus healed a man with a withered hand (Matt. 12:10–13; Mark 3:1–5; Luke 6:6–10), cast out an unclean spirit (Mark 1:21–26; Luke 4:31–35), healed the sick (Mark 6:2–5), healed a man with dropsy (Luke 14:1–6), healed a man who was ill for thirty-eight years (John 5:5–9), and healed a man born blind (John 9:14). He did all this on the Sabbath. Jesus's healing ministry on the Sabbath was both physical and spiritual—again, Jesus healed the "whole man." Likewise for us, Sabbath healing is spiritual, physical, emotional, social, and psychological. Sabbath ushers in the shalom of God that we all so desperately long for. Interestingly, Seventh-day Adventists are not allowed to work on the Sabbath unless one is a doctor, nurse, or in the health profession. The idea is that these occupations are Sabbath worthy because they are primarily about healing. Sabbath, for sure, is a day of great healing in which the Great Physician's best works are on display.

Norman Wirzba directly connects Jesus's Sabbath miracles to God making a world of shalom: "It becomes all the more significant for us to recall that Jesus performed many of his miracles on the Sabbath. . . . Was it simply to irritate the religious leaders of the day? A better explanation is to see the miracles as specific people—creation in miniature—being set right to be what God intends. In the miracles of healing, feeding, restoration, exorcism, and raising from the dead, Jesus is revealing creation's purpose and bringing it to completion."[21]

Do you find yourself resisting the Sabbath? You very well may. I certainly did. At their core, most Western people are deeply pragmatic. We will do something if it is practical and the result happens immediately. We rarely do things simply *because* God has invited us to do them. But the Sabbath is one of those things that we must enter into in obedience and the results of which will come down the road. We do not Sabbath in the same way that we start an exercise program; we Sabbath because the living God has invited us to. Indeed, the things of God are often found to be very difficult. The Sabbath *is* disruptive. It may seem unnatural. But would God ask us to do something that was impossible? As Gregory of Nyssa once wrote, "Would the Lord really command us to do something that is beyond our nature and issue a commandment whose enormity oversteps our human capacity? That is not possible. He would not order naturally wingless creatures to become birds, or creatures fitted for life on dry land to live under water."[22] God made us to work *and* rest.

Mental Sabbath: Rest for the Mind

If Sabbath is about entering God's shalom, should we not assume it has concrete effects on our minds? A few years ago, after a long and daunting season of spiritual wandering, a young man came to faith in our church. His conversion experience—similar to what I have seen in others—had a drastic effect on his entire life, including his mind. He explained how for the first time in his adult life he was feeling a sense of guilt and conviction over an addiction he struggled with. His regenerated spirit and mind no longer felt comfortable living in the same habits and patterns he had been. He soon began to *think* differently about the world, family, friends, and his moral responsibilities. He described how new life in Christ had birthed within him a renewed mind and conscience. That which he used to do unthinkingly no longer went unchallenged by his renewed, awakened conscience. Oddly enough, he began to sleep better. For the first time in his young life, he could put his head on his pillow unconcerned about some great abyss of nothingness or the incessant anxiety that had ruled him in the past—fears of a malevolent God who was eternally upset with him. He was finally at peace with God. There was literally nothing more powerful for his mind than being able to lay his head down at night knowing that the God of the universe loved him infinitely.

This illustrates the power faith has to affect one's psychological well-being. Just as salvation changes our minds, entering the Sabbath changes our minds. On the Sabbath, God's transcending peace reigns within our minds in a fresh way. In his gripping novel *Salvation*, Sholem Asch describes what he calls his two mothers: the weekday mother, whom he knew on the six days of work, and his *other* mother, the Sabbath mother. Asch cannot help but identify the effects of the Sabbath on his mother—it was as if she were two different people.[23] The Sabbath self is a different self. We become transformed from the weekday person to the Sabbath person with a seemingly new mindset. Anybody who has ever entered the Sabbath realizes that we were made to experience this rest. Again, there is a strong connection between Sabbath-keeping and psychological shalom.

A significant body of research suggests that even thinking about work is a stressful, anxiety-inducing activity.[24] The problem is that when we think about work, it becomes work in and of itself.[25] When we keep a Sabbath, it reorients the way that we think. Instead of thinking in terms of production, the day becomes about presence. Sabbath is not just ceasing from work, but ceasing to think about work.

Whenever I preach, I have an interesting sensation: my body gets tense, my hands sweat, and I lose any sense of hunger. Then, after preaching, I crave food and get incredibly tired. These are signs of an adrenaline letdown or even an adrenaline addiction. I have been preaching for so long now that my body is so used to the rush of adrenaline that when I take a month off from preaching in the summer (a practice I do each year), every Sunday at the same time my body goes through all the same symptoms, as though I were actually preaching.

In many ways, adrenaline gives us a kind of high. Over time, an addiction to adrenaline can have devastating effects on our well-being. Addiction to adrenaline can even create what is called *anhedonia*, the inability to feel pleasure. Anhedonia is what Archibald Hart has come to describe as no longer having anything in your life that "moves your heart." This comes from becoming addicted to forms of pleasure that are abnormal, or is the result of the purposes of God's good creation being usurped. Hart describes perfectly what happens to pastors over time who are addicted to adrenaline: "When [pastors] are young, just starting out on their calling and fresh from seminary, they could take great joy in what they were able to do for God. Every day was a thrilling adventure. But with time . . . something changed. Pleasure was lost. As one pastor said to me recently, 'I no longer feel any pleasure in my work as a pastor. I don't enjoy my wife and family. And the other night, it dawned on me that I don't even find any pleasure in God anymore.' An honest comment—but indicative of how widespread anhedonia has become."[26]

And the letdown can be dangerous. For me, the desire for sin and the proclivity for temptation seem to be greatly heightened on Sunday evenings after preaching. Many of my preacher friends experience the same thing. This is what many Catholic theologians have for years called a "near occasion of sin," a moment that we are particularly susceptible to temptations. This temptation may come in many forms for a preacher: an increased desire to view pornography, drink heavily, eat bad food, or go into an emotional coma. Whatever it may be, for many pastors Sunday evening can be the darkest night of the week.

This rush of adrenaline, or high, taxes our bodies. In fact, it is true that more people have heart attacks on Monday morning than any other day of the week.[27] Coming back to work, people's bodies are jolted back to adrenaline highs. In many cases, we are adrenaline addicts; we yearn for stimulation to bring about an emotional and psychological high.

The Sabbath gives our minds a chance to be at rest. While not everyone can do this, every Monday I go and sit at a Catholic monastery. I just sit there. I listen. I shut up. I am silent. At times the silence kills me. At times it liberates me. But in the time I've been doing this, one thing has changed. In the same way that my body knows when I am going to be preaching, it has come to know that the day after will be a day of rest and silence. This phenomenon is something mental health practitioners call "anticipatory brain"—when one's brain anticipates something because it has been trained to prepare for it. The psychological difference is astounding. My brain, body, and spirit have come to trust that a day of rest is coming. God gave us brains and minds to use to his glory. But to never give our minds a day to rest will have long-term implications.

The simple act of remembering the Sabbath changes our minds. We are often depressed because we do not give our minds, bodies, and spirits a day of rest to look forward to. Simply thinking about the Sabbath brings hope. Dreaming about it. Looking forward to it. Life is so much better when we know that we have a break coming up. I recall C. S. Lewis's depiction of the Hrossa in *Out of the Silent Planet*. The Hrossa love only one mate—no more. The central character, the human named Ransom, finds this strange, but he comes to the conclusion that the promiscuity of his race is what is strange. For the Hrossa, love is not the act alone but also the memory of the act. "A pleasure is full grown only when it is remembered. You are speaking, [human], as if the pleasure were one thing and the memory another. It is all one thing."[28] There is profound joy in the act of remembering the Sabbath.

As an experiment, sit with a child whom you know and recall a special time that you had with them. Watch as their face lights up with joy as they remember the experience. Thinking of the Sabbath, orienting our lives toward the Sabbath, is not worthless. Memory of the Sabbath is conditioning our anticipatory brain. The mind needs to know that there is a respite coming up, or we might just give up.

Why are we so tired? Unless we work in a rural context, more often than not our work is not of physical nature. Today, fewer and fewer people work the land as farmers. We no longer spend much time growing and gathering and preparing food. And because of it, our work has largely turned toward intellectual, artistic, city pursuits. How could we be so tired? Because our work is different. So much of our work is *mind work*. Most of our tiredness is mental exhaustion. Our brains need a Sabbath, especially from a content-driven culture in which we are bombarded with more ideas and information than at any other time in human history. Because of this, we are drowning in a deluge of information yet craving the cool waters of transformation. The words of Abraham Heschel ring true: "The higher goal of spiritual living is not to amass a wealth of information, but to face sacred moments."[29]

How important this is for writers, thinkers, teachers, and people who work with ideas all their life. As a theologian, to Sabbath is to *not* do theological inquiry that I have been doing all week long. I must put aside trying to acquire knowledge about God and simply learn to be with him. I should think of him, but not for the purpose of producing something. I may reflect but not construct. If I cannot reflect on God without having to produce or achieve, then something is very wrong. John Webster, a theologian, once reflected that "in regenerate theological activity, intellectual greed is replaced by hunger for divine instruction."[30] That is, theology is done improperly when it is to collect content rather than to be transformed. Christianity is not about information hoarding. It is about a community transformed into the image of Christ.

The silence of the Sabbath allows our mind time to kick up its feet and rest. Such a move may seem contrary to our idolatry of distraction. But in that silence we will find a kind of freedom that gives us space to apply our minds to the goodness and glories of the living God.

Physical Sabbath: Rest for the Body

Does the Sabbath relate to our bodies' well-being? Indeed it does. We must begin by recognizing that the role that the body plays for modern people is somewhat different from in previous generations. Part of this relates to the fact that technology has altered our relationship to time. I recall reading somewhere that in the ancient world, the average person spent something like 90 percent of their time producing food—growing, reaping, and cooking. For the vast majority of ancient society, life revolved around activities pertaining to food for purposes of survival. Today, with most of the world's population living in urban contexts, people are paid to do agriculture for them. As a result, many find themselves with more surplus time than at any point in history to do things other than hunting, gathering, and farming.

There are negatives that come with our sedentary lifestyles, particularly among younger people. With surplus time, we have almost become paralyzed by the amount of options life presents us. As the cliché goes: the young millennial stands terrorized in the cereal aisle for twenty minutes making a decision. This is why no one RSVPs for anything anymore. With mobility and accessibility, the world has grown smaller, and life's options have proliferated. I often wonder if this is why millennials have such angst, spending time and energy postponing career and relational choices in order to find the "perfect one" or the "perfect career" or even the "perfect church." We seem almost terrorized by the options of what we can do with our time. Again, most humans used to wake up, go work in the field, eat, and love their spouse—*whoever* they were. Often one could not even choose a spouse. Choice and individualism were a pipe dream.

This shift toward sedentary, self-selected living changed the way humans relate to their bodies. Ask yourself: How much of your day today consisted (or will consist) of growing, harvesting, or producing food? Yes, we buy it—but someone else did the labor. My best guess is somewhere around 3 to 5 percent of my life is given to food procurement. I doubt I'm alone. Work for me is sitting at a desk writing, grading papers, preparing a sermon, and meeting for coffee. It used to be that humans would spend their days working and sweating in the field and working and sweating to take care of their little homes. And this shift is changing the way we relate to each other. Urbanization, modernization, and the division of labor have caused divorce rates to skyrocket in the modern world.[31] My theory: when a person works the fields all day long, they do not have the energy for an affair. Physical life is exhausting life. Has all of this surplus time created space for us to do not-so-good things? I think in many ways it has. Not that we have surplus energy. The great irony is that we seem to be more tired than ever. It just so happens that the kind of exhaustion most feel today is not of a physical type but of an emotional and psychological type.

While we may not endure the same physical exhaustion people in the past did, our bodies still need rest—whatever rest that may be. Scientists remind us that the human body is limited and finite. Juan-Carlos Lerman, a researcher at the University of Arizona, examined the relationship between our physical work and rest. What Lerman's scientific research demonstrated was that the average human being needs *one day* of rest per seven days to function properly. Lerman's research is summarized by Marva Dawn: "According to Lerman's theory, failing to rest after six days of steady work will lead to insomnia or sleepiness, hormonal imbalances, fatigue, irritability, organ stress, and other increasingly serious physical and mental symptoms."[32] What we have here is a fascinating harmony between the biblical and scientific witness. This research illuminates a seemingly direct relationship between human well-being and the need for physical rest. In fact, when a person does not rest properly, their blood pressure will escalate to unhealthy levels.[33] In study after study, anecdote after anecdote, what is revealed is that without rest, humans cannot function as we were created to. We are finite, limited people.

The world's healthiest religious group is arguably the Seventh-day Adventists. This is due, in large part, to restrictions on consuming meat and alcohol, alongside a religious commitment to regular exercise. But most critical is their abiding pledge to a weekly Sabbath. While the Adventist approach toward Sabbath leans toward rigidity (Sabbath can *only* be Saturday), there remain clear indicators that their Sabbath practice offers remarkable health benefits.

Many religions practice some kind of day of rest. Among those, 72 percent of Jewish congregations reported a high emphasis on Sabbath-keeping, and 87 percent of Muslim communities reported the same thing.[34] Among Christians, however, there remains a great diversity around Sabbath observance: liberal Protestants had the lowest emphasis on Sabbath-keeping practices (24 percent); next were moderate Protestants (36 percent) and evangelicals (49 percent); and Catholic and Orthodox Christians had the highest percentage among Christians (84 percent).[35]

The difference is simple: the Seventh-day Adventists actually take a Sabbath. Consider the averages: a Seventh-day Adventist will live ten years longer than North American life expectancy.[36] Ten years! Perhaps obeying God is not a motivating factor for some, but living longer definitely is. At a time when Americans—for the first time since the 1980s—are living shorter lives, this stands out as a statistical anomaly. There is a direct, scientifically based connection between Sabbath-keeping and longer life expectancy. There is no health benefit from merely thinking or talking about Sabbath; the only benefit is in *doing* the Sabbath.[37]

Do not forget that physical rest is only one form of rest. Sabbath is about holistic healthy living, not just sleep or rest. God desires us to have spiritual, physical, mental, social, and emotional health. One can get all the physical sleep and rest one needs yet still be deeply drained spiritually. Or vice versa. That may mean that on the Sabbath day you need exercise. Again, in my own work of pastoral care, sweat is not a normal part of my job. If my heart rate goes up, it is the result of stress and anxiety. I do a lot of sitting, talking, listening, reading, and writing. Because a majority of my job is deskbound, I find that on the Sabbath day I need rest from my sedentary work by entering into some kind of physical activity. This may include spending time in the garden or playing basketball. I remember spending one Sabbath day picking up piles of wood that lay around our house. Such an activity, I agree, may seem ironic given the Old Testament admonition against picking up sticks on the Sabbath day. But that, for me, was the most restful thing I could do that day.

The principle is this: the Sabbath is opposite day. By that, I mean that it is wise to aim our Sabbath activities around what we do not ordinarily do for work. Maybe you will need to pick up sticks on the Sabbath. Maybe you work the land and need a day to sit and read. For those whose work is physically demanding, the Sabbath may be most restful when it does not include physical activity. For others whose work is more sedentary or mental, perhaps physical activity is what is needed. The Sabbath offers us a counterrhythm to whatever we have been doing for the workdays.

Emotional Sabbath: Rest from Burdens

One might wonder, isn't the Sabbath just religious escapism from the responsibilities and troubles of this world? An atheist friend once described his biggest frustration with Christians: because they think about heaven as much as they do, they have become essentially useless on earth. My friend, in many respects, is accurate. I do not disagree with him. Too often, Christians are "heavenly minded and no earthly good." Does this mean we stop thinking and hoping for heaven? Of course not. Rather, we must begin to critique any notion of heaven that is used as a distraction from the pain and difficulty of the world God has placed us in. Think about heaven—just make sure it makes you earthly good. It is certainly easy to think of heaven as a kind of escape from dealing with the realities of the world "below." But that is not what heaven is for. So while we may continue singing "I'll Fly Away," we must be careful not to make that our church vision statement.

Heaven is *why* we remain to serve the world around us. Heaven is not escapism. Neither is the Sabbath. Sabbath, if one desired, could easily be utilized as an escape hatch from reality. But it is not an escape from the chaos of our lives; rather, it is finding God in the chaos. The Sabbath is not a clever way to escape responsibility. It is not letting the world spin out of control into the oblivion of chaos. It is, however, taking a day to cease our work of trying to fix or control the world. We cannot "save" the world. To enjoy the Sabbath is to free ourselves from the temptation of total control over the world. To Sabbath is to crucify our desires for control over the world.

And so there is an emotional component to Sabbath rest. There are many kinds of stresses. There is good stress, which we call *eustress*, and bad stress, which we call *distress*. For example, a divorce is distress, while a marriage is eustress. A house fire causes distress, while renovating a home is eustress. One is a stress that builds up, and another is a stress that tears down. Both require energy and are taxing emotionally, mentally, and physically. Good stress is the kind of stress that is brought on by running a mile or doing a puzzle or working out an intellectual problem. Distress is the kind of stress that comes from our implicit belief that the future of the world depends on us saving it. Distress can be caused by thinking that if we were not here, continuing to work, fix, defend, mend, or maintain, the world would not continue. These kind of stresses do not build us up; they tear us down emotionally.

On the Sabbath, when you are no longer attending to the system of the world, you find that it keeps going on without you. There is a beautiful Christian tradition started early in the church that has often been called "holy indifference." One might call it "anointed irresponsibility." The Sabbath is an act of obedience to God to give up, for one day, carrying the burdens of the world and simply letting things be the way they are. When we enter the Sabbath, we become humbled by the fact that God cares far more for the broken world than we do. His lordship and care for the world do not cease when we choose to take a day to rest. We cannot help the world the way we are supposed to without moments of respite and holy indifference, when we turn our attention and compassion to the living God.

Because we do not often have any buffer against the distress of trying to care for the whole world, we quickly slip into compulsivity. Compulsivity is what happens when our impulses and actions become one—when there is no discernment about what we should or should not act on. Compulsivity is looking at the news two hundred times a day, sending texts with every thought, and getting work done whenever and wherever we are. But the Sabbath puts an end to that emotional crisis of compulsivity by protecting us from being enslaved to our instincts and impulses. If we had our way, we would continue to just do whatever we feel, "driven by every gust of enthusiasm," to borrow from Lesslie Newbigin.[38] The Sabbath is a boycott against human compulsivity.

Sabbath-keeping allows us to take a recess from emotional burdens by placing them into the hands of God, who desires to and is capable to care much more than we ever could. To Sabbath is to put into context the things that we think are important and to remember that they are not ultimate. God is ultimate. Our emotional burdens are not. When presented with an emotional burden on the Sabbath, I ask, *Can I put off caring about this issue for one day? Or does it require that I care today?* When a friend had a heart attack on the Sabbath, I could not put off caring for another day. However, when a parishioner has an issue with last week's sermon, I can postpone that emotional burden until the day after the Sabbath. This allows me, for one day a week, to not carry the emotional burdens that I carry the other six days. On the Sabbath, our irresponsibility to the whole world becomes anointed. We are returning to God the responsibilities that he has given us to hold for a time, and we are returning to God, whom our ultimate responsibility is toward.

Jesus cared. He cared deeply. And we should care too. Because of the news streams, social media, and constant communication, we are privy to the world's suffering at a moment's notice. We know much more information on a global scale than would have been possible to know a hundred years ago. That I can wake up to BBC news alerts on my phone letting me know that a plane went down, or that when we get in the car the first thing we hear on the radio is about a bomb going off in some remote country, is rather unnatural. News delivery in this age is unlike the way it used to spread more organically from person to person, or by a news story being printed and shared on a piece of paper of very limited size. The way we now receive news leads to "compassion fatigue," a real onset of exhaustion from the concerns of the world. Studies show how the flooding of news actually harms our ability to have real compassion and do something helpful.[39] We either end up hearing it all and become gripped with emotion and paralyzed by the weight of it, or we become numb so that we can just cope and carry on with our day-to-day activities.

We cannot carry all the cares of the world. "Come to me," Jesus said, "all you who are *weary* and *burdened*, and I will give you rest" (Matt. 11:28). We are a weary and burdened people, dragged down into owning the full weight of the world, trying to carry more than we can. It is easy, as Paul said, to "become weary in doing good" (Gal. 6:9). Doing good can drive us to exhaustion. And in order to sustainably continue doing the good that God desires, we must care for ourselves. William Wilberforce devoted incredible time and energy to put legislation through the British Parliament to end the evil practice of the slave trade—all out of faithfulness to follow Jesus. The good he did was so important its effects can still be felt today. Yet in all of Wilberforce's doing good, he still kept a regular Sabbath. He said, on that day, "ambition is stunted."[40] Had he not kept a Sabbath, one can only wonder whether he would have burned out before slave trade was made illegal in Britain. Sabbath gives us the rest we need to do the good Jesus calls us to do.

While escapism may seem bad, temporary escapism allows us to do our work better and more intentionally. Author J. R. R. Tolkien was accused of escapism by some of his critics. Tolkien responded in a prophetic tone, "Why should a man be scorned if, finding himself in prison, he tries to get out and go home? Or if, when he cannot do so, he thinks and talks about other topics than jailers and prison walls?"[41] One would never argue that slaves escaping are merely avoiding reality or living in some kind of false reality. In escaping, a slave becomes freed so that he or she might free others. Escapism is not altogether bad; it depends on what is being escaped. Sabbath is escapism from emotional slavery to our world, but it is not escapism from caring for the world.[42]

Sabbath is good escapism. It offers us a much-needed respite before being sent back to the world where we love God and serve others. There remains a long-standing Jewish tradition that strongly prohibits mourning on the Sabbath.[43] While there may be times to cry and mourn on a Sabbath, this prohibition puts into effect an allowance of time to lay down my heavy emotional burdens for a day. The rule is not arbitrary; its purpose is to guard us from carrying the world's weight on the Sabbath.

QUESTIONS
for Reflection

- Identify situations, environments, and relationships where you do not feel free to say no.
- How might saying yes indiscriminately be a way of avoiding taking a stand on what is actually close to your heart?
- What areas of your life are you confident God has spoken "yes" over?
- How might rhythms of rest bring life to your spirit, mind, body, and emotions?
- How might you be able to partner with God in bringing about the answer to your own prayer for rest?
- Can you recognize a time, either of success or failure, when you felt as though the result had depended entirely on you?
- Do you see areas of your own life where your habits may be what is preventing God's answer to prayer?
- Have you ever wearied of doing good?

PART 2

SABBATH
FOR OTHERS

4

Sabbath and Relationships

Our madly rushing, neurotic society needs the therapy of the silence and quietness that flows from a day kept holy, really holy. A day when our thoughts are of God, our actions are tempered by a desire to serve God and our families, a day that is so different from other days that it could make us different in our relationship to God and to our fellow men.

Ernest R. Palen, in Herbert E. Saunders, *The Sabbath*

Sabbath Community

Jerusalem can get a little crazy on a Friday night.

My friend Annalisa tells of her journey through the Holy Land during college. Her journey's final day happened to be a Friday in Jerusalem. Already busy with the hum of hustle and bustle, Jerusalem picks up to an even more frantic pace as Friday's sun begins to descend behind the breathtaking skyline. Hurry overtakes Jerusalem, she recounts. Cars zoom by faster than ever. Buses start moving before new passengers have a chance to sit down. Pedestrian paces pick up dramatically. All of a sudden, Jerusalem is in a flurry. Conservative Jewish men can be seen running so fast that their tightly wound Orthodox curls dropping from their temples flow far behind their heads as they race to home sweet home just in time for the sun to disappear into the night.

Why? What provokes the Jerusalem rush?

Of course, this very scene has been playing itself out for centuries every Friday night in the ancient city of Jerusalem. A Jerusalem before sundown is a city buzzing in anticipation for the weekly celebration—the Jewish Sabbath that begins as soon as Friday's sun descends. The sun's setting inaugurates a day of rest and joy and hope when an entire city once again finds itself wrapped in the arms of a God at rest. Week in, week out, for centuries, the city has made its way home once again to the sacred day of rest to rejoin God, synagogue, and family in celebration. Jerusalem is making its way home to light some candles, take its sigh of relief, and party with wine and laughter and the sweet taste of challah like it's the dawn of creation all over again.

The ancient Jewish rabbis have always seen the Sabbath as a kind of home-coming.[1] Sabbath is that perfectly timed day each week wherein God's people—prone to wander from the Lord their God—are once again welcomed back into the loving, eternal embrace of their Creator. Sabbath is not just a day of rest or family or good food. Sabbath, rather, is a structured reminder each week for *all* of God's people together to return to their God, to their Maker, who intricately crafted them with love. The Sabbath day is the day when we all together run back home to the presence of God in our sacred lives.

Jerusalem on Friday is a whole city coming home. A whole city entering rest. Soon the city will be shut down for a day. Can you imagine it? Years ago, a gentile journalist experienced a Jerusalem Sabbath, which left a dramatic impact on her: "The official beginning of the Sabbath is at sunset the previous evening, and a notice in the Friday paper tells exactly what time it is. After you've been through a few of them you can see why. They don't just close the stores; they shut down the whole city. Now that I'm used to it, I'm all for it and think if they'd shut down the whole world one day a week, we wouldn't be in the mess we're in."[2] An entire city resting together. Everyone. All of society. Every square block. Thank God it's Friday!

This chapter explores how Sabbath affects sociology—or, how to do Sabbath *in* relationship and *for* relationship with others. Indeed, as we have found, Sabbath is first about relationship to God. But the Sabbath is also about our relationship to each other. Leviticus 23 makes this crucial connection: "There are six days when you may work, but the seventh day is a day of sabbath rest, *a day of sacred assembly.* You are not to do any work; wherever you live, it is a sabbath to the LORD" (Lev. 23:3). The Sabbath, alongside other celebrations such as Passover, the Festival of Unleavened Bread, and the Festival of Weeks, was not celebrated individually or in isolation but was a sacred day for the community to gather. Such a rhythm offered a texture in the yearly and weekly calendar for people to enter into enriching, life-giving relationships around shared worship. Sabbath as such has never existed as individualism or isolationism. Particularly following the temple's destruction in 70 CE, the synagogue served as a central communal gathering place for the Sabbath-keeping Jews.

God's intention for the Sabbath was, and is, that we would be drawn into the richness of community. One observes this communal dimension of Sabbath in Matthew 12:9–14 as Jesus enters a synagogue on the Sabbath day to heal the man with a withered hand. The backdrop of the healing is Leviticus 23—they have gathered *together* at a synagogue. For the Hebrews, a Sabbath assumes community. And by God's design the Sabbath would draw us in toward each other to lean on and support each other. Sabbath, thus, is a day that draws us into the very nature of God. The Triune God—Father, Son, and Spirit—is not the relationship of three beings who at some point became friends and brought their powers together to create the world. The Triune Godhead is coeternal. God is, in himself, relational. The world was created by a triune relationship. Borrowing philosophical language, God is *ontologically* relationship—that is, God does not have relationships; God *is* relationship.

Years ago, one researcher discovered something interesting about Sabbath in Jewish communities: mortality rates plummet on the Sabbath. How could it be that fewer people die on the Sabbath? The researcher concluded that even the sick and terminally ill "rallied" for the Sabbath day because it was a chance to be with family and friends.[3] Sabbath creates a kind of community that we can look forward to. People waited a day to die because Sabbath community was so rich and meaningful to them that they did not want to miss it.

What does this mean for us, however, who live in a hyperindividualist society? In his book *Bowling Alone*, Robert Putnam describes the ways in which Western society is increasingly living in isolation and individualism. Putnam famously said that instead of having friends, we watch *Friends* on television. We no longer truly need each other. We think we can fulfill all our own needs with the click of a button. And in many cases we can. Because of this, we trade the kind of community that is forged around a Sabbath for a "sense" of community wherein we are not vulnerable to each other in real and tangible ways.[4] In many urban Jewish communities, one will observe far more people walking on the street on the Sabbath than on any other day of the week. Why? Because many Orthodox Jews believe driving a car on the Sabbath is work. While such a thought may seem arcane, it has a powerful social implication. On the Sabbath, one must walk with fellow worshipers to Sabbath services. David Jacobson illustrates the social dynamic in this: "It is . . . the fact that one group of people who live in separate homes are walking together to the same place at the same time. Try to think of another community that similarly walks together. This doesn't happen in very many churches anymore, nor does it happen for baseball games or grade school. Occasionally a neighborhood might have its own Fourth of July parade where people walk the streets together, but that's only once a year."[5]

For many Jews who opt to not drive on the Sabbath, it becomes a day to "walk together," to be alongside one another on their way to worship. Some Orthodox synagogues even have *Eruv* lines, boundaries within which Jewish families must settle to create a strong communal geography where rich relationships become a possibility.[6] So what kinds of relationships do Western, post-Christian, contemporary people form if they do not form it around the Sabbath as they used to—and particularly in a context where individuals no longer gather at the synagogue or in the church to discover community? Cultural philosopher Zygmunt Bauman has discussed the two kinds of community people often enter into in this modern world: "peg communities" and "ethical communities." Peg communities, Bauman writes, are communities forged by disconnected spectators around a mutually loved experience like a rock concert or a sporting match. Their participation is a feeling or a sense around something shared. Ethical communities, in stark contrast, are long-term commitments that are marked by the giving up of rights and service. In short, ethical communities are built on relationships of responsibilities.[7] These are relationships formed by commitment, love, covenant, and even familial fidelity. One of the fundamental shifts in our social matrix is that our relationships are increasingly made up of the peg communities rather than ethical communities. The latter, Bauman articulates, do not play the role they used to in the making of human society.

Let me contrast these two kinds of community. A book club is a peg community. In this community, we gather with others around a shared commitment to something we all enjoy. As long as we like books and feel that the book club is delivering something beneficial to each of us, then the community will continue. A marriage, however, is an ethical community. I am in it "till death do us part." If my wife were dying of cancer, I would stay. When things are hard, we work them out. We continue even when it is not the best emotional option. In peg community, I am in so long as it benefits me. In ethical community, however, we willingly give ourselves to a community whether it benefits us or not. Today, in a world where we can find whole communities of people who think like us, share our values, and have common likes, we are trading in our ethical relationships for peg relationships. The result is troubling: We do not really need to love anybody who is different if we do not feel like it. We can cower in the corner with all the people we agree with.

In a very real sense, the Sabbath gave a framework and context for the flourishing of ethical communities where a day shapes our relationships, not shared likes. The Sabbath drew people together not around shared likes or dislikes but around the commitment to God and each other. Remove the Sabbath and we are more likely to build our life on peg communities rather than ethical communities. Scripture, it turns out, has nothing to say about the building of peg communities, where we gather because of shared opinions. The church is the church that Christ builds, not our shared interests. And we are called to live in covenant community where we live and die for each other. A peg community is a place we go to feel alive. An ethical community is a place we go to die. The biblical picture of community—of ethical community—can best be illustrated by the early church community in Acts 2:42–47:

> They devoted themselves to the apostles' teaching and to fellowship, to the breaking of bread and to prayer. Everyone was filled with awe at the many wonders and signs performed by the apostles. All the believers were together and had everything in common. They sold property and possessions to give to anyone who had need. Every day they continued to meet together in the temple courts. They broke bread in their homes and ate together with glad and sincere hearts, praising God and enjoying the favor of all the people. And the Lord added to their number daily those who were being saved.

This expression of ethical community was costly, painful, and dangerous, only possible if people were willing to give up their rights and serve. John Gager once attributed the success of Christianity to this kind of community, "open to all, insistent on absolute and exclusive loyalty, and concerned for every aspect of the believer's life."[8] Christian community was radical community, not a radical "sense" of community of shared likes. Christianity was marked by people willing to die to self for the sake of the other because of the work of Christ.

There remains a big difference between finding a church we like and serving the church that Jesus calls us to love and lay down our lives for. The words of Dietrich Bonhoeffer should be written on the canvas of our hearts: "Every human wish dream that is injected into the Christian community is a hindrance to genuine community and must be banished if genuine community is to survive. He who loves his dream of a community more than the Christian community itself becomes a destroyer of the latter, even though his personal intentions may be ever so honest and earnest and sacrificial."[9] True community is not born of our efforts in creating a sense of community—it is the natural outcome from the act of loving other people.

As far as I can tell, in the Gospels, love leads to crucifixion.

I am convinced that the kind of community that we yearn for and need most is severely lacking in the church today—a place where we learn to love even the people we do not like. In that ethical community, Democrats and Republicans worship together, men and women serve together, and majority and minority can be reconciled. A Sabbath community is where commitment to each other becomes deeper than our commitment to shared desires and wants. In the Sabbath, we share space with the other whom God has placed before us. During World War II, Jewish philosopher Emmanuel Levinas was imprisoned by the Germans occupying France. Despite his feelings of rage and anger toward his Nazi captors, Levinas insisted on his obligation to the other: "To be able to see in the face of the other, in the face of those who would try and kill me, in the face of the criminal, *the face of God*, this is the hardest challenge of the religious enterprise."[10] The Sabbath opens up space for us to enter into community with the people of God whom we may or may not like, those in our family and our church whom Christ died for. In a world where we enter community as long as it is full of people we like, the Sabbath becomes a prophetic act of learning to love even those we deplore and dislike.

The Sabbath is the gateway to God's dream community.

A Church at Rest

Each year, our church corporately discusses a spiritual discipline that we are not particularly good at. Seven years into the church's founding, it was viscerally clear that our church was tired from the strain of the sustained efforts of ministry. In the fall of 2015, we decided to initiate a three-week conversation about Sabbath-keeping in the Bible. I was not prepared for what happened. Mind you, I have preached widely on sexuality, marijuana, polyamory, refugees, immigrants, and the unborn, alongside other topics that naturally make people upset. Still, I have never seen my people as hostile to my preaching than during those three sermons on the Sabbath. What is so threatening about a day of rest?

I learned much from the experience. The responses, for one, were intriguing. Generally, people asked me two main questions. The first was "What do I *do* on the Sabbath?" Such a question is very American, isn't it? What do I *do*? We are addicted to doing. *Being* is not even a category we are able to entertain. The second was "How do I make time for the Sabbath?" Again, we cannot make time. We are human. God makes time. And the assumption that we can make time is dangerously hurtful to our well-being. I have come to the conclusion that the topic of Sabbath-keeping is so hostile to American Christianity because Americans often worship their time. We think time is ours.

Our language is telling. We think we can *make* time and *kill* time.

Of course, many in our community began keeping the Sabbath—something worth celebrating. Some are doing it now who never did it before. Others tried and gave up. Some did not try. And some left the church. We decided to take it further. In an effort to model restful rhythms in the church body, we decided to take a monthlong break from public worship gatherings as a church that summer. No one preached. No musical worship. No children's ministry. Prayer and only prayer. We gathered in a field by our church building and prayed for the city and the world. It was a powerful experience. But nobody told me that I would be staying up, losing sleep, worried that people would start going to other churches because we were not putting our liturgical goods on the market. As a pastor, the experience scared me to death.

Following these experiences, I reflected a great deal on the hostility of American Christianity toward the Sabbath. In the midst of our Sabbath experiment, I was in a meeting with our church's financial board. Sitting there, it dawned on me that were I to cheat on my wife, I would lose my job. If I stole from the church, I would be run out of town. If I lied about the church finances, I would be in huge trouble. If I worshiped another god, I'd be removed. There are nine commandments that, if I chose to break, I might lose my ministry over. But if I did not keep a Sabbath day, I would probably get a raise.

We have forgotten we have *Ten* Commandments. Again, for the person who says that we no longer need to rest, I would be curious which of the other commandments they think are antiquated. Is the commandment against murder to be done away with? May we finally lie? Is adultery okay now? Is stealing okay now? We have basically changed a commandment into a suggestion.

As a pastor, praying in the field taught me an important lesson about church growth—namely, that church growth does not happen when you just gather in a field to pray. I wonder if Jesus's direction that "where two or three gather" was him setting our expectations right. When you pray, people run away. It isn't a mistake the Gospels tell us the disciples slept while Jesus prayed in Gethsemane. Americans generally want an experience, a product, the bells and whistles—God is simply not enough for us. In the field, our attendance tanked. In the end, the problem with the Sabbath is there are huge rewards and incentives for not actually doing it. Modern church growth has basically been built on *no* rest. Our church industrial complex generally rewards Sabbath-breaking as a rule.

It is important for pastors, including me, to deal with our own fears and neglect around the Sabbath. I am complicit in the church's Sabbath amnesia. If you are a pastor, you are complicit too. As scary as it is, the Sabbath causes me to examine in realistic terms the way in which we have been building the American church. I think of youth pastors whom, because of their youth, we subtly assume we can use, abuse, and overburden with responsibilities under the guise that it "builds character." Youth pastors are expendable, often unable to obey the Sabbath because if they did, they would lose their job. Add to this the plenty of young, more aggressive, Bible-college graduates who can quickly fill their position. Youth pastors are tasked with organizational responsibilities on top of relational ones; their work hours are unusual; their time is stretched thin. They are expected to do whatever is asked, whenever it is asked . . . "for God's kingdom." Sadly, that same expectation is rarely expected of the ones demanding it. Nor are youth pastors permitted to Sabbath, because their bosses never do. The system is toxic. And it is deadly.

Youth pastors especially should Sabbath because it is they who pass our current model of Christianity to the next generation. And the only way to do this is by modeling it. If there is a person who should be encouraged in the taking of the Sabbath, it is the youth pastor. Not to mention we should be training them for lifelong ministry. Sabbath-breaking, of course, cannot sustain lifelong ministry. "Start children off on the way they should go, and even when they are old they will not turn from it" (Prov. 22:6). That points us to the communal side of Sabbath-keeping. For we almost always pass along to others what we ourselves have received from others. This is for good and bad. There is no person more hostile to the notion of Sabbath-keeping than the minister who cut their teeth as a youth pastor who *never* got a break and worked tirelessly for "the kingdom." Because *they* did it that way, to do it otherwise is "lazy." Teach someone *not* to Sabbath and they will be hostile to it and pass that along to the next generation. Teach someone *to* Sabbath and you will raise up a generation that knows how to rest in the presence of God. We will always pass on our lifestyle to those who follow us.

What if the church became the best place in the world to learn how to rest? This is an exhausting world, friend. Everyone is weary. Anxiety is rampant. Whenever I'm preaching and I catch a glimpse of someone nodding off in the back, I cannot help but celebrate a little inside. That's okay. Nod off. This is the church. And there should be no safer place to rest than this. As pastors, we need to be okay with people actually resting while we talk about resting.

It has rightly been said that the Sabbath commandment is the only one we brag about *not* keeping. The test of time is not a litmus test for truth. That is, just because something is not believed anymore does not mean that it is not true. Just because everyone believes something does not make it true. Truth is truth. Scripture says that Sabbath is never antiquated, never old. The Sabbath is for us. Today. Hear the words of Hebrews: "Therefore since it still remains for some to enter that rest, and since those who formerly had the good news proclaimed to them did not go in because of their disobedience, God again set a certain day, calling it 'Today.' This he did when a long time later he spoke through David, as in the passage already quoted: 'Today, if you hear his voice, do not harden your hearts'" (Heb. 4:6–7).

I've slowly come to believe that if we do Sabbath and rest, God can (and may) surprise the church with miracles and even revival. There is a great story from the life of David Yonggi Cho, the Korean founder of the largest church in the world. During the church's establishment, Pastor Cho became deathly ill and bedridden. As he lay in his bed, unable to do anything other than pray, Cho feared for the church's future. But reports of the church's explosive growth continued to abound. In Cho's absence, the church grew exponentially. Thousands were turning to Jesus, and cell groups were multiplying. The growth was unexplainable and could not be contained. Whole families and cities were being changed. We often fear what will happen when we are absent. But we fail to recognize that our absence is not the absence of God, and that God loves his church more than we do. Jesus is the head of his church. Sometimes, in order for God to accomplish what he wants to accomplish, he needs us to get out of the way.

I sometimes wonder whether God is just waiting for me to get out of the way so that the revival can begin. It is interesting: Paul never stayed for long in a city where he started a church. Why? There is a terrific lesson about intentional absence in a little book by a missionary, Roland Allen, titled *Missionary Methods: St. Paul's or Ours?* Allen points out that when you examine the rhythms of Paul's pastoral life, he could easily be seen as one of the worst pastors in the world. Look at what Paul would do: he would start a church and then leave almost immediately to go elsewhere. But is this really Paul being a bad pastor? Allen makes a critical point about the life of Paul: Paul's absence was not a mistake or a sign of incompetent shepherding but was indeed intentional. Paul was aware that had he stayed, the new Christians would have soon begun to trust in Paul more than in the Holy Spirit. As a shepherd, Paul leaned on the Spirit in his absence.[11]

It is also worth noting that not one of the churches Paul is believed to have planted still exists today. But does that mean Paul's ministry was a failure? By no means. The organizations he helped start indeed died out. But the kingdom he was building will never die. Paul believed in what Tom Steffen calls "responsible disengagement."[12] The fact remains that as a pastor I am learning that my task is to lead people who are actually supposed to follow someone else: Jesus. That means getting out of the way every once in a while.

Do not forget that your Sabbath absence from everyone may mark the next great revival. What did Jesus do as he ascended to the Father? He sent the

Holy Spirit. "Very truly I tell you, it is for your good that I am going away," Jesus said. "Unless I go away, the Advocate will not come to you; but if I go, I will send him to you" (John 16:7). His going to the Father sent the church forward to receive the Holy Spirit. Even the way Jesus models revival is getting out of the way and sitting down at the right hand of the Father.

Sabbath Boundaries in Relationship

Rest can actually lead to peace between enemies. It was during the Oslo Accords of the 1990s that Jews, Muslims, and Christians gathered together in an effort to solve one of the world's biggest issues—the Middle East crisis. During their meetings, they immediately recognized a problem. Each Abrahamic tradition observed a different day of rest—Muslims celebrated Jumu'ah on Friday, Jews the Sabbath on Saturday, and Christians the Lord's Day on Sunday.[13] To accomplish the greater purposes of establishing long-term peace in the world, each side submitted to a decision to work through the weekend toward peace. They put aside their religious dogmas in order to bring about peace. They realized that peace was far more important than a weekend of rigid religious observance.[14]

The Sabbath helps us establish boundaries that give our relationships space to heal and flourish. Some might say they do not need boundaries based on Paul's strong words to the Philippians: "I can do *all things* through [Christ] who strengthens me" (Phil. 4:13 ESV). Is this not a prooftext that we have superhuman powers and can therefore do anything we want? The problem, of course, is that this kind of interpretation assumes that humans are created by God to do anything they wish. This is an entirely inadequate approach to understanding the human limits and boundaries that God has himself established. Dr. Richard Swenson, in lecturing about limits and boundaries, has discovered that well-meaning Christians often quote Paul's verse. Swenson's response? "Can you? Can you fly? Can you go six months without eating? Neither can you live a healthy life chronically overloaded. God did not intend this verse to represent a negation of life balance. . . . He did not work twenty-hour ministry days."[15] Jesus did not fly. Jesus had to eat. Even Jesus had boundaries.

Entering into Sabbath community invariably creates logistical and practical challenges. For example, if Sunday serves as someone's Sabbath day, should they volunteer with children's ministry at Sunday church? Or on the greeting team? Or does Sabbath preclude them from service? My experience dictates that there are some who love to serve on their Sabbath and others who cannot. For the former, serving children or cooking church meals blesses them and others deeply. For others, the same activity constitutes work. My task as a responsible pastor is to respect the Sabbath sensibilities of those in my church. If they *can* serve on their Sabbath and that service brings life to them and others, then I should support them. If they cannot, then I must learn to celebrate their boundaries and assist them in finding alternative ways to serve the church. Sometimes serving does not need to happen on a Sunday. Sometimes Sabbath does not need to happen on a Sunday. Experience has also taught me that if I respect *their* boundaries, they will respect *mine*.

Nobody can do "all things." We are human beings. There is an old saying: good boundaries make good neighbors. Similarly, good boundaries make good Christian community. To that end, Sabbath creates a context where healthy relationships between people in community can be established because there are healthy boundaries. As it is, there are only a certain number of trump cards in our culture that one can play to avoid going somewhere or doing something. That is, our list of acceptable excuses to say no is rather short. For example, if you have children, you quickly find that they are an acceptable trump card. If your child needs to be driven off for a soccer game or has a sickness, all bets are off. You can say no to something. Few parents are not guilty of using this trump card excessively. Another trump card is work. If an excuse has to do with work or making money, then it is perceived as an acceptable excuse. This is perhaps one of the most culturally respected trump cards. Work trumps everything.

Sabbath is not a culturally accepted trump card. It used to be, but it is not now. As an experiment, take a Sabbath day. People may invite you to some kind of engagement on that day. Now, if you say you have to work, people will understand. If you have to care for a child, you are off the hook. Try saying, "I cannot because I am keeping a Sabbath." The person to whom you speak may look at you as though you either hate them or have joined a cult. Sabbath is not a culturally acceptable reason to say no. When a friend asks you to do something on the Sabbath and all you can do is say, "I am spending time with God," you will hear the crickets. It is acceptable to have a scheduled appointment with someone else such as a family member or a friend. But even in Christian community, we are regarded as weird if we have something scheduled with God.

But it should not be that way—the Sabbath should not be an awkward excuse within Christian community. Sabbath is of utmost importance because it resists the boundaryless tendencies that are common in contemporary relationships. Jesus tells a parable in Luke 14:15–24 about a man who throws a party. A number of people had been invited to celebrate with the man but, alas, turn down the invitation because they have other things to do. One has just bought a piece of land that he is beginning to develop. One has just bought some cattle he wants to examine. Another just got married. All are full of excuses. What Jesus is speaking of here are the trump cards in social décor of which we have been speaking. Jesus paints a picture of people's excuses to not come and eat with God our King. The lesson is simple: there is no excuse for the one who is being invited to dine with God. The great irony of Sabbath-keeping is how hard it is for us to say no to people but how with such ease we say no to being at rest with God.

At times, it is essential to say no to others to be present to God.

Sabbath-keepers make for the best kinds of friends because they have come to humbly identify their own boundaries and can honor other's boundaries. If someone cannot still love us after hearing no, then the relationship's strength remains doubtful. Friendship without boundary is faux friendship. The Jews have a word for someone who "guards" or "protects" the Sabbath day—who puts a hedge of protection around it even from relational intruders. They call this person a *shomer shabbos*. They are the "protectors" of the Sabbath day. When we set a day apart for God, we will find ourselves deeply refreshed by the freedom of relationship. We are slowly freed from neurotic behaviors, obsessing to keep our relationships afloat and free of problems. When God is at his rightful place in our lives, our relationships with people become rightly ordered. But if our relationship to God is disordered, our relationships will follow suit.

Years ago, a series of studies sought to determine how a fence, a boundary, affected the cognition and behavior of children in a playground. The researchers constructed a playground with no fences. During the experiment, the children stayed in the center—almost in fear—and never ventured out beyond the playground structure. Then the researchers put up a fence. Immediately, the children's behavior changed. Instead of fearfully staying in the center of the playground, they roamed with freedom all the way to the fence, exploring and enjoying the entire space.[16] Ironically, fences brought freedom. It was the absence of fences that created fear and apprehension.

The depth of our relationships is directly correlated to our ability to set and maintain boundaries. Boundaries in relationship around Sabbath bring freedom, not constriction. One such necessary boundary regards the type of conversation that takes place. Because I live in intentional community with a number of housemates, I have asked each of them—who are members of the congregation I pastor—not to bring up questions about church or theology on the Sabbath day. While I am able to have conversations on just about anything on the Sabbath, I have found that even one question about leadership decisions in the church can cause my blood pressure to go through the roof.

Conversations that take place on the Sabbath must be guarded, for they can easily lead to work in heart and mind.

Sabbath boundaries must be flexible, especially if we Sabbath with others. In my marriage, introverts (me) and extroverts (my wife) prove to rest *very* differently. For me, a restful Sabbath is a day of silence, books, gardens, walks, and more silence. I am at peace, for that matter, sitting in a room by myself for days on end. But because my wife is a natural extrovert, she is drawn to people—friends, neighbors, and family. Our goal is a give-and-take where we balance what she wants and what I want. This may translate into taking the day's first part to quietly be at home with a book or watching a movie with my son. Then the evening might include entertaining friends or playing a family board game. I have had to come to terms with the reality that what is restful for me is not always what is most restful for my wife. And that difference is sacred.

Essentially, Sabbath community provides for us what we need but ultimately protects us from getting everything we want. When we Sabbath with others—be it in marriage, in family, in friendship, or in community—there must be a give-and-take that puts our narcissistic, "I get everything I want" tendency in its place. It is good when I do not always get what I want on the Sabbath. Jesus is the Lord of the Sabbath; my desires are not.

In the Gospels, we can see clearly that there was great disagreement over what was an acceptable Sabbath activity and what was not. For instance, on one occasion Jesus walks with his disciples through a field, picking heads of grain to eat on the Sabbath. The Pharisees stand there watching, disapproving. Jesus confronts them for their narrow religious perspective (Matt. 12:1–8). Two lessons can be learned from this story. First, it is not the work of the Spirit to stand and critique other people's activity on the Sabbath. If we ever spend our day of rest judging everyone else's activity, we have improperly understood the heart of the Sabbath. And second, what looked like work for some was actually rest and nourishment for others. Only Jesus is the judge. Jesus defended the disciples' activity on the Sabbath. Again, defining work and defining Sabbath rest is challenging and can only be discerned by listening to the Holy Spirit. It should be noted that to outsiders this was unclear in the life of Jesus. The work of Jesus is very different from the work of this world. This is seen in Luke 13:10–17. Jesus heals a woman. He says, "Woman, you are set free from your infirmity." The synagogue leader is angry because Jesus "worked" on the Sabbath. Jesus then criticizes the religious leaders for having untied their animals while he was willing to untie a woman. This is true: what is work for one is not work for another. What was work for the Pharisees was not work for Jesus.

Sabbath for Marriage and Families

Scripture drips with practical wisdom for marriage. Perhaps my favorite biblical marital principle is that ancient command in Deuteronomy 24:5: "If a
man has recently married, he must not be sent to war or have any other duty
laid on him. For one year he is to be free to stay at home and bring happiness
to the wife he has married." The aim of this command was to bring about
marital health—that the newly married couple could spend the beginning
of their marriage learning every lesson possible for lifelong marriage. The
Sabbath command has similar marital intents. While one may consider the
Sabbath for individual purposes, we must also consider its role in a collective
sense to strengthen marriages by offering one day a week to be together and
enjoy the relationship that God has established.

To be candid, my own marriage may not have survived had it not been for
our Sabbath commitment, which has helped us rethink boundaries with the
world and each other and even helped us cultivate intimacy. Sabbath is a gift
to marriages. But one would not learn this by reading many of the Puritans
who came to America. Many of their writings reflect a strict prohibition of
sexual contact on the Sabbath. To "sanctify" a Sabbath, one must not kiss,
fondle, or make love. There is one particular minister in Massachusetts who
refused to baptize babies who were born on the Sabbath, being well aware
that if they were born on the Sabbath, they probably were conceived on the
Sabbath. His policy continued until the minister's wife delivered a set of
twins—on the Sabbath.[17] Some Christian traditions, sadly, have offered a tepid
view of the connection between the Sabbath and sex. The Council of Rouen
in Gaul (650 CE) articulated the belief that sex on the day before the Sabbath
was prohibited. If a married couple had sex the night before the Sabbath, they
were not allowed at the Lord's Table.[18] Harsh, indeed.

The rabbis, thankfully, were not as prudish. In the Jewish tradition, Sabbath was a day to enjoy marital sex. In some orthodox communities, one was
obliged to have sex on the Sabbath.[19] Nancy Sleeth tells me of growing up in a
Jewish home and seeing her father come home on Friday night with a bunch
of flowers and a very large smile on his face; he had been looking forward to
the Sabbath all week.[20]

Sex does not count as work, praise God. Anecdotal evidence suggests, in
my experience, that Sabbath sex is the best. I imagine it has something to
do with the fact that it is the one day in a week that our hearts and minds
are fully present to each other. A recent study found a linear relationship
between frequency of sex and reported happiness up to a frequency of once
a week. In other words, couples' happiness and well-being increased with the

frequency of sex, but that level of happiness maxed out at the frequency of having sex about once a week.[21] Perhaps we might keep the Jewish tradition going: let there be lots and lots of Sabbath sex. You can just tell the kids it is "nap time."

This raises another issue: How does one Sabbath with children? Particularly for the spouse who gives most care and attention to the children—how can they actually even entertain Sabbath-keeping at home that is restful? Jewish communities often see the Sabbath as a *Mikdash Me'at*, or a "miniature sanctuary," where the home becomes a sanctuary "in which the parents [are] the priests and the family table [is] the altar."[22] The Sabbath home comes to be seen as a kind of miniature Noah's ark, which stands strong in the deluge of life, eventually resting on a mountaintop. The Sabbath is a day of family blessing. One Jewish author points to the tradition where the father blesses each child: "To the boys, 'May God make you into Ephraim and Manasseh.' And to the girls, 'May God make you like unto Sarah, Rebekah, Rachel, and Leah.'"[23] Very tender and sweet, indeed.

Scripture, however, does not address the issue of keeping Sabbath with children directly. One reason for this may be that when Scripture was written, it was assumed that Sabbath-keeping was being done *in* community. At that point, Sabbath-keeping as parents was more feasible because families lived in the general vicinity of each other and could spend the Sabbath together. In that case, there were grandparents and other family members in the community who could look after children. Today, Sabbath-keeping with children—in a culture where people rarely live near their families—is going to look very different. Parents do not always have the privilege of living near others who can help care for the children on a Sabbath. Removed from our family communities, many parents are the sole people who care for their children. This has definitely made Sabbath-keeping with children more challenging—but *never* impossible.

One way to keep a Sabbath with children is to cultivate what some in our church call an "intentional Sabbath community." Here, three or four families opt to set aside the same day for Sabbath. Taking turns, they share the responsibilities of leading a fun activity with the children, babysitting, and giving much-needed breaks to the parents. This cannot fully replace the beauty of a whole family unit with grandparents, aunts, uncles, and cousins, but it certainly can help.

Do not be surprised if the Sabbath seems like a day of unending boredom to some children. This is not unique to you. Rob Muthiah points to certain popular cultural icons such as *Little House on the Prairie* and *The Adventures of Huckleberry Finn* that many children have seen, in which the Sabbath is portrayed "as a day for wearing uncomfortable clothing and sitting still without smiling, laughing or playing. It was a day filled with boredom, which one endured as a sign of faithfulness. It was a day that everyone—especially kids—was eager to see come to an end."[24] Charles Dickens spoke of the Sabbath disparagingly: it "comes, and brings with it a day of general gloom and austerity. The man who has been toiling hard all the week, has been looking towards the Sabbath, not as to a day of rest from labour, and healthy recreation, but as one of grievous tyranny and grinding oppression."[25] In a text written by a Methodist missionary's kid titled *No Swimming on Sundays*, Sabbath is described as "another perfectly good day about to be ruined."[26]

No wonder the Sabbath may seem boring to some children. But increasingly, in a time when we never have time to be bored, perhaps we need to consider the holiness of a little boredom in their lives. I appreciate how many Jewish communities practice "Sabbath hour for the children," in which the parents recite a Sabbath story for the children. In the end, a child will not take a Sabbath unless the parents do. Someone must lead them. Someone must be willing to sit still long enough to tell the story.[27] As a family, we want the Sabbath to be a day of joy for our child. If he desires to watch a movie, and it is restful and done in the right spirit, we will let him watch a movie. (If we do it right, we will watch it together.) If he wants to be in his tree house in the back, and that is restful, there will he be.

The consequences of Sabbath boredom are far less than Sabbath nonobservance. In the end, the people who pay the biggest price for the pastors who are not released to take a day a week to rest are the people around them—spouses and their children. Year after year, these children watch their parents lay their lives down for the church. Soccer games are missed. Dinners are ignored. They never take time off. And we wonder why pastors' kids often hate the church? There is a whole generation of PKs who hate the church because they see the church as having stolen their mothers and fathers from them. And, often, it has. We say we no longer practice child sacrifice. But our actions are louder than words. Want kids to know Jesus? Tell them God said you have to be home on the Sabbath.

The Sabbath is good news to children. Recently, I was preaching at a nationally known church. The pastor was taking a sabbatical to rest and care for his soul. A number of families in the church had been taking public pot shots at him for being lazy and unfit for ministry. I preached on Sabbath-keeping and its importance for spiritual formation. Unbeknownst to me, the wife and children of the pastor had decided to come to church that Sunday. After the service, they approached me in the pastor's office. With tears in their eyes, the children hugged me and thanked me for granting their dad permission to come home and be with them.

Sabbath for the Single and the Widow

We have looked at issues related to church, friendship, and even marriage and children. But what about the single person who is either not married or no longer married? What does their Sabbath look like? Again, parents have a trump card. Even couples without kids can say no to other engagements because of plans with a spouse. But often single people feel as though they are at the whim of everyone else's requests and needs. Single people feel as though their time is everyone else's, that other people own their time. I have long appreciated what Eugene Peterson has said about his times of prayer and Sabbath-keeping. Peterson schedules times for prayer and meditation, dates with his wife, and even time to read books. And he schedules the Sabbath as well. When someone asks him to do something on the Sabbath, he will say, "The diary does not permit it."[28] This intention to schedule time and keep boundaries is particularly important for the single person. The single person should feel free to say no to other requests without having to fully explain. Ambiguity is not a sin. Not everything is everyone's business. Do not throw your pearls before swine. No matter your situation, God is always a worthy excuse to say no to something.

While I am not single, I do have many single friends and single parishioners. What I have seen is that the most daunting part of a Sabbath for them is the idea of spending the day alone when they have felt alone all week long. What the single person can learn is that one has freedom to do on the Sabbath what one's spirit and soul needs. If being with people is life giving, be with people. If being alone is life giving, be alone. For some singles, the Sabbath day is a perfect day to go out with friends, be with others, and even potentially go on a date. Because singleness in our present day often presents the difficulty of feeling alone, the Sabbath for a single person may look different from that of a married couple or family. A single person should not feel obliged to Sabbath in the same way others do. Resting and enjoying the Sabbath day should not entail a slavish commitment to solitude if it does not bring life. Again, ask, "Is it life giving?"

Another challenge is that people often take their Sabbath days on different days. This can make it especially hard for a single person to spend a Sabbath in community. The ideal picture of the Christian Sabbath would be that we all do it on the same day. On that occasion, our schedules would align. But, alas, this creates a problem for clergy. For there is no way Sunday could come even close to a day of rest. We need to accept that there is no such thing as a "perfect" Sabbath outside of our future hope in heaven.

QUESTIONS
for Reflection

- How might the Sabbath draw you into the richness of community?
- What kinds of relationships do you find you form if not ones formed around the Sabbath?
- What might it look like to give up seeking a "sense of community" and instead lovingly sacrifice, assume responsibility, and commit to love people? What is holding you back from living that way?
- In what ways have you seen the church reward workaholism?
- What would it look like for you to responsibly disengage? Have you had an experience of seeing God working in your absence?
- How could you partner with others in your community to Sabbath?

5

Sabbath, Economy, and Technology

A fanatic has been described as a person who, when unsure of his direction, doubles his speed.

Charles Hummel, *Freedom from Tyranny of the Urgent*

The Day of Preparation

In the first four chapters, we explored how the Sabbath affects our time, work, health, and relationships. Each of these generally represents areas of personal existence. Moving forward, we will pivot toward exploring ways the Sabbath affects the world around us and our relationship to it. In this chapter, we will particularly focus our attention on how the Sabbath brings God's shalom into the economic system of human society as well as our relationship to technology.

Can you imagine what the world's economy and marketplace would look like if by the stroke of a pen one entire day was set aside to rest? Can you dream of a world where 24/7 convenience stores became 24/6 convenience stores? Where websites stopped taking orders on Saturdays? Where restaurants closed down for a day? The ripple effects, indeed, would be far-reaching—workers would have a day to be with loved ones, society's bottom line would take into account the well-being of those in it, and we could not as easily imbibe in wanton consumerism.

That world would look nothing like this one.

Turning to Scripture, we find that God designed human economy to flourish around a Sabbath. As the earth orbits the sun, the economy of the world was to be oriented around the Sabbath. As Karen Burton Mains has perceptively written, every day of the week was to be transfixed and oriented around the Sabbath day. "Three days to look *forward* to Sabbath," Mains writes, "three days to *reflect back* on its wonder."[1] The entire workweek was set in this framework: we either find ourselves preparing for the next Sabbath or living in its glorious afterglow. Even the economy was Sabbathcentric—orbiting around the glory of God's day of Sabbath rest.[2]

Sabbath was to be the centerpiece of a society that reflected God's heart. But modern society is anything but Sabbathcentric. The result? Our society has become a place to produce, accumulate, save, and construct. But without a day of Sabbath, we are not able to enjoy our abundance. In other words, we make a living but have no time to live. We become like the grieving character from a Dutch novel who says, "If there were no Sunday . . . what would we live for?"[3] Indeed, Sabbath is not only a day to recharge for the six days of challenging work ahead. It is also the reason we endure six days of hard work.

Neither a Sabbath nor a Sabbathcentric society just happens. Intentionality is required. In the Bible, the spirit of intentionality and forethought is demonstrated as Israel wanders in the desert after their Egyptian captivity. In the wandering narrative, God miraculously provided through a daily portion of both *manna* (or, "what is it?") each morning as the dew lifted and quail in the evening as the sun descended. However, God placed just enough food on the desert floor for the needs of God's people and the cotravelers and animals who sojourned with them. This rich provision came with a command found in Exodus 16: everyone was to gather as much as they *needed*, not as much as they *wanted*. That society was based not on hoarding and stealing but on sharing and generosity.

In fact, hoarding was strictly prohibited. However, the food on the desert floor created a nagging challenge: If Israel kept a Sabbath in the desert but could not collect food on that day, what would they eat? On the day before the Sabbath, each family was instructed to gather just enough food for two days so that no one would go hungry on the Sabbath. Now, if the Israelites gathered more than their fair share on any normal day, "it was full of maggots and began to smell" (Exod. 16:20). But if they gathered extra manna for the Sabbath day, it would not rot and would be kept for the day of rest. The extra provision only went bad on the normal days, never on the Sabbath. Provision of the extra Sabbath manna is celebrated today by a white tablecloth used in the Sabbath ceremony, symbolizing God's rich and abundant provision in the desert wanderings.

This divinely orchestrated Sabbath preparation—or "day of preparation," as it later was called—guarded the Sabbath day against being consumed by work and productivity, providing a context for communal gratitude and contentment. Once arriving into the promised land, the day of preparation became normative for Israel. On Friday, Jews cooked meals in advance, cared for their animals' needs, and prepared homes for the Sabbath. The day of preparation fostered a whole new mindset, fundamentally contradicting any notion within the people that their task, their job, was to maximize productivity as an economic end. In the end, the Sabbath says the time for worship and enjoyment and rest should be a bottom line too.

While both the day of preparation and the Sabbath reorient how we might imagine our economy, they are extremely practical as well. We need rest. But we also must learn to *prepare* for rest. Truth is, things come up. Schedules get busy. Life happens. Our minds become distracted. We schedule our days to the max. The day of preparation gently reminds us that intentionality and mindfulness are part of authentic rest. Consider this: the first time Sabbath is mentioned by name in Scripture is in Exodus 20:8. There, Israel is commanded to "remember the Sabbath day by *keeping* it holy." What does "keeping" mean? Abraham Heschel illustrates that "keeping" (Hebrew *leqadesh*) something carries with it a sense of preparation as in a marriage preparation. More specifically, the word "to keep" was often used to describe a bride preparing for her wedding day. "To keep" was the same as "to betroth."[4] In fact, Jews speak of the Sabbath as a "bride" *and* a "queen"—we are her lover, but we are also ruled by her. What does a man do to prepare for his bride? He prepares a feast, makes a home, gets ready for her. What do you do if the queen comes to your house? You get the house ready. Both images are, in fact, about preparation.

Can you imagine a wedding ceremony without any work being put into its preparation? Can you imagine a bride throwing her wedding together the day of? Such an action is unimaginable, as the marriage day is such a sacred day. As it relates to the Sabbath, we should not aim to elope but aim for a wedding. And a wedding requires preparation. The marriage day requires months, even years, to prepare for. A day of preparation is the day that betroths the Sabbath. Godly rest, particularly in a 24/7 world, is never accidental and can only come when we have gone out of our way to prepare for it. We should take Jesus seriously: if we want to build a tower, we must willingly count the cost (Luke 14:28). Discipleship requires preparation. So does Sabbath-keeping.

Old rabbinic folklore tells of a man on his way home for the Sabbath. On the journey, he is accompanied by a good and a bad angel. If the man arrives home and finds it prepared for the Sabbath day, the good angel offers a blessing over the home, saying, "May this home always be an abode of happiness." But if the man arrives home and the candles are not lit and the home is unprepared, the bad angel will curse the home and say, "May this home never know the joy of Sabbath."[5] This illustrates how the work of preparing for the Sabbath is as important as the Sabbath itself. This is reflected by the author of Hebrews, who admonishes us to "make every *effort* [Greek *spoudazō*] to enter that rest" (Heb. 4:11).

Ironically, rest takes a lot of work to enjoy. Similarly, to create a new society in which Sabbath is the centerpiece will not come easily—it will require intentionality and forethought and may require us to think very differently about the way we live. How can we put effort into preparing for a Sabbath today? A great number of Sabbath practices in the Bible no longer have bearing on us. For example, we have no need to sweep out the yeast from our homes on the day of preparation. But the spirit of intentionality in Sabbath preparation still stands. What are creative ways in which we can prepare ourselves for the day of rest? Consider the following ideas as ways to help prepare to keep the Sabbath day holy:

- Take a half day (or even a couple of hours) before beginning your Sabbath to finish all housework. This may include mowing the lawn, trimming the roses, and watering the garden. If we do not intentionally do these things in advance, it can lead to work on the Sabbath and distract us from resting.

- Care for any animals in advance. Give the pets a double portion on the day before the Sabbath so they are free to have a day without needing your constant attention.

- If you are a student, plan your study schedule around the Sabbath and resist studying for that midterm for a day.

- Pay the bills, do the laundry, go to the bank, get your hair cut. Remember, the Sabbath is not a day to catch up.

- Get any and all shopping done, such as food, clothing, or filling the car with fuel.

- Clean house. Resting is difficult if you are thinking about cleaning the house on the Sabbath. Keep in mind: if you have too much stuff to take care of on the day of preparation, consider that you may own too much stuff. The Sabbath almost implies simplicity in the things we consume and own. To help, read Nancy Sleeth's *Almost Amish*.[6]

- Prepare a big meal for the night before the Sabbath so you have an abundance of leftovers for the Sabbath. This frees you from needing to cook or eat out on the Sabbath day.
- The Sabbath has deep economic ramifications. Sabbath living has implications on the lives of others. Ask yourself: Are there ways your Sabbath is forcing *other* people to work?
- Plan days where the church will be closed. Remember, whenever the doors are open, someone needs to be there.

Consider these, and any other, ways for you to prepare for the Sabbath. Be aware that it is easy to slip into neurotic modes of getting everything done before the Sabbath. Being neurotic is not sustainable, nor is it enjoyable for those around you. Perhaps make it your goal to enter the Sabbath with at least something on your to-do list so you do not become a taskmaster who must check everything off before the Sabbath. With that, take time to think through things that might cause you to stumble on the Sabbath. Remember, it is extremely rare for someone to *accidentally* rest in the twenty-first century. Forethought about the Sabbath should never be an afterthought.

Sabbath as Economic Justice

"Prosperity," stresses Walter Brueggemann, "breeds amnesia."[7] That is, those who have everything they want are often the ones most happy to overlook the importance of the Sabbath. When the bank account is full, abundant food sits in the fridge, business is booming, GDP is up, and everyone seems happy, we are tempted to keep our lives going the way they have been. Things are going well. Why would we need to change? While many countries in the West may be experiencing great financial upswings, we forget that those upswings are often built on the backs of the underprivileged and the poor. And that our national economy often booms on those who work too much or are paid too little.

That was, at least, the framework for Egypt's economy during biblical times. Pharaoh was a tyrant. "Pharaoh's slave drivers beat the Israelite overseers they had appointed," Exodus 5:14 describes, "demanding 'Why haven't you met your quota of bricks?'" Perhaps even more, Pharaoh was a shrewd businessman who understood how to grow an economy on the backs of oppressed slaves. Once they were enslaved, Pharaoh gave the Israelites despotic demands to fatten his profit. We see Pharaoh's greed mostly in his "store cities" (Exod. 1:11). These store cities existed as silos for goods and grains to be stored for the coming famine, when they could be leveraged at exorbitant prices. Then, as was the case in Genesis 47:13–27, the land of the poor was forced to be sold at rock-bottom prices to put food on the table. Pharaoh's intent is glaringly sinister: gouge the people during their worst famine and societal crisis. To accomplish this, Pharaoh enslaved Israelites to manufacture bricks to be used to build these storage facilities (Exod. 5). When Israel was downtrodden and exhausted from their slavery, they requested a chance to go and have a festival of worship to Yahweh. In sheer anger, Pharaoh made them work even harder (Exod. 5:1–9). All of this, of course, was largely a reflection of the Egyptian cultic religions, which believed the gods supported oppressive economic policies.[8] The interplay is terrorizing—slavery was the child of the economic system, and the economic system was a child of the Egyptian worship. In the end, we learn that time, economics, and worship cannot be neatly separated.

Pharaoh was obsessed with storage facilities. We are too. In the United States alone, we have somewhere north of 2.3 billion square feet of self-storage space. That works out to be something like 7.3 square feet of space for each one of the 317 million people who live in our nation.[9] Like Egypt, we are a nation of storage units. In this economy, our storage units are fuller than ever, and countless stomachs of children and the poor and the disadvantaged remain empty on a global scene. The rich are getting richer. The poor are getting poorer. And the disparity between the two is growing more and more every year.

Pharaoh would be proud.

Ours is a Pharaoh society. But what does this have to do with the Sabbath? The connection between the Sabbath and the economy of the world is a topic that has generated no small interest in recent years. An example of this is the Sabbath Economics Collaborative, a consortium of theologians, biblical scholars, and ethicists seeking to articulate how the Sabbath command might assist Christians in imagining the world's economic system and the church's role in supporting an ethical web for the flourishing of human life, for the rich *and* the poor. Beyond asking questions of pragmatics (how Sabbath is done), this effort seeks to ask the broader systemic questions: How does the Sabbath change the system of our economy? Does the Sabbath have anything to do with economy? Or with economic justice? The Sabbath Economics Collaborative contends that the Sabbath has a massive economic impact: "Sabbath Economics, then, concerns the theoretical, spiritual and practical task of imagining how we might limit and shape our economic activity in order to keep the gifts of creation circulating justly among all living communities."[10] As we think about creating a system that supports all of life on our planet, we must give keen attention to the Sabbath command as part of that flourishing system.

The Sabbath Economics Collaborative has offered valuable insights into the ways in which the Sabbath affects economic systems. But it would be a mistake to suggest that the Sabbath affects only the macro systems of economic order. Sabbath also has great influence on the economics of families and local communal systems. Our family has opted to live in intentional community for the last decade. My wife and I believe that part of our role as "parents" of the intentional community is to pass along some of the rhythms and practices that we have found to be transformative—including the keeping of the Sabbath. We want others who live with us to not only receive a taught theology of the Sabbath but to witness it in person. One of our former roommates, Daniel, expressed how odd it was to live in a home with a family that kept a Sabbath. He had to change his own rhythms around us out of sensitivity to our decision. Over time, he saw how important and life giving it was for our family. Daniel soon began to keep a Sabbath. Then he moved out and got married. He and his wife started keeping the Sabbath together. And now they have roommates in their home to whom they are teaching the Sabbath.

The Sabbath is never practiced in a vacuum—it has ripple effects in whatever system we live in. Sabbath-*keeping* is always Sabbath-*giving*; to keep it is to extend it as a gift to others who need it. To enter in oneself is to invite others to enter in as well. Indeed, Sabbath may necessitate taking a great risk, for someone has to do it first. Scary though it may be to begin to Sabbath, it can deeply bless those around the one willing to keep it.

In this light, the Sabbath must be seen as part and parcel of the church's work to serve and love the economically disadvantaged. Dorothy Day was the founder of the Catholic Workers Union. She was often asked how long the poor could stay in one of her houses. She always responded with "Forever." "They live with us," she would say, "they die with us, and we give them Christian burial. . . . Once they are taken in, they become members of the family. Or rather they always were members of the family. They are our brothers and sisters in Christ."[11] Day's hospitality toward the poor reflects the heart of God for the least of these. Likewise, Sabbath reflects God's heart for the poor and offers them scheduled opportunity to rest from their experience.

Many Christians throughout history have gone to great lengths to avoid contributing to the slavery of another. John Woolman (1720–72), for example, examined everything in his everyday life to ensure he did not contribute in any way to the global slave trade that was common in his day. To that end, Woolman, when invited to dinner at someone's home, would not eat with any kind of silver. Doing so, he believed, would be to comply with slave-trade economics. Woolman refused to eat or purchase sugar and certain kinds of rum, which likewise would have been supporting others' slavery. He also often walked barefoot as a protest against the mistreatment of postal horses.[12]

Embodying economic justice is thoughtfully choosing to practice a way of life that does not enslave others. Sabbath, undoubtedly, is part of God's economic justice that Christ calls us to. We see Sabbath-keeping as economic justice in the book of Exodus. As Israel is receiving instruction on Sabbath rhythms, God speaks to his people about how this day affects everyone: "For six years you are to sow your fields and harvest the crops, but during the seventh year let the land lie unplowed and unused. Then the poor among your people may get food from it, and the wild animals may eat what is left. Do the same with your vineyard and your olive grove" (Exod. 23:10–11). God continues to command that Sabbath rest should be extended so that "the foreigner living among you may be refreshed" (Exod. 23:12). Imagine the power in that! Imagine what it would be like if your religious tradition brought freedom and rest to those around you, even your enemies. Imagine that the convictions of your religion not merely blessed those observing the religious practices but had far-reaching implications for even those outside your faith system. For followers of Jesus, it turns out that it does. Every aspect of creation, not just the religious people themselves who keep it, should benefit from the keeping of the Sabbath.

Sabbath is scheduled social justice.[13] Ancient Jewish philosopher Philo, in his *On the Sabbath*, writes about the richness of the Sabbath for everyone in society: "On the seventh day there were spread before the people in every city innumerable lessons in prudence, justice and all other virtues . . . and so the lives of all are improved."[14] This way of blessing the nations around Israel was entirely contrary to the economic patterns of the other nations around them—most particularly Egypt.

But God did not call his people to live according to the patterns of Egyptian society. Rather, Israel was to be contrarian, reflecting the merciful and restful rhythms of Yahweh, whom the Israelites worshiped. Similarly, as a contrarian society, the church is called to depart from the economic mentality of whatever contemporary society it finds itself in. We are not to "conform to the pattern of this world," writes Paul (Rom. 12:2). While Egypt is perhaps a prototype of living under the curse, the church is to live in the rest that God created in Eden. The church is called to live in prophetic witness to our envious society by living simply. In a rat-race world where one is expected to climb over the dead bodies of those in competition, the church is called to holy simplicity and contentment.

The results of not building the Sabbath into economic systems should concern us. In Luke 16:19–30, Jesus tells the parable of the rich man and Lazarus. A rich man, Jesus narrates, lives extravagantly and has no compassion on the beggar who lies at the city gate. Notice the description of the rich man—he "was dressed in purple and fine linen and lived in luxury *every day*" (Luke 16:19). Biblical scholar Kenneth Bailey says this text is best translated as living "sumptuously every day." He points out that the ancient readers' eyes—particularly Sabbath-oriented Jews—would have immediately been transfixed on this phrase. Why? The rich man ate big meals *all* seven days of the week. Bailey describes the sin of the rich man: "He did not, therefore, observe the Sabbath. His servants were never given a day of rest, and therefore he publicly violated the Ten Commandments every week. His self-indulgent lifestyle was more important to him than the law of God. The injustice he inflicted on his staff meant nothing to him."[15] Here we are offered a graphic, heart-wrenching image—the image of what Jesus thinks about the one who lives in abundance and yet neglects to extend what he has been blessed with to his staff.

The rich man is judged by God.

Sabbath, we must remember, has ramifications for the world that go far deeper than we recognize at first glance. Sabbath is economic justice. While we enjoy life "sumptuously every day," others in our churches, neighborhoods, and schools go hungry, thirsty, and homeless. Statistics make this even more painful: the poor are often the most generous segment of society. Although the wealthiest 1 percent of Americans are to thank for nearly a quarter of all charitable giving, relative to their income the poor are much more generous. In 2011 those with earnings in the bottom 20 percent gave 3.2 percent of their income, while those with earnings in the top 20 percent gave only 1.3 percent of theirs.[16] It seems the richer one is, the less likely one is to give generously. Jesus's parable suggests that this kind of generosity aversion will be judged in the end.

Sabbath is a creative way to be radically generous with our time. And to rest is to invite others to share in the goodness of what we have been blessed with. In a world of Pharaohs, both our work *and* our rest should be a blessing. Miroslav Volf notes, "The stress on the pursuit of self-interest in modern societies is at odds with one of the most essential aspects of a Christian theology of work, which insists that one should not leave the well-being of other individuals and the community to the unintended consequences of self-interested activity, but should consciously and directly work for others."[17] His point directly relates to the Sabbath: the Sabbath undermines our systems of economy that are generally drunk on self-interest and turns them outward so that our work and rest are acts of service toward others. In a world where everything is about upward mobility, Sabbath becomes enacted *downward mobility*, where all work and rest become an act of service to fellow human beings. The Sabbath frees the slaves, feeds the poor, and restores the weak.

9/11, Black Friday, and Good Friday

In the sixth century, a letter titled the "Sunday Letter," purported to be written by Jesus Christ himself (again, purported), circulated throughout European churches. In the letter, Jesus condemns those who refused to observe a Sabbath day.[18] While having little to no historical credibility, the letter does reveal something about the role of the Sabbath by giving a snapshot into the cultural role Sabbath played in Christianized Europe. Before the Enlightenment, the Sabbath day was almost universally respected and honored in Christian societies and countries. The day served the purpose of bringing people together around worship. Today, the Sabbath has largely been replaced by activities centered on consumerism, sports, or recreation.

So important to Christian Europe was the Sabbath that it played a pivotal role in the formation of America and its developing economy. The Puritans who came to North America did so largely because of religious persecution and in order to practice a Sabbath that they felt the English to be lax and lazy about.[19] In coming to a land that was new to them, they sought to observe the Sabbath wholeheartedly, setting up a society and economy that was centered on the Sabbath. Sabbath became so central to American society that a naturalized American citizen who had immigrated from France once commented that the Sabbath was the only truly American and national characteristic.[20] That seems almost unimaginable today.

America was once a nation built on Sabbath. Tilden Edwards recalls walking around New York City as a child on a Sabbath day, finding it completely quiet—everyone was worshiping together at church.[21] Until fairly recently, people did not need to be as intentional about rest as we do now. Sabbath, in large part, was legislated in the United States. Until the 1960s, "blue laws" required that businesses shut down on Sundays, providing a context for people to go to church, be with family, and rest.[22] Imagine having one day a week that you would not be permitted to work, shop, or get your iPhone fixed. Regrettably, as North America moved into the era of post-Christianity in which the Judeo-Christian ethic was being unsettled, blue laws were eased and eventually erased, and societal rest was effectively lost in our culture.

Now, of course, blue laws are a historical relic. And this is not entirely a negative—true rest cannot be forced or legislated by laws or fiat. And it is actually when the laws do not reflect one's values that one's commitment to such values becomes clear. Still, Sabbath is incredibly difficult to protect and maintain in any culture. Historians would be quick to point out that Sabbath has equally been displaced among Jewish people today. Fewer and fewer Jewish communities keep the Sabbath day as they used to. Why? One Jewish historian laments this loss and identifies the loss of Sabbath in Jewish culture as a result of Jews increasingly living in places where they are a minority.[23] As Jews settled throughout the world, it became more and more challenging to justify taking a day of rest when the rest of the world existed in a different economy and timeline. Their Sabbath practice came to be seen as hostile to the economic systems around them. In order to survive, Jews had to work on the Sabbath. In the system of the world, if they did not work, they would lack the ability to earn a decent wage.

Now we live in a 24/7 world. I can, at any hour, go to the grocery store and purchase what I need. I can email a colleague late at night and most likely get a response before sunrise. I can go to the noodle stand down the street and eat whatever I want—*whenever* I want. I can get anything, anytime, at my leisure. With all of this convenience, it is easy to forget the price tag of such conveniences: *others*. A 24/7 world requires a 24/7 workforce. The result is a kind of Sabbath inequality where some rest and some cannot. And how disastrous this can be. I am thirty-six years old. In my short thirty-six years, the closest resemblance to Sabbath I've seen in American society was on September 11, 2001. On that fateful day, when those two planes flew into the Twin Towers, the Pentagon was hit, and a plane careened into a Pennsylvanian field, everyone went home. Everyone stopped flying. The markets shut down. And we all called the people we love the most. Manhattan used to go quiet for the Sabbath. Now the only thing that makes Manhattan pause is a catastrophe. In a 24/7 world, we only Sabbath when we are forced to by circumstance.

As Judith Shulevitz prophetically writes, "Americans, once the most Sabbatarian people in the earth, are now the most ambivalent on the subject."[24] As a nation, we have replaced Good Friday with Black Friday, replaced Sabbath with consumerism. We are a people defined no longer by the grace of Christ but by the consumeristic ways of the world. Cultural critic Daniel Harris has gone so far as to argue that as Christian faith has been displaced, consumerism has taken its place as the one thing that draws us all together: "In a fragmented society in which major institutions like the church and the community no longer play the same role in bringing people together, owning identity possessions becomes one of their chief ways in which we experience community, overcoming our isolation through shared patterns of consumption."[25] Eventually, this kind of society defined by consumerism creates a whole new caste system. Those without smartphones, computers, wireless, the latest technology, a keen fashion sense, or cultural nuance are the lepers of this consumer society.

In consumer society, we have been duped into thinking that life is about stuff. "The luggage is for the journey," writes Jesuit Gerard Hughes, "not the journey for luggage."[26] Consumerism equates the journey with the luggage. If the rhythms and values of the world had their way, we would become slaves to a system whose sole purpose is to amass wealth. The bottom line of this system is composed of what promises pleasure, comfort, security, or power. But the Sabbath undoes this entire ideology by standing firm that the bottom line and the real rewards are much more complicated. Sabbath creates an important corrective to the world's way of doing business. If the bottom line makes money for a few and the rest are being hurt because of it, we must critique that economic system. Sabbath does just that. When we integrate Sabbath rest into our lives, we are going against the kind of bottom-line thinking that says making money is the only objective. "Sabbath," contends Jarrod Longbons, "implies that humans value other beings and use them within a proper limit."[27] Our belief that we are limitless people who can either work endlessly or have others work endlessly for us without harmful consequences is wrong. Sabbath reminds us that the bottom line is more than making money, having experiences, and obtaining cultural power. Sabbath is also about nurturing and caring for people. The Sabbath is a form of resistance against the powers of this world that say that people are mere cogs in a machine.

I once read about a shopkeeper whose business was kept open every day of the year except for one. The shopkeeper had always heard "the customer is always right." That one day he shut down each year was an act of resistance. It was his way of saying that the customer is not the one who is always right—God is always right, not the customer.[28]

It is one thing to shut down one day a year. But what about one day a week? B&H Photo Video is located on Ninth Avenue in New York City. Other than Yodobashi Camera in downtown Tokyo, it is the largest nonchain photo and video store in the world—up to nine thousand people pass through on a given workday. But this is a unique organization. B&H is operated and owned by a community of Hasidic Jews who dress as their eighteenth-century Eastern European descendants did. And their practices almost seem as ancient. At 1:00 p.m. on Friday, their doors close for the next twenty-four-hour period so that their employees may honor the Sabbath rest. Even more, customers may peruse the online store on the Sabbath, but look is all they can do. One cannot purchase anything from the online store on the Sabbath. When asked why the company disallows purchasing on those days, along with Black Friday, the day after Thanksgiving, the director replied, "We respond to a higher authority."[29]

This spirit and commitment reflects the prophet Amos, who sharply critiqued those who wanted the Sabbath to end so that they could get back to robbing the poor. "Hear this," Amos writes, "you who trample on the needy and do away with the poor of the land, saying, 'When will the New Moon be over that we may sell grain, and the Sabbath be ended that we may market wheat?'" (Amos 8:4–6). The wicked ask when Sabbath will finally be over so that people may return to valuing profits over people. The Sabbath reverses that economic principle—people *always* take precedence over profit.

While not all of us have a business that we can shut down one day a week, we all have the power to take a day a week from spending and purchasing. Such a practice, as difficult as it may seem, not only serves those who work in business but also helps to guard our minds and souls against the corrosive dangers of consumer idolatry. Consumerism, in the end, is the devil's sacrament. And Black Friday is his liturgy. Black Friday is the Good Friday of consumerism—it is the day that we worship the gods of consumerism, greed, and opulence by atoning for the "sins" of simplicity and locality and generosity by self-indulging in uncontrolled, limitless spending. We need a *Good* Friday economy in which the bottom line is people. Jesus came to create not a kingdom of slaves to consumerism but a kingdom of friends.

Some organizations have recognized their responsibility to their employees, customers, the environment, and the rest of society by intentionally closing their doors. Beginning in 2015, REI, one of the world's largest outdoor clothing and supply stores, opted to shut down its stores nationwide and instructed people to get outside for Black Friday. Other companies have also stopped Black Friday shopping. In response to the recent trend of Black Friday encroaching on Thanksgiving Day, Staples, Costco, GameStop, and T. J. Maxx have closed their doors on Thanksgiving to give people a chance to go home and enjoy family. For a time, Northwestern Mutual Life Insurance had a "quiet day" on Wednesdays, when phones were routed to the receptionist so that employees could work in quiet. Likewise, Hobby Lobby has long shut down on Sundays for employees to be able to have a day home with their families.

Jesus's first sermon—preached on the Sabbath day—was about freeing the oppressed (Luke 4:14–30). Jesus knew he was the second Moses. The exodus foreshadowed a time when people would no longer be slaves. Jesus came to lead this exodus. Sabbath helps us undo the common consumer drives that keep people in slavery. Sabbath allows us to walk in the freedom that Jesus offers.[30]

A Technological Sabbath

Throughout this chapter, we have discussed how Sabbath potentially undoes unjust structures within our economic system alongside provoking those practicing Sabbath to embody more responsible and restrained consumerism and material simplicity. However, the relationship between Sabbath and economics cannot be fully addressed without also discussing technology, the medium by which most modern people tap into this economic system.

We are just awakening to how newer technologies—such as social media and smartphones—are changing our lives. There are many benefits to new technologies. We should be thankful for penicillin and heart surgery and flu shots and emergency crews who can save lives. We should be thankful for mass food production that feeds more people. There are many technological benefits. Still, the problem remains that we so readily, and uncritically, accept *every* technological evolution—deeming it "good"—without carefully considering the repercussions of these so-called progresses. We assume technological newness equates with progress. But as Wendell Berry laments, "The aims of production, profit, efficiency, economic growth, and technological process imply, as I have said, no social or ecological standards, and in practice they submit to none."[31] Berry's point? Not all new technologies are progress. A technological society blindly celebrates every technological advance, turning a blind eye to the effects technologies have on creation and the people around us.

The negative impacts of social media on our psychological well-being, for one, are becoming clearer and clearer. Reputable studies are suggesting, for instance, that constant social media use has the same effect on our brains as gambling. In gambling and social media, the user seeks a hit of some kind from the external reward.[32] What was once the chime of a slot machine is now a notification of a post that has been liked or retweeted. This can lead to a whole new kind of addiction and obsession. Five hundred years of video are uploaded to Facebook every day.[33] One hundred hours of video are uploaded to YouTube every minute.[34] The average person checks their phone 150 times a day.[35] And that is an average! With blistering speed, we can learn anything about anything or anyone, so long as our iPhone is charged and we have a decent wireless connection. This kind of compulsivity has led to a new kind of slavery that Joseph Ratzinger (aka Pope Benedict XVI) calls "a slavery of activity."[36]

If you remain unconvinced that society has grown addicted to telecommunication and social media, try turning your phone off for a day. Finger trembling, hold that power button down on your iPhone for a few brief seconds. As though still in the garden of Eden, you might even imagine that apple with a bite taken out of it asking, "Are you sure you want to die?" A new apple tempts us, seeking to pull us from the life of intimacy with God and each other. After the phone blinks off, one cannot help but feel life has just ended. The world goes on without you. You are naked. And ashamed. This is the beginning of your death. Truth be told, we continue to happily eat from the tree of *knowledge* of good and evil.

The internet has become the altar where we worship our god of information. In 1978 Aleksandr Solzhenitsyn, a prophetic revolutionary who had experienced firsthand the evils of the Russian gulags and had boldly confronted the communism of his motherland, delivered a commencement address at Harvard University titled "A World Split Apart." Solzhenitsyn was new to America, and from that fresh perspective he railed against Americans, who wrongly believed they were entitled to false "freedoms." He suggested that Americans falsely believed they had the freedom to look into everyone else's life. He writes, "We witness shameless intrusions on the privacy of well-known people under the slogan: 'everyone is entitled to know everything.' But this is a false slogan, characteristic of a false era: people also have the right *not to know*, and it is a much more valuable one. The right not to have our divine souls stuffed with gossip, nonsense, and vain talk. A person who leads a meaningful life does not need the excessive burdening flow of information." Solzhenitsyn—freshly emancipated from totalitarian communism—used the Harvard stage to stand against oppression masked as personal freedom. He was saying that what we call "freedom" is often nothing more than oppression with better packaging. By implying that the land of the free might actually be a land of great oppression, his address shocked many.

"Everyone is entitled to know everything." This is the motto of a technological society. Through hypertext and the internet, everything and anyone and any experience is a mere click away. Again, to be sure, a technological society has many positives. But what should interest the church most is how newly welcomed technologies are changing how people relate to one another. A number of years ago, a friend died. Throughout the time I was at the hospital after his tragic death, family members came to grieve together in the room his body occupied. The room was diverse: a number of older folks, boomers, and millennials. What I observed could have given a sociologist a decade of material to write about: different generations grieving together in very different ways. The difference between the generations? The older family members hugged one another while talking and crying with each other. The millennials, indeed, cried as well. But they were largely silent, grieving as they looked down at their phones, posting on Facebook and texting their friends. We all grieve in our own way; nobody bemoans that. But until that day I had not suspected just how substantially technology affects relationships.

In a world where the way people relate is changing and information rules, what does the Sabbath have to say? To begin, the Sabbath invites us to a healthy posture of criticism toward normative technologies. It is said that one in three people is overworked.[37] That very well may be true. But this statistic only reflects recorded, scheduled hours where the person is *at* work. When we live with our world in our pockets—by virtue of the smartphone—we carry our work around with us everywhere we go. In unprecedented fashion, we can work whenever we desire because phones, personal computers, and Wi-Fi go with us wherever we go. Work is now in our pockets. In fact, 75 percent of those who work more than forty hours a week in a white-collar job in America work on the weekends.[38] How is this possible? Through the ability to do work from our computers at home or our smartphones. There is a social dimension to this as well. Dozens of millennials in our church community have expressed to me how texting seems to make turning the phone off almost impossible, either out of fear of missing out or worrying what others will think when they do not receive an immediate response. One friend told me that once when he went camping in a place where there was no cell service, people were worried he had gotten lost or had been kidnapped when he did not respond to a text for *one evening.*

A Sabbath also questions our commitment to information as a means to salvation. A technological society essentially replaces relationship with information. I wonder whether our ability to consume information is actually alienating us from people. How many times, when a person comes to mind, do we go to Facebook or Instagram to get our information rather than pray for them or call them? Smartphones allow us to get information without having to engage in actual relationships.

But a Sabbath restores relationship back to its proper place. On the Sabbath, we turn our hearts and lives from the consumption and gluttony of knowledge toward each other. I love the words of Wayne Muller: "We are every day becoming aware of the costs of a life without rest. Increasingly, social workers, courts and probation officers are raising our children, rescuing them from the unintentional wasteland of our hyperactivity."[39] We know something is wrong. Deep down, we know that information does not save us. Hyperactivity is not true life. The kind of hyperactivity associated with having the world in our pockets is catching up to us. Sabbath settles us down. Meditate on the words of Richard Swenson: "Chronic overloading is not a spiritual prerequisite for authentic Christianity."[40] We do not need to know *everything.* Sabbath tells us it is okay. Ignorance can be good.

Sabbath dismantles the tyranny of multitasking. Many in Western society increasingly spend their time multitasking, which is made possible by "time-saving" devices such as washing machines, computers, and dishwashers.[41] Eventually, chronic multitasking can lead to what is called "hurry sickness," where we get sick doing a hundred things at once. In some cases of "hurry sickness," individuals wear chairs out faster, having no ability to sit still in them.[42] While our dishes and clothes are being washed, we have time to go online and buy those pants we want while we listen to music as we respond to emails. One could argue that every single one of us has some level of attention deficit disorder.

I was teaching at a Christian university on the topic of Sabbath-keeping when a professor approached me and explained how difficult it is to Sabbath as a professor. He said that students used to come to "office hours"—those hours in which a student could seek out the professor for counsel, questions, or help—to find the assistance they needed. However, now that students are equipped with technological capabilities to email or text at any point throughout the day, the rhythms of teaching have changed, he expressed to me nearly in tears. Nowadays, professors are expected to respond day or night with immediacy. After hearing the professor that day, I got up on the big stage to address the student body. I told them that the Sabbath was important for them as students, that they should not wait until they had everything figured out to begin Sabbath-keeping. "Start now," I said, "right where you are." I told them it was important for their minds, their bodies, even their spirits to give themselves rest from their academic pursuits. I paused and then told them it was important for their *professors* as well. I told the student body that perhaps the best thing they could do would be to *not* email the professor late at night on Sunday and expect an answer right away. They could actually give their professor a gift, a modern apple on the desk.

Sabbath disconnects our technologies so that we might reconnect to our Creator. "Being connected" is not a metaphor new to our technological society—Jesus utilized the metaphor quite powerfully. In John 15 he says we are to be "connected" to the vine. His agrarian metaphor conveys the idea that the central identity of being a Christian is not having mere information about Christ but being in *deep relationship* with Christ. In fact, as we learn from the Pharisees, one can have all the information but be disconnected from the life of Christ. Jesus deeply desires for us to be connected to him, to be on the vine, as it were. In our technological society, being connected to the internet often distracts us from opportune times to be connected to Christ in relationship. We surround ourselves with devices that help us connect with other people and websites anywhere and at any time. We keep up with the Kardashians better than we do the Holy Spirit.

Just before takeoff, a flight attendant instructs passengers to put phones on "airplane mode." I swear, some of my most intimate moments with God have come as I fly across the country in prayer, reflection, and quiet. On occasion, I have caught myself wanting to fly somewhere just so I can go back on airplane mode. That is what hyperactivity does to us. Yet we can experience this period of peace each week through God's original airplane mode—the Sabbath. All minus the high cost and heavy carbon footprint! We do not have to get on a plane to commune with God; we can commune with God right here and right now. Soon we will start so craving every God-ordained moment that we *cannot* use our smartphone.

Consider this Sabbath technology principle: the Sabbath prefers natural light to artificial light.[43] Have one day a week free of light bulbs and screens that do not respect natural life rhythms. The Sabbath returns us to natural light—to the established rhythms of God—and honors sunlight over iPhone light. Meditate on these practicalities regarding technology and the Sabbath:

- Set up email auto-reply for the Sabbath so others will not have to worry about your whereabouts. This helps others think critically about their own rest rhythms.

- If your work demands the care of people, ensure your auto-reply has contact information to reach help if there is an actual emergency.

- Relentlessly "eliminate hurry from your life," writes John Ortberg. "Hurry is not just a disordered schedule. Hurry is a disordered heart."[44] If you are hurrying, ask: What drives this?

- Ask permission from your boss to have one day each week that you are not reachable by phone or email.

- Turn off the television. Gift your mind and heart space to process what has happened during the week.

- Have a Netflix-free day. The Psalms invite us to quietly reflect on God's goodness when we lie on our beds (Ps. 4:4). Binge-watching our favorite show prevents us from following this beautiful instruction.

- Aim to spend time out of doors. The average teen spends nine hours a day using media for enjoyment.[45] This has led to "Nature-Deficit Disorder."[46] We were not made for screens alone. We were made to get outside.

QUESTIONS
for Reflection

- If there is no Sabbath, what are you living for?

- In what ways have you experienced true joy or delight in faithful obedience?

- What might it look like for you to prepare for the Sabbath?

- How might your Sabbath practice free others from oppressive economic systems?
- In what ways might God be leading you to change your consumption habits?
- How may God be leading you to change your business practices?
- How might you create margin by changing your technology habits?

6

Sabbath and the Marginalized

Yes, child of suffering, thou may'st well be sure;
He who ordain'd the Sabbath loves the poor.

Oliver Wendell Holmes, *Urania*

A Weekly Jubilee

All people matter to God. And they should, as well, to us. When Columbus stepped foot on New World soil in 1492, it was unclear to him and his fellow travelers whether the native peoples they encountered were indeed human beings or not. They looked, believed, and acted differently, speaking in unknown languages. In his uncertainty, Columbus did not treat them as human beings, worthy of love and respect. In fact, it was not until 1537 that Pope Paul III issued an edict declaring that the natives were indeed human beings on the basis that they could be converted to Christianity and receive the sacraments.[1] We are pained by this historical tale—yet we are often like Columbus toward other people. We often treat people with respect and dignity so long as they make sense to us or can soon become like us. Should Christ's love only be extended to those who make sense to us or who look like us? Never. We are sent to love without question.

Being a Christian means being a blessing to the whole world. Notice God "blesses" the seventh day, the Sabbath, in the beginning. God, it turns out, continues blessing the cosmos, the critters, and Abram, Isaac, and Jacob throughout Scripture. Indeed, God is a blessing God. What is pivotal here is that God's default relationship to *all* of creation is not that of some mean-spirited deity delighting in withholding love, mercy, and blessing. God's love, as John later reflects, is "lavished on us" (1 John 3:1). God's divine posture is not primarily one of curse; rather, God's posture toward his world is one of relentless, generous blessing.

God desires to bless the whole world, not just his people. This is why we see God declaring Abram to "be a blessing" (Gen. 12:2–3) to the world around him. God blesses Abraham to be a blessing to the whole world. God likewise blesses Isaac, Jacob, and David to bless the world. And God blesses us with the mercies of Christ that we, his church, might bless the world. "Love one another," said Jesus, "as I have loved you" (John 13:34). Therefore, no blessing from God should be bottled up. The church is a conduit, mediating generously that which it has received. This means that the litmus test for true Christian ethics is how those who follow Christ love and serve and bless those who do not.

Our awareness of this should greatly affect our rationale for Sabbath-keeping. Sabbath is not a gift from insiders to insiders. Sabbath is a blessing for *all* people—not only the ones we understand or who might become like us. The Sabbath has universal application. This raises some questions. First, what does the church at Sabbath mean for the poor, the alien, the underemployed, the disabled, and the marginalized? Second, how do the poor, the marginalized, and the "least of these" actually enter that rest themselves? Is the Sabbath a day only for the wealthy? Is the Sabbath a product of class or privilege? Should (or can) the underemployed enter the Sabbath? This chapter examines how the Sabbath principle has tremendous potential to help Christ's church begin to undo the festering effects of sin and darkness that create tremendous hurt, oppression, and abuse.

The very "weekend" we enjoy would seem foreign to the Jews during their Egyptian slavery. Why? There were no Sabbaths or sabbaticals in Egypt—Israelites worked seven days a week for forty years. One of the first things God initiates as he frees his people is new norms for societal life under his rule. God prepares Israel to enter the promised land by instructing them to have a sabbatical year every seventh year, in which the land itself enjoyed a respite. During that rest, no sowing, reaping, or gathering was allowed. The implication had huge import for human society: if the land rests, so do the people. There is no work to be done. And vice versa: if the people rest, so does the land.

Sabbaticals are fundamentally a biblical exhortation. Although common in contemporary society, sabbaticals are generally reserved for academics, some clergy, and those in the higher echelon of the business world. Grocery store greeters do not generally get sabbaticals. Nor adjunct professors. Can you imagine a burger flipper requesting a sabbatical? Ironically, corporate workers at McDonald's *can* take a paid sabbatical once they have worked there for ten years.[2] The sad truth is that McDonald's often does sabbaticals better than the church. Still, the sabbatical commands in the Bible would have included *everyone*: grocery store greeters, adjunct professors, burger flippers, and even the land. The biblical narrative insists that the Sabbath rhythm is for society—for *everyone* in it, not just the rich.

That would have been a different kind of society, wouldn't it? Clearly, God's sabbatical society runs squarely against any society based on endless work and toil—societies ominously marked with the devil's fingerprints. If social media has accomplished anything, it is this: sin and evil are not figments of our imagination. We can see them. We have the videos. Sin and evil are *real*. And not just systems of evil—Satan himself is personal and real. And the devil does not Sabbath. Scripture refuses to mince words about the power of darkness and its tireless work in our world. Satan, in the piercing words of Paul, is the "god of this age" (2 Cor. 4:4) and "the ruler of the kingdom of the air" (Eph. 2:2). John further asserts that "the whole world is under the control of the evil one" (1 John 5:19). Control. That is a strong word, is it not? Theologically speaking, Jesus has not yet fully entered his rule in this domain, as he soon will in the coming age. The kingdom of Christ is both here and not yet. Satan controls this present world and asserts his power to destroy God's dreams for the world. But God is still sovereign and ultimately the one who will have his way. In God's sovereignty, he actually grants freedom to Satan, his allies, and our dark world to exercise autonomy until the reconciliation of all things. Satan's control is dependent and limited.

As a pastor, I find this awareness of Satan's authority to be extremely helpful in responding to those who wrestle with questions about how God can be simultaneously good and in control of a world in which there is evil. While being sovereign, God is not fully in control of this world. Satan controls the world—for now. God was sovereign during the Holocaust. That is a disturbing paradox for a Christian to deal with. God has willingly given freedom to humans to do the destructive things they do. The truth remains that this is a world ruled by powers of darkness and oppression at present until Christ comes to rule again. Evil exists because God is not yet fully occupying the throne of human authority. That *will* change. For now, however, we must remember that all the evil and sin in the world is not God's fault. The devil has his way in this world. Blame for suffering is on his shoulders, not God's. The world we now see is a world where Satan has *his* way. No one can say with a straight face that this world looks like a world where God is in control. Rather, this is a world that looks like humanity has abdicated its authority to Satan.

In the devil's reign, society is established and ruled by power and dominance, not service and love. As we saw earlier, Adam's relationship to his work and the woman was altered by obeying the words of the serpent. Genesis 3 further describes similar trajectories: Cain kills Abel, and Lamech becomes a polygamist. The rest of Scripture, one could say, is history. Men have tried ruling women with iron fists. The rich have abused the poor. One race has enslaved another. One class has stolen from another. Sin tempts us to rule *over* each other rather than serve one another, as God would desire. Relating this to the Sabbath, one must not overlook the subtle fact that God instructed *both* men and women to rest together. God never wanted Adam to rest while Eve slaved away in the kitchen and took out the garbage. In a world hardened by male rule, the command for women to Sabbath is deeply significant and reflects God's heart.

Broken systems ultimately break people. A broken humanity that listens to and follows the devil's advice can only make a broken system, and our systems have massive effects on the people who live within them. In Aleppo, Syria, mass concrete production has led to severe drought. With more than a million farmers losing their livelihood, cities have become crowded with people scrounging to get by. Hunger, unemployment, and overcrowding have made fertile grounds for extremist organizations.[3] Climate scientists consider climate change as a threat multiplier when studying the connection between climate and conflict. Even Defense Secretary Chuck Hagel said in 2014, "Rising global temperatures, changing precipitation patterns, climbing sea levels and more extreme weather events will intensify the challenges of global instability, hunger, poverty and conflict."[4] With increasing temperatures, fewer and fewer freshwater sources are available, leading to more competition and increased tension and conflict among governments and peoples.[5] Broken systems affect real people in real ways.

We *are* affected by the systems and environments we create. How can we honestly think that a society without Sabbath will not affect people? Do we really think we can create a society that treats people as commodities, machines, and slaves who never rest and expect that the systems we are creating will *not* have an impact on us? There is a connection. What if so much of the strife we are experiencing is the result of the lack of Sabbath? I have often wondered whether people in this 24/7 age are more emotionally and psychologically drained than at any other time in history—we say the regrettable, we do the unthinkable, and we are more reticent to forgive. Could it be possible that our exhaustion is driving us all to spiral further down into violence and hopelessness?

As this chapter was being written, my newsfeed was flooded with stories unpacking two weeks of racial strife, violence, and unrest in urban America. There are two sides to the news. More young black men have been gunned down as they have attempted to surrender to authorities. Simultaneously, police officers have been shot in retaliation. In many respects, these stories do not reveal a new societal problem. Instead, these defects of the human heart that breed violence have existed since humanity's fall. What is new is social media's incredible power to deliver this news into our pockets at lightning speed. And every story is a punch to the gut. No wonder so many simply choose not to care.

These stories seem to come daily now. I wonder whether part of our pain is exacerbated by the fact that we are simply exhausted. Can we truly love, forgive, and be patient with others *without* entering the Sabbath? In his book *Margin*, Dr. Richard Swenson makes a compelling connection between broken relationships and our lack of rest. He argues that relational strife and unrest take place largely because of overload.[6] When we do too much and take on far more than we can handle, we greatly increase the chances of not living peaceably with each other. We are tired, we are unfulfilled, we are frustrated, and we are hopeless.

Do not misunderstand this: sin is not atoned for by a day of rest. Nor is discrimination on the basis of age, disability, race, sex, or marital status a result merely of a lack of Sabbath in our culture. But our unwillingness to rest and find respite in Christ is negatively affecting the way we treat each other. I would strongly argue that the Sabbath commandment is one step forward in undoing systemic evils that our world has been enslaved by since the fall. I know this: I can best serve, love, forgive, embrace, and welcome others when I am at peace in my heart and my own body.

When the church embraces the Sabbath, our society *will* change. God's heart for a society built on Sabbath is reflected in the Jubilee commands (Lev. 25). Every seventh day, God's people were to rest. Every seventh year, the land was to rest, giving it a chance to heal, breathe, and recover from human toil. Then there was the Jubilee. While Sabbath may already seem extreme, every fiftieth year was to be a complete societal overhaul. Debts would be canceled. Land would be returned to its original owner. And the poor would be released from exorbitant burdens. The Jubilee commandment would drastically alter the economic system. Many rabbis who reflected on the Jubilee also believed that every fence should be removed from the land to blur the lines of personal ownership.[7] It was as though, in the Jubilee, everything returned to God. Animals could roam freely. This land was not our land. It was God's land.

Imagine the consequences of this. The rich would no longer be able to rule the poor with exorbitant taxes or rents. All bad debts would be null and void. And any land taken away from you would be returned. The poor would sing in the streets. One almost hears in Mary, celebrating over her baby Jesus, a sense that she saw him as the Jubilee:

> He has performed mighty deeds with his arm;
>> he has scattered those who are proud in their inmost thoughts.
> He has brought down rulers from their thrones
>> but has lifted up the humble.
> He has filled the hungry with good things
>> but has sent the rich away empty. (Luke 1:51–53)

One can only imagine that such a new arrangement was welcomed by the poor and humble but would be perceived as horrible news for the rich and powerful.

The sad matter remains: it is largely believed that no one actually kept the Jubilee command in its totality. Certainly, elements of it may have been attempted from time to time, but there is no evidence the Jubilee year ever actually happened. Such a dramatic societal shift would have literally turned the world upside down. So radical, ideal, and different in its scope would it have been that any economy that gave preference to the rich over the poor would have most likely crumbled at its very core if Jubilee were established. And I think God would have been okay with it. What kind of God spends his time propping up systems that push people down? A Jubilee society would have been an alternative society to Egyptian ways of life.

A Sabbath society reflects God's compassion to all people. Does God care about systems? Without question! Systems affect those God came to redeem. Only an absentee, absentminded God could *not* care about the systems that affect the people and creation he made. Jesus cares about the systems of our society precisely because Jesus cares about people. The intrinsic worth of each human leads us to understand that God cares about anything and everything that affects human beings. If anything hurts people—even those in society we give little attention to—God cares. Sabbath is about a pro-life God who cares for all vulnerable life—refugees, immigrants, migrant workers, the elderly, the rich, the poor, and the unborn. If it is a life, God is pro-it. On the Sabbath, the pregnant mother rests alongside the child within her. As she enters Sabbath, she extends rest to the truly vulnerable. Her unborn child—that tiny, vulnerable child being formed by the caring Creator—is allowed to rest as well and sit in the tranquility of that Sabbath womb. An abortion, in the end, is a violation of God's original safe space, the womb. An abortion ends the Sabbath rest of the most vulnerable child among us.

In Luke 6:1–11, Jesus and his disciples walk through grainfields on a Sabbath. To the consternation of the Jewish leaders who look on, Jesus and his disciples pick and eat the grain. Is Jesus stealing? Why can they eat grain that is not theirs? But in Jewish culture the outside layer of one's grainfield was to go unharvested so that the poor had something to eat, a practice called "gleaning." The lesson is profound: Jesus gleaned from someone else's field. Even Jesus reaped the rewards of a farmer honoring God's commands. Everyone, even Jesus, benefits from biblical living. The religious, of course, take issue—seeing the Sabbath day in terms of rules, not graciousness, generosity, and kindness to others. But God incarnate chose to live vulnerably as a poor man, gleaning from another's field, existing on the generosity of others.

"Sabbath," quips Samuel Dresner, "is the great equalizer."[8] Sabbath breaks down false walls and powers and any rationale that leads to social stratification wherein one is perceived as more valuable than another. At the Sabbath, like the cross, everyone stands on equal footing and gets a break. We realize that we are all loved and embraced by the love of God as we rest in his presence. Everyone, not just the privileged, is invited into the rich feast of mercy that has been theirs since the creation of the world.

A Sabbath is a weekly Jubilee during which the powerful are humbled and brought low, and the poor and lowly are gifted space, love, and generosity.

Sabbath as *Hesed*

A Sabbath is an act of love toward other people. Jesus was asked, "Which is the greatest commandment in the Law?" His response, albeit a little evasive, communicated a great truth. "Jesus replied: 'Love the Lord your God with all your heart and with all your soul and with all your mind.' This is the first and greatest commandment. And the second is like it: 'Love your neighbor as yourself'" (Matt. 22:35–39). As is often pointed out, Jesus's questioner asked for *one* commandment. For Jesus, however, the greatest commandment was summed up not in one command but two: love God *and* neighbor. The way of Jesus is that one cannot worship God properly without loving one's neighbor. Likewise, one cannot love a neighbor appropriately if one is not loving God. Love of God and love of neighbor are never mutually exclusive.

Paul writes, "Whoever loves others has fulfilled the law" (Rom. 13:8). Thus, the totality of Old Testament law is beautifully fulfilled in the actions of loving the neighbor. Look at the Ten Commandments. Some, particularly the first three, detail ways we love God—worship, rejecting idols, not taking

God's name in vain. The last six, however, concern themselves with love of neighbor—no stealing, no murder, no adultery, honor your parents, no lying, and no jealousy. Yet one command remains unclear as to its purpose—the Sabbath. Is the Sabbath about loving God, or is it about loving the neighbor? This is why it has been called "the bridge commandment." For tradition holds that it is the one command explicitly concerned with loving God *and* neighbor simultaneously. When one enters the Sabbath, it is as though we are loving God *and* those around us.

One Puritan thinker, in antiquated English, stresses that worship of God and love of neighbor always culminate in the practice of the Sabbath: "Religion is just as the Sabbath is, and decayes and growes as the Sabbath is esteemed: the immediate honour and worship of God which is brought forth and swaddle in the first three Commandments, is nurst up and suckled in the bosome of the Sabbath."[9]

But Jesus does something remarkable: he comes up with a new commandment, one not listed in the original Ten Commandments. In Mark 10:17–22, Jesus responds to the rich young ruler who asks him what he must do to inherit eternal life: "You know the commands: 'You shall not murder, you shall not commit adultery, you shall not steal, you shall not give false testimony, you shall not defraud, honor your mother and your father'" (v. 19). Jesus lists those commandments concerning loving a neighbor. However, Jesus adds one: "You shall not defraud." Was this one of the Ten Commandments? It was not. Jesus is speaking to a rich young man who most likely made his fortune from the high debt percentages he was charging to the poor who borrowed from him. Jesus demands that the rich man cease doing such work. To the young man, the thought of not living off of the backs of those from whom he is stealing is unthinkable, so he walks away from Jesus, downcast.

The lesson is potent: to love God is to cease sinning against one's neighbor. Loving God is done not only directly but also *indirectly* by loving the neighbor. In Matthew 25, Jesus tells the parable of the sheep and the goats, contrasting those entering God's glory (sheep) and those entering judgment (goats). Speaking of the future judgment, Jesus commends the sheep for giving *him* a glass of water, visiting *him* in prison, and giving *him* clothing. But for the goats, he condemns them for not giving *him* a glass of water, not visiting *him* in prison, and not giving *him* clothing. Both parties are surprised. The sheep say, "When did we do these things?" Jesus says, "Whenever you did this to the least of these." The goats are surprised as well, saying, "When did we *not* do these things?" Jesus says, "When you did not do these to the least of these, you did not do it to me." The parable is convicting and weighty—for when we care for others, we are caring for Jesus himself.

Another example of this kind of "indirect worship" is seen in Hebrews 6:10, where the author encourages Christ followers who have shown great love to others in the church: "God is not unjust; he will not forget your work and the love you have shown *him* as you have helped his people and continue to help them." Here, the author of Hebrews says that caring for the needs of those in the church *is* loving God.

Think of it this way: imagine that my six-year-old son were kidnapped and kept alive in some hole in the ground far from my embrace. Then imagine that you, the reader, stumble upon that hole in the ground, see my son, and fight off his kidnappers. You rescue him and bring him to me. In that moment, it is as though you are helping me. Why? Because anyone who helps my son is actually helping me. With the Sabbath, we see in one single command what it is like to love God and love others at the same time. All in one. In loving people with the Sabbath, we are loving God. And vice versa. What we do for them, we do for him. That is *hesed* love: unbounded love toward the other as an expression of love for God himself. George Forell wisely illustrates *hesed* in his book *Faith Active in Love*. In *hesed* love, God says to us, "If you want to love and serve me, do it through your neighbor; *he needs your help, I don't.*"[10]

Sabbath is an extension of *hesed* to those around us. In Exodus 20, as the Sabbath command is being described, its loving orientation toward the other is seen. All are to rest—sons and daughters, slaves, oxen, donkeys, livestock, immigrants. Walter Brueggemann writes, "Sabbath is the great day of equality when all are equally at rest. Not all are equal in production. Some perform much more effectively than others."[11] On the Sabbath, all get to rest! We are freed to not have to do more, sell more, control more, know more, be involved in more, focus on our appearance more, or score more. The Sabbath changes our relationship to others and breaks us from one-upmanship.

The Sabbath for Stay-at-Home Moms, the Poor, and the Imprisoned

Inevitably, someone will propose some practical, philosophical, and theological rebuttal to Sabbath on the grounds that the "least of these" cannot Sabbath: What about the person in abject poverty who works seven days a week? Or the stay-at-home parent who works eighty hours a week to put food on the table for five children? Or the imprisoned man who cannot control his schedule? These questions matter greatly because the Sabbath is not meant to be a mark of any kind of privilege. Sabbath should not be for those with time, space, energy, and money to do so. God desires Sabbath for *all* people. Would God command something unattainable by the "least of these," whom he dearly loves?

Time and again for the Jews, Sabbath welcomed adversity, be it through exile, cultural assimilation, or economic pressure. During the Babylonian exile, for example, Sabbath came under great attack as God's people lived in a foreign land. Jewish communities struggled to Sabbath during the Middle Ages, often putting their lives at risk to do so. Even while the leaders of the Spanish Inquisition had their military leaders stand on the tallest building of the city in winter to see whether any home did not have smoke coming out of the chimneys—a sign of a hiding Jewish family who was not lighting any fires on the Sabbath—the Jews endeavored to keep Sabbath. Sabbath rarely seems to find a welcome home in this world.

Perhaps no greater challenge arose than during the Holocaust, when Jewish families went to extremes to keep Sabbath. A great deal, in fact, has been written about how the Jewish people kept a Sabbath even while in the concentration camps and ghettos under the Nazi regime. One particular story recounts how German gestapo soldiers sought to undermine the Jewish Sabbath because they knew it brought comfort and community to those who kept it. In one ghetto, German soldiers gave out food rations on Sundays—the day *following* the Jewish Sabbath—hoping that Jewish families would run out of food by the following Saturday, being forced to abandon their day of rest.[12] These oft-forgotten stories remind us that Sabbath obstacles will arise. There is rarely an ideal Sabbath. But the presence of problems has never historically been reason to ignore the Sabbath. Again, I wonder whether adversity is the sign that we are doing something right. The Sabbath is always subversive.

We should expect difficulty to arise for ourselves when we Sabbath. But our Sabbath should not create problems for others. There are horrific historical instances when one's Sabbath became another's slavery. For example, a class of gentiles during the Old Testament period, the *Shabbos Goyim*, were hired to provide rest for Israel. That was not Sabbath—that was slavery. Here is the working principle: it is not a true Sabbath if my rest becomes another's slavery. In most cases, the rich must take the first step to use their power, resources, and influence to provide Sabbath on others' behalf. In the end, if the rich do not Sabbath, neither can the poor. A society's most well off have a disproportionate responsibility to keep Sabbath so that the poor might also. Too often, our systems do not provide people with one whole day completely off. And so the poor are prevented from resting—especially those who have to work seven days a week just to put food on the table. In many cases, the poor literally cannot afford to rest.[13]

To illustrate, I remember a group project during my freshman year of college. Our self-selected team was to prepare a presentation. Our ragtag group of highly motivated undergrads worked around the clock to finish what we perceived to be a top-notch product before presentation day. There was one problem: I was the weakest link in the group. Everyone was far more motivated and skilled than I. So, because it required me to work extra hard to keep up with the intellectually privileged in the group, I was forced to work whenever anyone else did and twice as hard when they did not. As long as the others worked, I was on the clock. We finished the project, exhausted. That experience illustrates the principle of why the privileged must rest. The biblical command to allow rest means that as long as the privileged in society are working, the less-than-privileged must as well—if not harder just to keep up.

I find it interesting that academics—a group, mind you, who often get a sabbatical every seven years—can be the quickest to critique the Sabbath on the grounds that it remains an activity of privilege. Is it hypocritical to advocate for Sabbath rhythms for self but not for others? If we get Sabbath, we have a responsibility to advocate for others. We should not feel shame when we get a Sabbath. Rather, we should turn and advocate for others as well. Nor should we feel shame for not keeping an ideal Sabbath. When I first began teaching on the Sabbath, I was struck that those who resisted the most were mothers with children. Ultimately, their concern was that we were inviting people into something that was not practical or possible for them. Many of those mothers felt shamed for staying at home and caring for a family and then, on top of it, felt shamed for not having a Sabbath in place in their home.

Sabbath is not honored through shame or guilt. Put simply, shame is work—tedious work to be exact. Shame and rest are mutually exclusive realities.[14] If Sabbath becomes about heaping shame on anyone else, then we have failed to practice the rich grace of the Sabbath. If we feel shameful about keeping a Sabbath, we are not understanding it properly. Nor will coercion ever lead to authentic rest. To be clearer, it is guilt that so often motivates us to work eighty hours a week and produce like we work for Pharaoh. Guilt does not motivate us to rest. Life does. As the old saying goes: never teach a man how to build a ship; rather, teach him a love of the sea. We cannot force someone to rest, but we can inspire them to love life as it is supposed to be lived.

We must embody a Sabbath way that, first, makes Sabbath possible for all and, second, never forces it on anyone. The words of Nelson Mandela ring true: "For to be free is not merely to cast off one's chains, but to live in a way that respects and enhances the freedom of others."[15] One's Sabbath, one's freedom, must extend to all for it to be considered real freedom. For the Jewish people, this is reflected in the principle of *kavod habriyot*—that we have a duty to honor *every* living being. For the way in which we treat the least in our society is how we treat God. Sabbath for the poor, the underemployed, and the stay-at-home mom becomes a litmus test of the health and justice of a society. Should the Sabbath also count for those who have been imprisoned? Absolutely it should. In many societies, those in prison are forgotten. But the Sabbath command should be extended to them as well.[16]

Years ago I heard John Goldingay, a professor of Old Testament at Fuller Theological Seminary, lecture on the commands and laws of God in the Hebrew Bible. He talked about how they represented God's dream for the world, an idealistic picture of what humanity is supposed to be like. God, for example, envisioned a world where there was no sexual violation or perversion. He dreamed of a world free of lying, gossip, and jealousy. His world was to be one free of murder and oppression and torture. God dreamed of a world where humans could rest. Throughout history, people have chosen autonomy over God's ideals, which are for the flourishing of community. People have confused license with freedom. License is for personal satisfaction. Obedience, however, results in freedom for the whole community.

An illustration may help. Children often need to clean their rooms. It is not uncommon for a parent to see the disaster that is a child's room and inform them that they need to pick up. Every time children clean up, parents stand and look at the clean room and enjoy the ideal picture. The room, however, is rarely in that ideal state. I often remind my son: You remember what your room is supposed to look like? I communicate the ideal. He knows the ideal. But as a good parent, I never kick my son out when the ideal is not met. That is true of God: when the ideal is not met, God still enters in and loves us. And it is when we seek to live the ideals of God, to care about the things he cares deeply about, that we meet him.

Goldingay calls this a "theology of ideal and condescension."[17] Simultaneously, God has ideals that he expects of and desires for us, *and* God knows we cannot meet them and so he seeks to meet us in the moments that we try to keep his ideals, even imperfectly.

As it relates to the poor, the stay-at-home dad, the person in prison, the disabled, or any person who is in a place of life where Sabbath is excruciatingly problematic, what matters most is not that they do a Sabbath perfectly but that they try their best in whatever context they find themselves in. While the ideal is to rest one day a week, some simply cannot. And for the person who risks to take a four-hour window of rest, the Lord will be present with him or her in the midst of the attempt. For the stay-at-home mom who can give one hour of quiet and solitude to God after putting her children down to sleep, God will meet her in her intentional rest.

God never intended what he gave to us as a gift to become a tool of shame or guilt. The Sabbath is for us. We are not for the Sabbath. And in that reality we can experience freedom and joy. Remember Paul's words: "Therefore do not let anyone judge you by what you eat or drink, or with regard to a religious festival, a New Moon celebration or a Sabbath day" (Col. 2:16). Do not be judged, friend. Remember, no one has ever, save Jesus, kept a Sabbath perfectly. There is grace. Endless grace. All we have to do is "make every effort" to enter the Sabbath.

Practically, how can you begin if you find yourself in a challenging situation? Do this: begin with a half-day Sabbath. Just half a day. Turn your phone off. Make some pancakes. Go on a walk. Pray. Pull out your journal. Read a psalm out loud. God will meet you. And as you enter into the Sabbath rest that God eternally beckons you into, you will find that your heart is being slowly transformed. You may just find yourself hooked. God will provide in some way. Never forget all the "booty stories" in the Bible. Every time God sends his people on a journey—be it through the desert, on the way to the promised land, as disciples with Jesus—he provides for them in unique and special ways. As Israel leaves Egypt to enter the journey to freedom, they receive riches and provisions (booty) from the Egyptians as they leave. They never went on a journey without provision. That is the God we follow. He sends us into the desert with a provision of rest.

My gut tells me that you will not be able to stop. In a decade of Sabbath-keeping, I have never met someone who *used to* Sabbath. Nor have I met someone who wished they had kept fewer Sabbaths. Once you start, you probably won't stop. It is profoundly life giving.

Change is hard. Do not expect Sabbath to come easily overnight. But the act of trying to do it is the most important thing. I taught a class once at a local university on ecopsychology, an area of study that relates ecology (the study of organisms in an environment) and psychology (the scientific study of the human mind). In the class, I presented some rather startling research on the relationship between our minds and the environment around us. The research asked what causes one to embrace a sustainable lifestyle. What the research revealed was that there is literally zero connection between formal education on the matter and caring for God's creation. That is, people did not begin to care for creation because they took a class on it or read a book about it. Rather, the most foundational thing that helped someone care for creation was their experience of actually doing it and being in creation.[18] The lesson: you cannot love something you do not personally know. The Sabbath cannot be loved as an idea: it must be loved in the doing.

When we look at the Gospels or the writings of Paul, St. Augustine, and even Aristotle, we get a skybox view of the *real* problem of humanity's unwillingness to change: sin.[19] Laura Ruth Yordy once wrote, "Human sinfulness, unfortunately, proves highly resistant to cognitive cures."[20] Her point? Sin is not fixed through mere cognitive education. Sabbath is not an education issue; it is an obedience issue. The results of the Sabbath affect so many people and places. We can be aware of this, and yet the thing that matters is not whether we have that knowledge in our heads. What is important is that we take action, that we practice it, that we try it, that we give it a shot.

I love the old African proverb "Truth is but a rumor until it lives in our bones." We must start to *try* truth—we must do it. How do we start keeping a Sabbath? Start here and start now. The problem is not the need for more education and more information. We need to begin to try it out—to experience it. We change as we do what God invites us into. I did not begin caring for God's creation because I read Genesis 1 or heard a lecture on the topic. I began caring for creation because I hiked the woods outside Birmingham during my PhD studies in Britain and came to love it. I did not start sharing my newfound Christian faith in high school because I read a book on evangelism; I began sharing my faith because I loved my friend whom I shared a locker with. Hatred is overcome the same way—not by reading books about friendship but by making friends. I would venture a guess that former white supremacists did not begin to love and respect African Americans by becoming "educated" on the topic alone. Rather, in most cases, former white supremacists' *experience* of having an African American friend caused them to see and act differently. True life change does not come by simply knowing the facts. True life change comes by beginning to live out truth in a context of great grace.

"God's *kindness* is intended to lead you to repentance," Paul writes in Romans 2:4. Guilt trips do not lead to repentance. Neither does shame. Or more information. Repentance is the result of God's sheer grace and mercy alone—nothing else. When you know you are loved even if you never change, then true change is possible.

QUESTIONS
for Reflection

- If the church is a conduit for God's blessings, what could it look like to extend the blessing of Sabbath to others (who may not even keep a Sabbath)?
- How might Sabbath enable you to become a person of service?
- Are there areas of your family, community, workplace, or the world where you can observe that a lack of Sabbath causes strife?

- How might you embody the spirit of Jubilee?
- What might it look like for you to "make every effort" to enter Sabbath rest?
- How will you begin to Sabbath this week?
- How does the knowledge that you are known and loved completely, even if you never change, speak to you?

PART 3

SABBATH
FOR CREATION

7

Sabbath and Creation

We now understand God's rest to be at the same time the rest of his creation.

Dietrich Bonhoeffer, *Creation and Fall; Temptation*

A String Holding It Together

In this chapter, we will look at the relationship between Sabbath-keeping and our call to care for God's creation. Most important, I want to discuss how keeping a Sabbath actually helps heal a creation that is "groaning" (Rom. 8:22). Indeed, when we forget the Sabbath, the well-being of the planet is put at risk.

What happens when we do not Sabbath? In the news, we encounter stories of individuals who have been physically hurt while serving in our nation's armed forces. One particular story of a young man who fought in Iraq caught my attention. During battle he was shot, eventually losing a limb. The veteran described a surprising phenomenon years later: although his leg was gone, deep pain could still be felt in the place where it once was. This happens, it turns out, often. Those who lose limbs often feel excruciating pain for years to come at the very place where something has been lost. Doctors call this "phantom pain."[1]

Creation was created perfectly. Everything that it needed in order to function properly was included. God created an environment perfectly suited for life to thrive. Examining the biblical account, we see that the Sabbath is an integral part of God's creation. Although done on the final day, Sabbath remains as much a part of creation as light, water, the sun, food, livestock, microorganisms, chickens, the garden, and people. Can you imagine, for a brief moment, what our planet would look like if we no longer had water? Or light? Or food? What if we decided trees were unnecessary and cut them all down? In the end, remove any of these elements from creation and assuredly creation would not continue as a place suitable for life. The world would start to fall apart. So why do we think we can have a world without Sabbath and all will be well and fine? In creation, everything is affected by everything else because the perfect Creator knew what he was doing when he made the planet. By ignoring the Sabbath, the world suffers tragic consequences. Creation suffers great pains because of what we have essentially cut out. The Sabbath is as integral to the sustaining of our planet as water, light, and all the green things. Without the Sabbath, the world would begin to crumble.

What would happen if everyone in the world stopped Sabbath-keeping altogether? In his book 24/6, Dr. Matthew Sleeth illustrates this with a story from his residency program. One day, his attending supervisor showed him an X-ray of a sick patient. The supervisor asked, "What is wrong with this patient?" Investigating the X-ray, Sleeth could not see anything that looked wrong—no lumps, shadows, or seemingly concerning issues appeared in the X-ray. The problem, it turned out, was not what was there but what was *not* there. Dr. Sleeth soon learned a crucial lesson about health and well-being. The patient was missing her left clavicle, almost certainly eaten away by cancer. Sleeth stresses that this is how we must think about the Sabbath. What often hurts creation the most is not what is there but what is *not* there.[2] By leaving out the Sabbath from our lives, the very earth God has put us up on suffers devastating consequences.

Like the creation story, the earth is created to have rhythms of rest and respite. The land needs a break from productivity. Certain animals need to hibernate. The ocean needs breaks for fish populations to be replenished. Like human beings, when creation is robbed of a chance to rest, it quickly begins to communicate its exhaustion to us. The earth is a lot like our own bodies. To stay healthy, I am committed to regular check-ins with a professional counselor and a spiritual director. During an appointment with my counselor, Raymond, he taught me how to listen to my body as a way of helping me discern how my spiritual life is going. He suggested that the first place where the by-products of my false worship and idolatry will reveal themselves is in my body—increased blood pressure, headaches, and exhaustion. Raymond taught me how to listen to, and respect, my body's cry for sleep, good food, and quiet. The body is a good thing to listen to. It knows me best. The body God has made knows what it is doing. The problem remains: we rarely listen to it.

My body, Raymond explained, is a kind of prophet in my life, telling me what I most need to hear. Raymond calls this the "sovereignty of the body." As a theologian, I am reluctant to think of anything as sovereign other than God. Still, I have come to understand his point. Our bodies know what they are doing and remain apt communicators. They tell us what we need to hear when we need to hear it. Rather than ignoring exhaustion, hunger, pain, and anxiety, we should pay attention to it and ask ourselves what our body is speaking to us. The body speaks clearly. It is God's gift to speak truth to us.

The earth speaks truthfully to us as well. Over the better part of ten years, I focused my academic pursuits on studying what is transpiring in creation and considering what our biblical responsibility is in response. I have studied and written a great deal about all kinds of issues, such as climate change, ecological sustainability, and creation care. And at the end of the day, I can say with confidence that so much of the ecological issues we face are a direct result of the fact that we have ignored the Sabbath. We never give creation a break. And like a body screaming that it needs sleep, the earth is screaming at us that something is wrong. When God's creation stops working the way it is supposed to, it is because it is quietly (or loudly) telling us that we are not treating it appropriately. When cancer rates skyrocket, our bodies are telling us we are using too many pesticides. When consuming unhealthy foods leaves us in poor health or obese, our bodies are crying out to us that we need to rethink the importance of health. When earthquakes become commonplace in Oklahoma, the earth is speaking to us that fracking is not life giving to God's good order. And so on and so forth. Just as our bodies speak to us to alert us, the earth speaks to us to guide and correct us.

God's creation is a sensitive environment designed to support the flourishing of life. In fact, God spends five *entire days* creating the world *before* Adam and Eve are even introduced to the environment. Before creating humanity, God creates the great beasts of the world. Some of these beasts our text calls "livestock." What are livestock for? Livestock are specific animals that are good for—I daresay made for—the purpose of helping to support human flourishing. All before humans had been made. The text explicitly states that before human beings are introduced into creation, God is strategically creating a space where human flourishing could be possible. God did not just create people; God created a whole system of air, water, plants, animals, and livestock that made human flourishing possible. Again, imagine if God left light out. Or air. Or trees. Humanity would long be gone.

As the psalmist writes, God actively causes the grass to grow for the cattle God has made (Ps. 104:14).[3] God does not create accidentally. He creates intentionally. God made a system *for* life, not just a system *of* life. It is an intricate system with Sabbath built into it. In this system, everything is dependent on something else to thrive. The system must be protected—or tragic things begin to happen.

The sensitive interconnectivity of creation is powerfully illustrated in a fascinating story from the mid-twentieth century. During the Great Leaps Forward between 1958 and 1962, Chinese ruler Chairman Mao went to great lengths to increase the productivity of the rural rice-growing industry. To that end, Mao initiated what was called the Four Pests Campaign.[4] This campaign was initiated, in short, as a result of Mao's desire to rid the landscape of what he perceived to be pests—rats, flies, mosquitoes, and sparrows—that he believed were getting in the way of a better rice industry. The idea was simple: remove the pests, and the landscape would become pristine and more productive.

Radical measures were implemented. The populace was encouraged to make excessive noise by banging pots and pans to keep the sparrows from ever landing to rest or nurture their young or protect their eggs. If a sparrow nest was found, it was to be immediately destroyed. It was reported that the sparrows would fly until they ran out of energy, dropping to the ground in sheer exhaustion. Rewards were given to those who killed the most "pests." As a result, the Eurasian tree sparrow nearly went extinct in China. Populations are still recovering to this day. And something else went wrong. Mao failed to account for the fact that sparrows, which could eat upward of ten pounds of grain each year, could *also* eat hundreds of pounds of crop-eating insects each year. In cutting out the "pests," crops were also destroyed. Rather than grain production increasing, it radically decreased, because the sparrows were a natural predator to crop-destroying insects. Some twenty million Chinese died as a result. The campaign is remembered as perhaps the worst environmental disaster in world history.

Creation cannot exist without even pests. This story illustrates the interconnected nature of God's creation—that creation needs all its parts to function properly. While God made each part of creation "good," creation was not complete—or "very good" (Gen. 1:31)—until all parts of the ecosystem were finished and worked in harmony with one another. Rather than seeing creation the way that we should—as a set of interconnected parts absolutely in need of one another—we get tricked into thinking that cutting off a foot will not affect anything else. In God's creation, even the Eurasian tree sparrow is necessary for human life to flourish.

John Muir once boiled this principle down: "When we try to pick out anything by itself, we find it hitched to everything else in the universe."[5] Creation is like a piece of clothing that, if we pull a string, will keep pulling, pulling, and pulling until the entire thing comes undone. This is the principle of all ecology at its core.[6] Perhaps my favorite definition of ecology comes from G. Tyler Miller, who says it means everyone and everything is *downwind* from everyone and everything else.[7] That is, nothing is isolated. What a powerful way to describe the created order. Physicists further define this as "quantum entanglement," the idea that every breath of air we breathe is actually air that has been breathed a million times before us. In fact, the breath of air you last took is most likely filled with atoms and molecules that Chairman Mao or even Jesus Christ himself previously breathed in. The air we breathe is not new. We breathe used air. Even our very breath is dependent on others. We are entangled with everything else in creation.

This perfect interconnectivity is both impressive and immensely humbling. My friend Steve Fitch runs an organization called Eden Reforestation Project. Steve has spent his life serving Jesus by planting millions of trees around the world for the purposes of creating jobs and helping the well-being of the planet. As it turns out, when we do not have trees, we do not have air. Trees are the earth's lungs. Steve was explaining to me a theory that people in the tree business have had for a long time. Do you know when the last ice age was? It was in the late 1770s. Do you remember that painting of George Washington crossing Valley Forge on his horse in the snow? That was a picture of the spring. Why was it snowing in spring? And what preceded this ice age? Years earlier had been the plague, which wiped out millions and millions of people from Europe. When the people were wiped out, whole communities disappeared. As horrible as that was, one good thing happened: *people stopped cutting down trees*. With millions of new trees growing, much more fresh oxygen was made. All the new oxygen, many theorize, caused the last known mini ice age.

Down-to-Earth Sabbath

When we look at this world, we clearly see that it is indeed a world marred by human sinfulness. This is summed up by Danny Glover's character, Simon, in the movie *Grand Canyon*: "Everything's s'pposed to be different than what it is."[8] For Christian philosopher Cornelius Plantinga, Simon's words capture the very essence of sin.[9] Few would disagree with the statement: creation is not operating the way it's supposed to. Through abuse, misuse, and selfishness, humans have been consumers rather than stewards of the created world. As a result, the well-being of creation, its shalom, is harmed. We must be cognizant that things are in disrepair and that humans are the only part of creation capable of reversing the damage done.

How does Sabbath play into the broken creation? In their book *Making Peace with the Land*, Fred Bahnson and Norman Wirzba expound on the idea that God is the Gardener of creation—the One who loves, cares for, and sustains creation. Convinced that the concept of Sabbath unlocks "creation's deep and inner meaning," Bahnson and Wirzba ask, "Why does God rest?" They contend that Sabbath is not God's escape from the world (for if God escaped creation, we would cease to exist) but rather an intimate immersion into it. In other words, when God practices Sabbath, God delights in what God has made. Likewise, when humanity participates in the Sabbath, humanity is to "soak it up, be fully present to it and cherish the goodness of the world God has made."[10] Thus the opposite of rest is not work but restlessness. Humanity has become restless in its consumption, which "leads directly to the neglect of the places we are in and the people we are with."[11]

When humans Sabbath, we intentionally immerse ourselves, as God did, into the creation order. And, as we have seen, this is reflected in the fact that Sabbath is not for humans alone but also for livestock, land, vineyards, and fields. Sabbath had far-reaching implications beyond humans to all nonhuman creation. Sabbath is, at its core, an ecological principle. This is not accidental. God intentionally designed and created the world in a manner that would allow for the flourishing of all. There were no mistakes in his created realm. Long before we started burning out, long before the land started dying, long before disaster struck—there was God! The world that God created is beautiful, intricate, and interconnected. And part of that interconnected beauty is the need for rest.

When we ignore the Sabbath, we become a little like Chairman Mao—we proudly believe we can eliminate from this finely tuned environment something that God created. Like getting rid of the pests, we think we can ignore the one-day-in-seven Sabbath and everything will go along the way it should. But in so doing, we fail to recognize that this is messing with the creative rhythm that God made for the benefit of humanity and the rest of the world. A world with no Sabbath is a genetically modified world. Even if we do not suffer the consequences personally, even if we are more productive and make more money and go about our lives happily, creation pays a massive price—and the damages are often irreversible. As Jewish ethicist Jonathan Sacks writes, "We know too much about ecological systems to suppose that you can remove one element and leave the rest unchanged. There is, if you like, a God-shaped hole in our ozone layer."[12] Sabbath is like the ozone. Without it, creation will simply not work the way it is created to.

Global surface temperatures, species loss, rising sea levels, loss of drinking water—these ecologic tragedies are a direct result of human sinfulness. Some well-intended Christians do not believe God would allow us to destroy our planet. Yet I wonder how we could have the capacity to run away from and destroy our relationship with God in the garden of Eden but lack the capability to destroy the garden itself. Could that be possible? Unlikely. Overconsumption, greed, selfishness, and, yes, the environmental crisis are, above all, the result of human sinfulness. Why would God let us have the freedom to go to hell but not to affect the climate?

One thing was forgotten in the "progress" of the Industrial Revolution—Sabbath. Like the sparrow during the time of Mao, creation has no space to rest. The world is too loud. That sparrow, along with the rest of creation, is beginning to fall to the ground in exhaustion. No longer a functioning society, we are an *over*functioning society. We do not cease. Therefore, creation gets no rest.

Sabbath is a string holding everything together.

But there is more. Sabbath reminds us of our own humanity. We are not, as it were, above creation. We are an integral part of creation and, like the rest of creation, are dependent on God's rest to survive. As we have discussed, one mark of technocratic cultures is the ability to know more and more information at an increasing rate. But instead of nurturing peace in our hearts and minds, informational overloading has led to a kind of gloominess wherein we no longer experience the world as a mysterious world imbued with God's mystery. As Thomas Merton once remarked, "Man's unhappiness seems to have grown in proportion to his power over the exterior world."[13] That is, the more power we have (or feel like we have) over the world around us, the less happy we become. The world is not ours. It is a wild world far outside our control. We have not been fulfilled by what control we do have. In fact, this kind of information overload is crushing us and depressing us. In the words of Bertrand Russell and Albert Einstein, "We have found that the men who know the most are the most gloomy."[14]

Sabbath dethrones humanity from its self-aggrandized place of lordship over creation by handing authority of the world back to the One to whom it already belongs. The Sabbath brings us back down to earth. In our insane curiosity to gain knowledge and have power *over* the world, we have minimized the world. I once heard that physicists are far more likely than biologists to believe in God. Why? I have a theory—the biologist looks *down* at really small things while the physicist looks *up* at big things. Ours is becoming a biologist culture—we look down at a world that we think we can completely understand and control. This is God's wild world. He ordained purpose for all parts of the created order. While holding a deep love for learning, we must also recognize that our seemingly never-filled lust for knowledge and information comes up short on its promises to make us happier and humbler people; rather, it has the capacity to cause us to believe that we are *over* the world and in control of it. Arrogance such as this does not acknowledge or respect God's design.

Sabbath-Keeping as Earth-Keeping

Just as we can see in our bodies signs that we need to rest, we need to begin to pay attention to the earth in the same manner. We need, in the words of Simone Weil, to learn to "read nature" and pay close attention to it and what it is experiencing.[15] Evidence points to the fact that the earth, the land, and the creation are deeply exhausted. If we were to pay attention, we would see that what we are doing to the planet is not advantageous to its health—and by extension, to our own.

"The earth is the LORD's," writes the psalmist, "and everything in it" (Ps. 24:1). It is not *ours*. Every part of this world was made by the Creator. This includes the beautiful parts that we love to take pictures of and put on Instagram as well as the parts of creation that seem scary or disgusting. Wendell Berry rightly states, "We will discover that God made not only the parts of Creation that we humans understand and approve but *all of it*."[16] Our call as Christians is not to *control* creation (as though we could) but to *care for* creation. All of it. Each little part of it.

One cannot read the pages of the Bible and fail to recognize, from page one, God's deep affection and love for what he has made. The love of God for creation, as one scholar describes it, "springs off the pages of the Bible."[17] The Bible is chock-full of text after text describing God's love for the created realm. Of course, it is not uncommon to run across someone who argues, from a profoundly errant reading of the Bible, that the world exists only for human consumption and for human usage. Or another may claim that no biblical texts provide an ethic that teaches we should recycle or drive less. It is true, the Bible does not explicitly use language of "environmental care" as we have come to call it. But ecological principles—about storms, agriculture, and animal life—are nevertheless found throughout the entire Bible. It should also be remembered that the biblical books were written in the context of agrarian societies almost entirely free from the kind of soil erosion, pollution, and species degradation that are commonplace today. There was, of course, a word for creation care and environmental living in biblical societies: life. Scripture does not speak about "environmentalism" as we do, because to live as a person in the ancient world was to live an environmentally friendly life.

We care for creation because God cares for his creation. I want to be cautious to not allow this call to care for creation to become just one more guilt trip. Yes, we "ought to care."[18] But for the Christian, our rationale for caring is far different from the rest of the world's. Our rationale for caring is directly linked to God's caring. To illustrate: When my son was younger, he had a set of little stuffed animals that he took meticulous care of. On many occasions he would bring those animals to me and ask me to tuck them into bed with me during the night to keep them safe. I admit, it felt awkward sleeping with stuffed animals in my early thirties. But I did it. Why? Because I loved the stuffed animals? No. I cared for those animals because my son loved them.

A Christian cares for the things God cares for. I call this "borrowed compassion." The original compassion is not ours. It is God's compassion. We care because God cares. And compassion is connected to pain, not comfort. Jesus had compassion on people and felt the pain that they felt. When we watch the news and see stories about how creation is being harmed by the way we live, we should feel pain. We should hurt. We should groan. In leading our church community, when I feel the pain of the decisions of people who have chosen themselves over others, who have chosen sin over righteousness, who have chosen selfishness over service, I should hurt. Christianity is never about arriving at a place in life where we are insulated and free from the pain of the world. We need to feel it. Compassion is feeling the pain of God in our guts and being moved to actually do something about it. In fact, I think our obsessive, overworked lives are situated in such a way that we do not have to feel the pain of the world. In insulating ourselves so, we do the world a disservice. We do what Douglas John Hall calls "psychic numbing"—we surround ourselves with activity to protect our hearts and minds from having to feel the compassion of Jesus for this world.[19]

Sabbath-keeping *is* earth-keeping. Often, when we realize our responsibility in caring for creation, we feel overwhelmed by the fact that there is so much to do. Whenever I am teaching on creation care, a student will always ask what they can do *right now* that will have an impact on the world. Certainly, there are many things. We should limit how much beef we eat, because the amount of water, fossil fuel, and grain it takes to procure one pound of beef is nearly unimaginable. We should recycle. And precycle—buy things that have as little packaging as possible. We should do our best to walk and take public transportation and offset our fuel by giving generously to those who are helping plant trees around the world through organizations such as the Eden Project. But perhaps the most important thing we can do immediately to positively impact the health of the planet is to begin to take a Sabbath. If we work six days a week, it very well may be that we can limit one-seventh of our carbon footprint because we are not commuting on that day.

Paul speaks to the fact that creation is oriented toward a future time when it will be "liberated from its bondage to decay and brought into the freedom and glory of the children of God" (Rom. 8:21). Creation cannot wait for that moment. I once read a piece by a writer who spent considerable time with prisoners. He wrote about how people who are incarcerated for extended periods of time do not necessarily have clocks or timepieces to guide their days. Moreover, their relationship to time is not one of minutes and hours—it is of months and years.[20] Time is different in prison. In prison, all time is oriented around a future moment—a time of release. In a similar way, the biblical paradigm of time is oriented around Sabbath, which, in the long run, is actually the culmination and fulfillment of all time. The weekly Sabbath day is intended to be an appetizer for the fulfillment of Christ's work in the world. It points to our liberation, our freedom. And in a very real way, our honoring of the Sabbath gives the created realm a sense of hope and anticipation for the future freedom to which it looks.

QUESTIONS
for Reflection

- What would happen if everyone in the world stopped Sabbath-keeping altogether?
- What might we be able to tell about the health of the planet if we listen?
- How might we honor God as the designer of both individual organisms and entire ecosystems?
- How might Sabbath be part of reinstating Jesus as head in your own life?
- How could your Sabbath practice liberate creation from its bondage to decay?
- Can you recall a time God spoke to you meaningfully in creation?
- What would it look like for you to spend more time in creation as a way of connecting with God and being struck with awe and wonder at his glory?

8

Sabbath and the Land

If you keep a bow always bent, it will break presently; but if you
let it go slack, it will be the fitter for use when you want it.

Aesop's Fables

Land Sabbaths

As we have discovered, God created each and every part of this world to
be interconnected and interdependent. Part of that interconnectivity is the
need for Sabbath. A world without the Sabbath would be a world in great
dysfunction. We have examined how this Sabbath principle might actually
harbor deep connections to the health and well-being of the created realm of
which we are a part, particularly as it relates to the creation-care mandate.
But we must not be tempted to end there. In this chapter, we will examine
how keeping the Sabbath actually changes, and even heals in a substantive
way, our relationship to the very land on which we live.

To begin, the Sabbath offers the physical land in creation a scheduled and
intentional opportunity for rest, respite, and restoration. When we journey
through the Old Testament and examine such land laws as those found in
Leviticus 26, a fascinating connection is established between God's people
keeping the Sabbath and the well-being of the land. With the Sabbath command implied, God says, "If you . . . are careful to obey my commands, I will
send you rain in its season, and the ground will yield its crops and the trees

their fruit. Your threshing will continue until grape harvest and the grape harvest will continue until planting, and you will eat all the food you want and live in safety in your land" (Lev. 26:3–5). The word of God was to shape Israel's conception of how the Sabbath was an act of obedience and also how such obedience was a blessing to the land. As long as God's people faithfully kept the Sabbath principle that God had established—including resting one day a week—the land would be fruitful and inhabitable. In the same chapter, however, God warns them that if they ignore the Sabbath, he will "scatter" them and their land will be "laid waste." "Then the land," God says, "will enjoy its Sabbath years all the time that it lies desolate and you are in the country of your enemies; then the land will rest and enjoy its sabbaths" (Lev. 26:33–34). The land would flourish if the Israelites kept the Sabbath. But the land would reject them if they refused to.

Of course, our eyes are drawn to one of the more interesting insights of this text: the land will "enjoy its sabbaths." Creation rests, recuperates, and even enjoys the day of rest that God is asking his people to obey and embrace. Look at this: What did the land do while Israel experienced their years of exile in Babylon? Read the powerful words of 2 Chronicles 36:21: "The land *enjoyed* its sabbath rests; all the time of its desolation it rested, until the seventy years were completed in fulfillment of the word of the LORD spoken by Jeremiah." When the Israelites were exiled, the land finally got what it needed: Sabbath rest. The land "enjoyed" its newfound lease on life because it kept a Sabbath. The land ceased. It got the break God so desired it to have. The implication, of course, is that the Israelites did not give the land a Sabbath when they occupied it. They stole from the land. And they stole from the land by not taking any breaks. Because they never ceased, the land could never cease. Thus, because of their workaholism, Israel was sent into exile.

What these texts reveal is that the land not only needs rest but, when it finally gets it, "enjoys" the rest it receives. As it rests, the land heals and flourishes. The land, it turns out, is incredibly productive when left alone. The creation narrative uses the word *teem* to describe an Edenic environment wherein life not only survives but also thrives (Gen. 1:20). What exactly does *teeming* mean? Two illustrations come to mind. Every August, our family goes on a two-week vacation, forcing us to leave our garden unattended. Returning to the Pacific Northwest, we arrive to find the garden having literally gone wild in our absence—tomato plants have doubled in size, weeds have proliferated, and strawberries have ripened. All in our absence. That is teeming, when creation flourishes and thrives even without human effort. The land has a chance to restore itself in the absence of its human caretakers. A second illustration arises from one of the most diverse bioregions, where there are more species of plants, animals, and other creatures than almost any other place in the world. Can you guess where it is? It is that parcel of land between North and South Korea known as the "demilitarized zone," the DMZ. That parcel of land has been given space between two warring peoples. Space and rest from humans breeds life in abundance. When we give space to the land, life miraculously begins to bud.

Stepping away from the land can help the land heal. In the absence of human occupants, intentional or not, the land begins to teem again the way it did in the creation story. It turns out that the best agricultural practices are based on this. When farmers give intentional breaks to their land as a way to restore it, the land is stronger the year after. Letting the land lie fallow is common practice among many to this day. As the biblical command establishes, when the land is given a year of rest every seven years, it will be more fruitful and productive. If we love the land, the land will love us back. The Sabbath gives the land a day, even a year, without us. A number of years ago, Alan Weisman's *The World without Us* examined what would happen if the world continued on without human beings because of some cataclysmic societal collapse that caused humans to go extinct. Weisman's argument, in sum, was that the world and all of creation would basically continue on just fine without us.[1] In fact, many modern ecologists are confident that even if we managed to completely annihilate our own species, the world would continue on without us. While humans are as much a part of creation as any other part of creation—the light, the sun, the water, and even the Sabbath—there is an element of truth to Weisman's argument. The Sabbath provides a day a week where the land exists without us. When humanity follows God, the land and creation is blessed.[2]

All of this helps us establish a healthier relationship with the land. In previous generations, the language of marriage was used for our relationship with the land—*husbandry*. And any healthy marriage must entail both intimacy *and* distinction. The two, Scripture says, are to become one. This relational arrangement protects simultaneously the unique identities of those involved and the intimacy they have entered into. By contrast, when a marriage has only intimacy but no difference, there ceases to be two people in the marriage. One might call this a codependent relationship. The act of two becoming one has ceased to protect the unique identity of each. When there is difference without intimacy, we would call that a separation or divorce. The one has become two. But a marriage is the two being one. A healthy relationship needs both intimacy and difference, an attribute of the Father, the Son, and the Spirit, who are all fully God but remain distinct, unique persons.

The relationship of humanity to the land—husbandry—is to be modeled after this kind of relationship. Humans were made to be intimate with the land. But humans are also different from the land and the animal orders. To function as God has desired it to, the land needs humanity to care for it *and* it needs to have a day to rest from the toil and work of humanity. In turn, humanity gets rest and is restored as well. We might see a Sabbath as having the same effects on the land as one of our times of vacation—space is created for restoration and renewal. When we are constantly present and at work with the land, it gets sick in the same way that we get sick when we overwork.

This becomes a powerful opportunity to care for the land as we rest. I spend a good deal of my vocation caring for creation and helping other Christians care for it. I believe creation care is part of God's call on all of our lives and not some accidental part of the Christian walk. A well-known environmentalist in our city heard about the environmental work our church was doing and wanted to take me out to breakfast. We set a time and met. She sat in front of me as a secular, non-Christian environmentalist telling me about the work she does. She explained how she has given her life to try to help save the planet from the coming ecological disaster. At a point in our conversation, she began to cry. I looked at her and asked her a simple question: "What is wrong with the world?"

She looked at me with a sense of great seriousness and said that the world is greedy and that if people were less greedy, the world would be okay. I pressed again and asked her how we can change the greed in the world. She began to respond hopelessly, as she knew that what was about to come out of her mouth was not going to solve the problem.

We needed new laws, she said.

I jumped in. I expressed that laws have never been able to change the human heart and that we need far more than a new set of laws. What the world needs is for hearts to be changed, and that cannot be legislated.

The environmentalist's attitude reflects so much of the environmental movement, which can lead to what my friend Dan Stiegerwald calls "shame-based activism."[3] In this approach to caring for the world, guilt and shame become our motivating factors to get others to change. And while laws can play a powerful role in a society, they are external motivators rather than internal motivators that stem from a changed heart. The world is not always changed for the better by doing more activity. Sabbath, however, offers a different way. It says that we can care for the world and the land not by doing more but actually by doing less. Who would have ever thought one day of rest a week would help heal the land?

We must recognize that God's statement "Be still, and know that I am God" (Ps. 46:10) applies to creation as well. Sometimes the best thing we can do for the healing of creation is nothing at all. "Who can make muddy water clear?" Laozi writes in the Tao Te Ching. "But if allowed to remain still, it will gradually become clear of itself."[4]

Be still. Let God do some work. Our culture says that healing can only come by doing. Scripture tells a different story. The world is healed by our stopping. The Sabbath reverses this notion and invites us to see the process of healing through silence and nonaction. Just by being, we allow God to heal us and the land. The Sabbath helps us understand that our role in bringing about God's peace in the world is not to be understood *only* in what we do; rather, sometimes it is by ceasing our doing that we usher in God's kingdom and help heal the land.

Sabbath and Returning to the Land

The Jubilee command requires that land be returned to its original owner. The radical implication of this is that *none of us own the land we live on.* All land is God's land. Humans are mere tenants, not the owners, of the land God has placed us in.

In the Old Testament, priests were not permitted to own land (Deut. 18), and thus they could not farm food or raise livestock. But the priests still needed to eat and be cared for. To remedy this, a portion of the sacrifices given to God was for the priest. The New Testament calls each believer a priest in the royal priesthood of God's kingdom. I have often wondered whether our priestly function should be a reminder to Christians that we do not own any land. Jesus is Lord of all the earth; we are merely tenants of the land beneath us.

Humans are largely growing estranged from the land. As part of this narrative, more and more people in the modern world are transitioning from living in rural contexts to urban contexts. The dramatic migration to the city is testified to in a series of headlines that appeared in *Time* magazine throughout recent decades. In 1955, one cover read, "The Rebirth of the City." In 1962, *Time* ran a story on the rebirth and "renaissance" of city life. This was followed in 1981 by a front cover headline that read, "Cities Are Fun!" Yet another, in 1987, read, "Bringing the City Back to Life."[5] The urban swell that *Time* chronicled has been matched in dramatic demographic shifts: 39 percent of the total population of America lived in cities in 1890, 53 percent in 1940, 73 percent in 1970, and 75 percent in 1990.[6] It has grown since. These migrations to the city for work and relationship often leave us feeling, and being, disconnected from the land.

Cities are growing. And they are growing fast. A contemporary city is generally defined as a population center of twenty-five thousand or more people. And settlements fitting this qualification are added by the week.[7] Today, three-quarters of the world lives in metropolitan centers.[8] In fact, the single largest move of people in human history is taking place as I write this: rural Chinese are migrating to major cities almost exclusively for the purpose of employment. In seemingly every corner of the world, urbanization is swelling with little sign of slowing down. In the West, the vast majority of people increasingly locate their home and workplace in urban centers, working, living, and playing in the city.

This urban migration has changed the way people relate to wild places, and it has created a divide between urban and rural living that has shown tremendous potential to bring about strong cultural resentments. As illustrated in the 2016 presidential election between Hillary Clinton and Donald Trump, there is a growing chasm between urban and rural ways of life within American culture, a chasm seeming to cause a kind of visceral pain and anger.

My context is an urban one. My own work as a pastor, professor, and author takes place in the context of a sprawling city. Listening has been remarkably important for our church work. When my family originally moved to the city, our goal for the first few years was to learn to listen to the needs of the people in the neighborhood that we sought to serve. This meant sitting for a few years, listening and paying close attention to the neighborhood. One thing we noticed was that everyone in Portland spends inordinate amounts of time outdoors. People's connection to the great outdoors is not simply recreational. People equally care for the land. As one might remember, it was in the Pacific Northwest that the spotted owl controversy played itself out. A group of concerned people petitioned the US Fish and Wildlife Service to declare the spotted owl an endangered species and so bar the timber industry from clearing these old-growth forests.[9] Portlanders care about the land. But this desire to care for and enjoy the land does not seem unique to Portland. As I travel our country, I constantly encounter people who are hungry to understand the gospel as it relates to the great outdoors. People have a deep, innate longing to be connected to the land.

I have long accepted that God has called me to serve the city of Portland. Rather than ignoring or resisting this deep longing in the human heart, I have been engaging ways in which the gospel might connect us to Christ *and* reconnect us with the land as an extension of his kingdom work. In short, as a missionary I have sensed that part of my role is not only helping connect people to the life of Jesus but also connecting them to the land that Jesus created. There is a reason people are hungry to reconnect to the land. And this is not something we should resist as missionaries in the twenty-first century.

Moreover, engagement with the land actually becomes a creative way to preach the love of Christ to those in the city. A friend who attends our church and does inner-city ministry in Portland learned this same lesson. Serving inner-city youth in their high-school settings, he found it challenging to help them encounter the message of Jesus. Then it dawned on him—these kids have never seen the raw beauty of the land or the stars of heaven; they live in the city. So he experimented with something. He took inner-city kids camping in the rugged Oregon landscape. What he discovered was mind-blowing: kids got God. Turns out, when you show inner-city kids the sheer beauty of God's creation, they start asking really big questions about themselves, the universe, and eventually God. It is kind of like how God takes Abraham outside to explain his promises to him (Gen. 14).

One of the difficulties that has transpired with society's move from rural contexts to urban ones is a kind of homelessness where we no longer live in husbandry to the land. In their book *Beyond Homelessness*, Steven Bouma-Prediger and Brian Walsh take a sustained look at our relationship to the land in a new and promising way: through the lens of homelessness.[10] We have, through our constant mobility, become ecologically homeless. Less and less are we connected to a certain place for a long period of time. Our culture has experienced a loss of husbandry in agricultural life; we no longer have a lifelong relationship with a given place, like humanity did in ages past.

But the ultimate problem with this kind of land homelessness is that it limits our awareness of responsibility to a place. Allow me to illustrate. When my wife and I purchased our home, we had no idea what we had gotten ourselves into. After countless hours of walk-throughs, prayer, counsel from family and friends, and talks with the real estate agent, we were certain we were buying the best house we could in the neighborhood; everything looked perfect. After scrounging together a down payment, we bought the house and moved in with the excitement of any new homeowner. But before too long, it became evident there were many hidden ailments with the house. Lights stopped working, the dishwasher continually broke down, the gate fell off its hinges countless times—I cannot list all the problems. Doing some homework revealed that the previous owners had flipped the house for great profit.[11]

You do not flip something you plan on living in. And yet, truth be told, for generations humanity has been flipping creation. Real work has been postponed. Decade after decade, for this or that excuse, we have abdicated real responsibility and real care for the integrity of the earth, leaving our children and grandchildren with the tasks that we have put off. In trading stewardship and husbandry of the land for quick profit, we have come to a crossroads. The consequences of our irresponsibility are upon us. Things are starting to fall apart. How could we have done this? Could it be that we have assumed we would never have to live in *that* place again, that we could just move on to another space? If the people who flipped our house had been forced to live on the property for the next three decades, they would have made different choices in caring for it. We might think of it like this: Because of sin, humanity has increasingly exhibited a short-term, utilitarian relationship with the land, the same way that many of us treat a hotel room. We stay for a short time, make a mess, pack up, and go somewhere else, all the while expecting someone else to clean up after us.

In ancient cultures, generation after generation lived on the same piece of land. That meant that anything negative they did to the land was something the next generation would pay the price for. But our mobility and loss of connection to one place greatly blurs our sense of responsibility to care for the land. I have moved some ten times in my lifetime. While I have powerful memories from each place I have lived, I did not stay in any of them long enough to really fall in love with them. And because of that, I did not feel the need to give great care and attention to those places. I became like a military kid whom I knew who moved every six months as a child. Because he was always on the move, he could never make any true and lasting friendships. And because he knew that he could never make true and lasting friendships, he never gave effort to do so. Our relationship to the land, as people homeless from the land, is the same. Because of our mobility, we are never anywhere long enough to love the land. And because we know we are probably going to be leaving, there is no reason to care for the land.

Treating the land like a hotel room, we rarely suffer the consequences of what we do to the place. In a hotel, there is someone we pay to clean up our messes. In the land, however, no one is paid to clean up our messes—and some of them cannot be cleaned up at all. We all pay the price with a creation that is harmed. We can murder the land, completely annihilate it, tear it up, skin it, and do whatever we wish—and have no remorse. Paul Brooks wrote a provocative little book in 1971 titled *The Pursuit of Wilderness*. In it, he laments the self-selected things that we consider a violation of the natural order: "In America today you can murder the land for private profit. . . . You can leave the corpse for all to see, and nobody calls the cops."[12]

There is a massive price to be paid for our disengaged relationship to the land as society has increasingly moved from the land to the city. The more and more disengaged from the creation we become, the less likely it becomes that we will recognize our innate responsibility to the land.

Sabbath and the Beauty of the Land

Sabbath opens a door for humans to appreciate and celebrate the land God has made, and it also restrains us from using it or demanding anything from it. Humans are to be intimate with the land. But humans are also distinct from the land. As we saw in the creation texts of Genesis, humanity's very existence is, in a primal sense, connected to the earth. The wordplay in the Hebrew text echoes our interconnectedness to the land and our work within it. *Adam* (the person "Adam") and *adamah* (the "ground") illustrate the intimate relationship humanity was to have with the earth. Tragically, sin damages this intimacy. And it continues to keep us away from the ground, the earth, and the land.

While humans are intimately related to the land, the Sabbath protects us from becoming parasites of the land. Have you ever had a friend who always wants something from you and can never just be a friend? Such a parasitic relationship may work in the short term, but long term it will ultimately cause the relationship to be ruined. Humans are, of course, not parasites on the land. And the land cannot endlessly give to us without receiving love and care itself. While the other six days of the week may be given to growing food, building, and working the land, there is to be one day when we can only *appreciate* the land for what it is—a gift from God.

The Sabbath helps us to stop and smell the roses, as it were—to cease from our hustle and bustle, going here and there, uprooted and disconnected from the places we call home. The Sabbath is an interval in which we can admire beauty around us, to take it in and enjoy it, appreciating the work God has done in the land. "The Sabbath asks us to notice," writes Norman Wirzba.[13] The words of Jürgen Moltmann help us capture the significance of creating space to take in the beauty around us: "The true meaning of Sabbath is ecological. Related to it is also an aesthetic aspect: Only someone who comes to rest and has nothing planned is able to perceive the beauty of things. He or she sees the flowers and the sunset, a painting or a vase or a beloved person with unintentional/unexpected pleasure."[14] Do we not need time to breathe in what is made by God? If we do not take time to really see creation, we buzz past it at speeds we never wanted. I love that Harvey Cox translates the word *Sabbath* as "to catch one's breath."[15]

There is an aesthetic quality of creation that undoubtedly is intended by God to draw us back to himself. Neil Armstrong and Buzz Aldrin, just before taking their first steps on the moon, broke out a Bible, read, and took Communion. Is it not powerful that the first human act on the moon was a Communion service? Another astronaut, Frank Borman, was the first space commander to lead a team outside Earth's orbit. His first radio transmission some 250,000 miles from Earth was a reading of Genesis 1. Later Borman described feeling the presence of God as he looked down on Earth. In 1971 James Irwin walked on the moon. Soon after returning, Irwin became an evangelical minister. He described his walk on the moon: "I felt the power of

God as I'd never felt it before."[16] Because we have no space in our lives, we often do not even see the land anymore. But when we do stop to see the land, the creation, the effect can be deeply transformative. I am all but certain that that is precisely why one astronaut converted to Christianity because of an experience in space looking down over the world.

This planet is simply beautiful. The land is precious, beautiful, and glorious in its own way. This beautiful and spacious land that the Creator has imagined in love and fashioned by his own fingers is magnificent, overwhelming, and breathtaking—that is, to the person who takes the time to bask in it. Creation, writes Paul, reveals the "invisible qualities" of the Creator (Rom. 1:20). When we look with intent and forethought at what God has made, we can learn a great deal about God's nature and character. The soil, birds, sunsets, potato bugs, clouds, whirlwinds, waters—each part of creation whispers to us one indelible aspect of the One who made them. We should be greatly saddened by extinction, erosion, and elimination. Each part of creation teaches us about God. Scripture, in fact, witnesses to this at countless points. Job, for example, writes,

> Ask the animals, and they will teach you,
>   or the birds in the sky, and they will tell you;
> or speak to the earth, and it will teach you,
>   or let the fish in the sea inform you.
> Which of all these does not know
>   that the hand of the Lord has done this?
> In his hand is the life of every creature
>   and the breath of all mankind. (Job 12:7–10)

Likewise, the psalmist reminds us of the beauty of God in creation in explicit terms. "The heavens declare the glory of God; the skies proclaim the work of his hands. . . . They pour forth speech" (Ps. 19:1–2). The Lord's name is "majestic . . . in all the earth," and he has "set [his] glory in the heavens" (Ps. 8:1). Even the sea creatures praise the Creator (Ps. 148:7).

The land even teaches us of the wisdom and goodness of God. God sustains the land by his love. Theologically speaking, we must not believe that God created this beautiful expanse only to step back and watch it spin into chaotic oblivion, as deists would have us believe. Christian orthodoxy argues that God *continues* to be the ongoing creator and sustainer of all the land. God is the initial creator, but God does not stop creating. Rather, God continues to make creation and hold it together, which we call *creatio continua*. This idea is depicted in the book of Hebrews: Jesus "holds everything together"

(Heb. 1:3 GW). One may even consider the physical ramifications of this—it is literally the love of Christ that holds the land together. We see in Scripture that God loves the land and cares for it. God is not portrayed as some absentee landlord. God makes his creation to display his beauty and then continues to regenerate the land over and over again.

If all of creation is continued by God and marked by the fingerprints of a Creator, why is it that atheists and agnostics do not come to believe in God every time they go on a hike? The land is so abundantly full of beauty and majesty—dripping with revelation—that it is astounding that people can still reject God even as they delight in his creation. As St. Augustine taught, the land is so profoundly beautiful that we almost seem to be over-whelmed by it. He spoke of the "daily miracles" that happen constantly all around us. A daily miracle, he writes, is so "excessively common it has lost its power to strike wonder, and by its very frequency has become com-monplace."[17] The beautiful and wondrous parts of creation have become so exceedingly common for us that we fail to even recognize them for what they are—miracles.

Instead of being drawn to God by the beauty of the land, we walk by it unthinkingly. I have come to call this "beauty exhaustion"—having experienced something beautiful long enough that you begin to forget how beautiful it is. I remember a moment of beauty exhaustion a few years back, when my wife and I walked through the London Museum of History. We saw piece after piece of absolutely unbelievable ancient artifacts. After six or seven hours, we were overwhelmed. Soon we were just walking past "one more artifact" that told the story of all of Western civilization. Perhaps you have experienced that: that moment when you are walking around a museum, looking at countless pieces of the greatest art known to humanity, and you walk mindlessly from a piece by Monet to a piece by Renoir, not recognizing the beauty of what you are looking at or realizing who made it.

Every time we do truly recognize the gift of beauty, the artistry, the skill required, the imagination to create something so life giving, we cannot help but see the grace of God all around us. But our busyness keeps us from all of this. Our frantic multitasking causes us to continue to walk through this life inattentive to the beauty all around us. We walk by in our busyness, without margin in our lives to pay attention. We do not stop to smell the roses. Or even if we do smell the roses, we view God's land as some kind of product. It is like watching a film: we often think merely about the story line, the dialogue, or the themes. But when we begin to realize how the screenwriters employed rhetorical devices in the script, how lighting was used in a particular way, what effects colors in the costuming have, we appreciate the film much more. The knowledge of the care and forethought allows us to see it as artistry. Then we begin to become aware of the artists behind the film.

What if we do the same with the land? We look at it and appreciate it to the extent that it is visually appealing in an Instagram photo, or we enjoy the smell of the roses, but rarely do we contemplate the forethought that went into the design of both the smallest details and the largest systems, such as how beautiful flowers are pollinators for vegetable gardens and how flowers and herbs often help to keep away pests. It would seem at first that the utilitarian thing to do would be to just plant vegetables, but we find that God is far more inventive than we originally supposed. He gives us that which not only has a practical purpose but also is beautiful in more ways than one. We might see and smell lavender and appreciate it, but we so often miss beauty's invitation to admire how purposeful, interconnected, and well designed it is, let alone how it reflects the One behind the work of art.

St. Bonaventure once said, "Whoever is not enlightened by the splendor of created things is blind; whoever is not aroused by the sound of their voice is deaf; whoever does not praise God for all these creatures is mute; whoever after so much evidence does not recognize the Maker of all things, is an idiot."[18]

The Sabbath teaches us to appreciate the land for what it is, not for what it can do for us. I find the "fields" of Scripture a fascinating case study of this. Indeed, there are places where "fields" are good—such as the grainfield where Ruth and Boaz meet and the field in which Isaac is meditating when he meets Rebekah. But there are two fields in particular that are portrayed in a very negative light. The field of Cain and the field of Judas are both depicted as wicked land. I have often wondered whether a "field" is a place where humans have sought to control and force their will on the land. But we must see the land in a new light. For the land is not good only inasmuch as it gives us what we need. "It is not allowable to love the Creation according to the purposes one has for it," writes Wendell Berry, "any more than it is allowable to love one's neighbor in order to borrow his tools."[19] The Sabbath undoes our use of the field and lets it return to the care of the Creator.

The Sabbath gives us restorative time to catch up to all this beauty that we see in the land but have no time to stand in wonder over. John O'Donahue, in his book *Anam Ċara*, recounts an old story of a European explorer who brought along with him some African helpers. After three long days of travel, the Africans said to the explorer, "We have moved too quickly to reach here; now we need to wait to give our spirits a chance to catch up with us."[20] That is us—we move too quickly. Our minds and hearts are not given the chance to catch up to the warp speed at which our bodies are going; we fail to see the sacredness of God and the land. God's presence cannot be fully enjoyed if we are constantly checking the time or running to our next appointment. Enjoyment of beauty should not be rushed.

QUESTIONS
for Reflection

- If when the land is overworked it gets sick, how might you be able to help keep it healthy or help it recover?
- How might your treatment of land change as you grow in the understanding that you do not own it?
- How might the land receive rest when you Sabbath?
- In what ways might you be responsible to land (whether or not you physically occupy much of it)?
- If you were going to dwell in this place for eternity, would you treat the land differently? If yes, how so?
- How might taking time to smell the roses allow you to connect with the Creator?
- How might Sabbath allow you to connect with the land?

9

Sabbath and Critters

Let us consider the way in which we spend our lives. This world is a place of business. What an infinite bustle. . . . It interrupts my dreams. There is no Sabbath.

Henry David Thoreau, *Life without Principle*

Good News for Critters

Cows are beautiful creatures. Sadly, so much of our economic system has developed an unhealthy dependence on them—and their misuse and abuse. In the natural order, cows get pregnant when they are in heat. But in modern agricultural practice, cows are artificially inseminated while still secreting milk from their last pregnancy. Why? So that they can be milked nearly without break. In industrial dairy practices, cows are milked for ten months out of the year compared to just five to six in places where traditional dairy farming is practiced, such as Mongolia. Our cows are given almost no rest between pregnancies, *and* they are being milked during most of their pregnancy. It turns out that when cows are not allowed to rest, human health is put at risk. Pregnant cows' milk contains significantly higher amounts of sex hormones than milk from cows that are not pregnant. Studies have indicated that the increase in sex hormones may actually affect cancer rates as well as human development in puberty.[1]

On top of this, livestock are often given steroid hormone implants used for growth. One of these, estradiol, is listed as the naturally occurring sex hormone estrogen on the Food and Drug Administration's website.[2] This is a misnomer, however, as estradiol is a synthetic sex hormone that is an endocrine disrupter by nature.[3] This and other steroids, which regulate hormones and the reproductive system, are given to livestock to increase dairy production. As a result, large amounts of synthetic estrogens are excreted in manure and then spread on fields, eventually ending up in our water supplies.[4] Because sex hormones are not removed from wastewater before it heads from sewage treatment to our rivers and seas, fish populations are harmed.[5] Along the Potomac, Columbia, Colorado, and Mississippi Rivers, fish are found to be "gender swapping" as a result of the presence of sex hormones.[6] These intersex fish exhibit sex traits of both male and female fish and in extreme cases are found to have been made sterile.[7] If this is the effect endocrine disruptors have on fish, one might wonder what effect they could have on humans.[8]

Turns out when a cow is given the rest it needs, these large doses of dangerous sex hormones do not end up in our milk, our water, or our streams, thus protecting everyone, from fish to humans to cows. This chapter examines a side of Sabbath-keeping that would be tempting to overlook: how the Sabbath is integral to the well-being and flourishing of the animal kingdom. We will begin by looking at the importance of animal welfare in Scripture and how it applies to our society, where animals are often abused, neglected, or misused for human purposes. Then we will make the connection between animal welfare and the Sabbath command.

To begin, take a moment and recall the fourth commandment: "Remember the Sabbath. . . . On it you shall not do any work . . . nor your animals" (Exod. 20:8, 10). The original Sabbath command as found in the Mosaic covenant immediately connects the dots between our rest and the rest of the animals that we depend on and are responsible to care for. The Bible's perspective on the Sabbath reveals that it is a day of rest extended to humans *and* nonhuman creatures of God's creation.

A note about our theology: the critter kingdom sadly receives sparse, if any, attention in the contemporary church's theology, thinking, practice, or preaching. I have never heard nor preached a sermon on animal welfare. The argument is often made that in a world of sin, disease, unrest, and societal breakdown, why should the critters even matter all that much? As a Bible-believing, Jesus-is-the-only-way-to-God, theologically traditional follower of Christ, I have encountered little from my tribe regarding our responsibility as Christians to care for the critters of the world, largely because we believe there are more important things to be doing. Moreover, it seems almost assumed that animal welfare is a distraction from the real issues of Christian living: evangelism, preaching, repentance, and right doctrine.

But this attitude does not reflect the Bible's attitude. "The righteous," Proverbs 12:10 tells us, "care for the needs of their animals." My faith—*our* faith—should reach so far as to change the way that we treat the animals God has made. But in the tribal church of our time, it is often assumed that progressive and conservative Christians have different interests: one cares for animals, and one does not, at least not as a point of doctrine. It is assumed that the work of evangelism and preaching and doctrine are the things that conservative Christians care deeply about and that issues of justice and activism and politics are the issues with which liberals are concerned. But why should conservatives *not* do justice? Why should liberals *not* do evangelism? Justice and evangelism cannot be done without the other. The gospel is hypocritical without the social gospel, and the social gospel hollow without the gospel. But since the early twentieth century, this bifurcated logic has set the agenda for large parts of the church and has caused division, strife, and misunderstanding. Is one called to *preach* the gospel and another to *do* the gospel?

I remember reading a story told by Ronald Sider, founder of Evangelicals for Social Action, that illustrates this very sentiment of some doing and others preaching the gospel. In 1979, Sider traveled abroad and spent a couple of weeks lecturing in South Africa during apartheid. During his time there, Sider met a young man he calls "James." James did not identify as a Christian. Rather, he identified as a Jewish student who had traveled to hear Sider teach on Jesus's commitment and love for the poor, as well as God's heart for those trapped and oppressed under apartheid. One evening, James and Ronald sat down and had a three-hour conversation. James expressed how it had been personally difficult to labor for social justice on behalf of those who were being oppressed by apartheid.

"Ron," James said, "I'm burned out." Sider listened as James explained how his activism efforts were nearly killing him. He sensed the young man's consternation and shared the good news of Jesus with him in hopes that it would meet him in his present need. During the interchange, the young Jewish student said something to Ron that stuck with him. He said, "I don't want to be like these white Christians here. They sing about the love of Jesus and the joy of heaven, but they don't care about justice in South Africa. If I become a Christian, will I have to give up the struggle?"[9] Indeed, the work of justice was part of what Jesus asked this young man to do. After Ron affirmed to him the call of God to fight for the freedom of those suffering under apartheid, James came to faith in Christ.

James's words exemplify the lamentable separation in our understanding of what a Christian is to do: that the conservatives sing about Jesus and heaven while the liberals do the work down here. But can the two really be separated?

"It is my own conviction that the church," writes Nicholas Wolterstorff, "and humanity at large, neglects inwardness at its own peril. It seems to me that amidst its intense activism, the Western world is starved for contemplation."[10] Our call, of course, as committed followers of Jesus Christ, is to do activism *and* prayer and contemplation. Why should I not sing of Jesus and of the joys of heaven while standing up for the poor and the oppressed? Why should those two things not happen together? What is separating these two parts with the same aim—namely, to serve Christ and the world? I see a generation of young Christians who are tired of such a dichotomy. I can speak for myself: I want to believe in Jesus, believe in the Bible, and preach the good news all the while submitting my life to justice, mercy, and life for all living beings. Sider calls the form of Christianity in which some preach Jesus and some live out the life of Jesus a "lopsided Christianity."[11] Doing justice is, indeed, the thing that makes our evangelism come to life.

I am not convinced that one can believe in the gospel and *not* do justice in the world. Any attempt to translate our otherworldliness into irresponsibility is catastrophic. Jesus wants heaven to come to earth. God's justice matters. I take the words of Jesus literally. And by reading them literally, I *literally* am compelled to do them. Love the poor. Pray for the enemy. Face all my addictions. Forgive. Speak truth. Be sexually pure. Repent. Embody generosity. And care for the animals well. I have no permission to select which words of Jesus I must obey and which to drop by the wayside. I am bound to *all* of Jesus's words. The gospel—the good news that Jesus lived, died, and was resurrected to save humanity from its sins—very well better change the ethical structures of our lives.

What does the gospel have to say about genetically modified crops? Refugees? Bioethics? Sexuality? Money and economics? Politics? Even caring for God's critters?

If nothing is exempt from God's purview, then neither are animals. And that brings us to another question: What does the message of the Sabbath have to do with the welfare of animals? These questions may seem like they lie outside the scope of the gospel, but no part of creation is outside the breadth of what the gospel has to say, because there is nothing outside the scope of God's concern. God desires for life to flourish.

The gospel—along with the Sabbath, we will soon see—very much *does* matter for the well-being of God's critters. I have met two particular individuals who have shown me the connection of Christian discipleship and our relationship to the animal kingdom: Susan and Sarah. I first met Susan over coffee. Susan's story is quite remarkable. For the better part of twenty years, she has given her life to serve the Oregon Department of Fish and Wildlife.

More specifically, she has given her career to caring for the turtle population in the state of Oregon. While her job description does not actually articulate it, Susan does her work to care for turtles because she believes that the gospel has something profound to do with the well-being of turtles. "If God so loves the *world*," she told me, "shouldn't that mean that God's love extends to turtles as well?" Susan's love and passionate fight for turtles and her commitment to see them protected could not have come at a better time. Illegal transportation and poaching of turtles in and through our state has been rampant for years. The black market has swelled. So, as a follower of Jesus, Susan serves the population of Oregon turtles.

I met Sarah a few years ago over breakfast as she traveled through our state. Sarah spends her life teaching Christians around the world about the welfare of animals and how God cares deeply about the way we treat every creature God has ever made. In fact, Sarah spent some time working at PETA (People for the Ethical Treatment of Animals). Detailing her time at PETA, she described how difficult it was given how few Christians worked in the area of animal welfare. Often she felt belittled by her Christian friends for entering into the work of caring for animals, and she also felt ridiculed by her non-Christian friends who worked in animal welfare for being a Christian in the first place. Now Sarah runs an organization to help inspire the ethical treatment of animals based on the biblical narrative and sound orthodox theology.

Both of these women have connected the dots for me. Both women believe Jesus is the only way to God. Both read and believe in the Bible wholeheartedly. Both worship God in a local church. Both give generously of their time and money. The point? Their work to care for the well-being of animals is not somehow antithetical to their faith. What both Susan and Sarah have taught me is of endless value: believing in Jesus should actually cause us to care for nonhuman creation—because God made it. They taught me that caring for the *whole* world is part and parcel of the Christ follower's work in this world.

Critters in the Bible

Scripture clearly and pointedly lends voice to the nonhuman, critter kingdom. A colleague of mine once undertook the task of listing all of creation's characters mentioned in the life of Jesus. In the Gospels, Jesus mentions sparrows, sheep, oxen, donkeys, foxes, fish, snakes, sea monsters, worms, scorpions, moths, birds, salt, figs, grapes, eggs, fruit, oil, wheat, mustard seeds, nests, fig trees, branches, wood, logs, lilies, grass, grain, shrubs, bramble bushes, thorns, thistles, weeds, soils, land, rocky ground, deserts, gardens, fields, vineyards, fire, earth, wind, water, seas, lakes, rivers, rain, floods, stones, rocks, pearls, sand, sun, moon, stars, sky, clouds, and the weather. Indeed, Scripture canonizes creation's splendor into its sacred pages.

But what does Scripture reveal about God's attitude toward all that God created? Here I will identify three main issues that Scripture voices concerning God's love and care for the critters. First, the Bible consistently teaches that God created all the critters—the beasts, the insects, the birds, the sea creatures—and that God made them "good" (Gen. 1:25). Not only did God create each of the critters, but God created each of them *before* creating humanity on the day before Sabbath rest. I have written elsewhere that I believe this simple fact should lead to great human humility—as humans, we must remember that God made the dung beetle before he made us.[12] In Genesis 1, the critters of the earth are made on days five and six of the creation week. On day five, we learn, God creates the winged creatures and the creatures of the sea. Then on day six, immediately before humanity's creation, God creates the critters of the land and the creeping insects. The text speaks of their beauty and goodness: "God made the wild animals according to their kinds, the livestock according to their kinds, and all the creatures that move along the ground according to their kinds. And God saw that it was good" (Gen. 1:25). Later, we find that within all of the creatures God has made is the "breath of life," the same breath of life God breathed into Adam and Eve (Gen. 7:15).

Second, God deeply cares for each of these critters. The critters are "good." But even more than that, God opts to establish a personal relationship with the critters he has made. This relationship is illustrated by a number of biblical texts. For example, in the story of Noah's ark, we find that two of every creature came into the ark just before the flood, as God had desired. However, there is one thing missing from the story—Noah himself never went out and gathered the critters. Rather, the critters *came on their own* (Gen. 7:8–9). Noah's task was to make space for them in the boat, not go out and get them all. This raises a question: How did the animals know to come into the ark? The story seems to suggest that God himself went and spoke to the animals, calling them to advance to Noah and the ark. The implication of this is that God has a unique way of communicating with the critters he has made.

God also makes covenants with the critters. In the covenant that God establishes with Noah after the flood, God promises every living thing on the earth (including the critters) that never again would he flood the earth with a downpour of rain (Gen. 9:11–17). The covenant was accompanied with the sign of a rainbow. What is most fascinating is that this covenant is established not just with humanity but also with the critters who had been in Noah's boat. Other stories abound of God communicating directly to animals. For example, God commanded the ravens to bring Elijah food while he was in the desert east of the Jordan River (1 Kings 17:4–6). God, we see, has a relationship with and a desire to communicate with animals.

Not only does God enter into relationship with the critters—and even make covenants with them—but God's love and compassion extends to them as well. As Jonah preaches to the people in distant Nineveh, God reminds the prophet that alongside the 120,000 people who have been spared God's judgment, there were "many animals" who were spared by his mercy as well (Jon. 4:11). Likewise, Jesus speaks lovingly of the critters. In the iconic text of Matthew 10:28–31, Jesus speaks of God's care for people, but the lesson is not merely about human beings. Jesus states, "Do not be afraid of those who kill the body but cannot kill the soul. Rather, be afraid of the One who can destroy both soul and body in hell. Are not two sparrows sold for a penny? Yet not one of them will fall to the ground outside your Father's care" (vv. 28–29). Of course, to the ancient person, sparrows were seen as worthless entities.[13]

Jesus's lesson is powerful. If God deeply cared for something the world deemed worthless, how much more does he care for humans! As Denis Edwards has aptly articulated, in keeping with his loving embrace to hold the universe together, God's love has even the capacity to love the sparrow and take care of its needs.[14] We cannot get our heads around just how much God loves *us*, because we are often blind to how much God loves the sparrow. Jesus's words here would have had dramatic impact on the imaginations of a group of first-century men.

Third, the critters reveal a great deal to us about God's nature. We must be cautious here not to oversentimentalize the critters—the natural world is not composed solely of furry bunnies, nice kitties, and friendly dogs. Some critters are gentle and loving, and others are ferocious and violent. For instance, certain pelicans will hatch two chicks, the younger of which serves as a kind of backup in case the elder chick does not survive. Eventually, the younger will be pushed out of the nest and starve to death if the elder chick survives. This is not something we can Instagram. This is painful. It is violent. It is harsh.

Other parts of creation speak to God's sheer wisdom and brilliance. Thomas Reimchen is a research biologist who studies the relationship between salmon and bears. In his research he discovered something very interesting. When you look at the tree rings in forests of the Pacific Northwest, stable nitrogen isotopes can be found. Where does the nitrogen come from? Reimchen believes the answer lies in bears and salmon. In essence, the bears catch salmon and carry them into the forest. There, under the trees, they eat the salmon, thus delivering much-needed nitrogen for the trees to flourish. Thus, one ecosystem (the ocean) provides for another ecosystem (the forest).[15] This reveals to us God's incredible ability to create a world where not only are there innumerable biological processes happening within one ecosystem but also, in the interaction between ecosystems, one system is able to meet the needs of another. How intricate the world is! How deeply God loves it!

All of the radical diversity within the critter kingdom speaks of the full spectrum of God's nature. Indeed, God is generous and kind, but God is also powerful and unimaginably wild. The critters even demonstrate to us our hope in God. Consider how many times in the biblical story God's hope is delivered through the birds. It was by a dove that Noah discovered that a new world awaited. It was in the form of a dove that the Spirit descended on Jesus in his baptism and ushered him into his public ministry. And it was "worthless" sparrows that reminded the disciples they were loved and cared for by God.

"Let everything that has breath praise the LORD," Psalm 150:6 says. Animals have breath, and with that breath they praise the Lord. They can even speak with a voice—a lesson we learn from Balaam's donkey, which also had the capacity to see angels (Num. 22:21–33). Even the things that do not have breath have the capacity to sing the praises of the Creator. Jesus says that even if we did not worship God, the rocks would cry out in praise (Luke 19:40). God will be praised with or without us—for God was praised even before our creation. As Dietrich Bonhoeffer writes, "God is worshipped first by the earth which was without form and void. He does not need us men to prepare his glory; he creates worship himself from the silent world which slumbers, resting mute and formless in his will."[16]

As we survey these biblical precedents, we come face-to-face with the fact that God deeply cares for the critter realm and calls us to contend for its welfare. This whole world is not for just us; God has his hand in caring for the rest of creation as well.

Sabbath for the Critters

How does the Sabbath affect the critters?

Angelus Silesius once wrote, "If God stopped thinking of me, He would cease to exist."[17] God is "glad" with all of his works, the psalmist writes (Ps. 104:31). And in his gladness, God thinks of the critters. God thinks about the animals and desires them to be well—and so should we. But what is the relationship between the Sabbath and all of God's critters?

As we discussed in previous chapters, the Sabbath is largely about freedom, flourishing, and setting a context in which creation can be nourished. This freedom is not only for human beings and the land but is for the critters as well. Once again, hear the fourth commandment:

> Remember the Sabbath day by keeping it holy. Six days you shall labor and do all your work, but the seventh day is a Sabbath to the LORD your God. On it you shall not do any work, neither you, nor your son or daughter, nor your male or female servant, *nor your animals*, nor any foreigner residing in your towns. For in six days the LORD made the heavens and the earth, the sea, and all that is in them, but he rested on the seventh day. Therefore the LORD blessed the Sabbath day and made it holy. (Exod. 20:8–11)

On the Sabbath, the animals are to get a day of rest as well. In context, "animals" refers to all domestic livestock. The animals on the Sabbath, writes Norman Wirzba, "must have freedom to come out from under our unremitting demands, as when animals are left to rest and refresh themselves or fields are left to lie fallow. As we cease from our steady toil, we learn the valuable lesson that the whole of creation does not exist exclusively for us and to meet our desires."[18]

Animals in Israel were to be treated fairly. In the same way that a human worker was worthy of wages, one could not muzzle an ox while it was working in the field (Deut. 25:4). And animals were allowed to eat the fruit and vegetables from the fields lying fallow during a sabbatical year (Exod. 23:11). In line with this high view of animals comes the Sabbath command. Animals were required to rest one day a week unto God. God's command for animals to have rest reveals to us that the Jewish tradition is extremely committed to the care of animals, perhaps more than any other ancient religion. Jesus even taught about putting aside a perfect Sabbath day to care for the needs of an ox who had fallen into a hole in the ground (Luke 14:5).

Sabbath-keeping honors the God-created rhythms of rest. Do critters need rest? Yes, they do. Whole species of critters rest for eight months out of the year in certain climates—a season called "hibernation."[19] Research has shown that when animals do not hibernate or get the rest they need, their lives are greatly changed in negative ways. When the global surface temperature rises, there is less snowpack, thus affecting those animals that normally hibernate in the snowpack. Evidence suggests that this is harming many species whose season of hibernation has been shortened dramatically.[20] Animals need hibernation. They need sleep as well. Some animals (cats, for example) sleep far more than even humans do. The sleep and rest of animals is God ordained just as much as it is for human beings.

Have you ever considered the joy of God's critters? The Scriptures point out that the sea creature Leviathan *plays* in the sea (Ps. 104:26) and that the beasts *play* in their surroundings (Job 40:20). The Hebrew word for "play" is the same word used for David's celebration of the return of the ark to Jerusalem (2 Sam. 6:21).[21] Job similarly says that the ostrich flaps its wings "joyfully" (Job 39:13). I wonder whether the Sabbath day for the animals in the Old Testament was received as a day of joy, of play.

Yes, animals help humans flourish in certain ways by providing food, clothing, and transportation. In many ways, animals are critical to human life. But that does not mean that we can disregard animals' well-being. God's intention is not that we use the animals in such a way that we destroy their kingdom and species. If our use of anything in God's garden destroys or annihilates that thing, then we are improperly using it. To Sabbath is to extend the joy of the Lord to the *whole* of God's garden, not just the human occupants.

How we treat the animals that God has put into our lives matters to the Creator. Proverbs 12:10 reads, "The righteous care for the needs of their animals, but the kindest acts of the wicked are cruel." There is a Jewish tradition that permits someone to have a pet—a dog, a cat, or other animals. Those household pets can bring joy to the lives of any home. The person who cares for a pet should learn to extend the day of rest to the pet as well. One particular writer goes so far as to suggest that if one has a dog, the dog should not be required to get the newspaper from the front of the house on the day of the Sabbath.[22] I think it is important, if we have any animals in our homes or in our given context, that we consider what a day of rest might look like for them. What might it look like to give our pets a Sabbath? What do our livestock need on the Sabbath to receive special rest on that day?

Letting Our Chickens Sabbath

There is a story of one Linda Henderson. Linda, a horse racer, wanted to take seriously the Sabbath command for the horses she competed with. Her policy was simple: she would compete six days out of seven. If a competition was on a Saturday—the day she honored the Sabbath—she and her horse would get the day off. Because of her commitment, she often finished as runner-up when events were scheduled over the whole weekend. On the Sabbath day, as all the other horses were racing, Henderson would put a sign on the stall of her horse. The sign simply said "Rest."[23]

Linda's story is remarkable. It takes serious forethought and intention not only to enter into rest but to bring animals into that rest as well. She is not the only one to give this some thought. The Jewish Sabbath laws outline a few basic principles regarding the day of rest. Feeding is permitted on the Sabbath. In fact, this is the spirit behind Deuteronomy 11:15, which states that you should take care of the needs of your animals *before* you take care of your own. However, "trapping," the act of restricting the freedom of your animal, is strictly prohibited. A Sabbath for an animal should be a day that they can run around, stretch their legs, and experience a sense of freedom perhaps foreign to them on the other days. The Sabbath laws also permit one to walk a pet on the day of rest so long as one avoids carrying the animal. Finally, many believe petting an animal on the Sabbath is not permissible.[24] Many other commands exist, such as the command against intentionally killing any insect on the Sabbath day.[25]

Of course, the Christian is not bound by nonbiblical Sabbath laws. But these laws reveal deep thought and intention—something Christians should aspire to as well. We must learn to see the Sabbath as not only a day of rest for humanity but also a day of holy respite for the animal kingdom. The Christ follower has the responsibility to serve the well-being of the animal kingdom. I am reminded that William Wilberforce, while fighting the slave trade in nineteenth-century England, simultaneously opposed cockfighting and animal fighting for sport. Wilberforce was not the only Christian forebear whose life stands as a testimony to the goodness of the animal kingdom. Jerry Root, a professor at Wheaton College and perhaps the most influential C. S. Lewis scholar in North America, has written an excellent piece examining the compassionate approach toward animals in C. S. Lewis's life. Lewis, the magnanimous and groundbreaking theologian, had a deep love for animals. Root tells two stories about Lewis. On one occasion, a school administrator at Oxford wished to trap a mouse, to which Lewis pushed back. The mouse, Lewis said, very well may be somebody's mother. On another occasion, Lewis came upon a fox caught in a thicket. At that very moment, Root recounts, some foxhunters approached. When they asked Lewis whether he had seen a fox, Lewis pointed the opposite direction in an effort to protect the wounded fox.[26]

The Sabbath is an important day for our critters at home as well. A few years ago, our family adopted three tiny, trembling baby chicks from a local urban farm store. We had always dreamt of having our own chickens in the backyard. We hoped that in six months' time these three chicks would mature into the best egg-laying chickens in all of Portland, the kind neighbors would peek through fences to gawk over. The dream has been fulfilled.

Adopting these chickens has been a welcome disruption to our family's rhythm. Above all, it had a dramatic impact on our son. Tucking him into his bed each night, my wife and I sit in front of him on the floor, offering a concise litany of predictable prayers that a child can grasp—prayer for the day, friends, family, a safe night of sleep, and health for his doll Elmo. He lights up when we pray for Elmo. Up until recently, however, he would only watch, silently refusing to verbally pray, either out of fear or embarrassment or sheer stubbornness. We do not know why. But everything seemed to change when Elliot offered his first prayer, a little prayer for our three chickens. In the humble piety that only a child could embody, Elliot prayed that his new friends would "sleep good and be safe outside." A fitting prayer. A prayer we guess all of heaven melted at.

Elliot is not the only one in Christian history to have prayed for chickens. Stanley Hauerwas once wrote a prayer titled "A Plea for Peace with Chickens":

> Sovereign of All Life, we pray that you will give us the patience to stay still long enough to witness the beauty of your creation. Help us live at peace with your world, especially with our brothers and sisters in and without the church. Help us to live at peace with those creatures not like us—that is, dogs, pigs and even, God help us, chickens. And help us to live in peace with ourselves. Amen.[27]

Praying for chickens. Who prays for chickens? If I were to guess, all this poultry prayer will make a great many Christian readers squirm with some modicum of discomfort. *Praying for a chicken seems unfitting for someone seriously committed to the gospel of Jesus Christ. This kind of prayer smacks too close to the all-too-evil sin of creation worship.* Why pray for chickens? What does God care about a chicken? The truth is, if praying for chickens is discomforting, we are going to have to deal with the fact that some of our most revered Christian heroes prayed for animals (e.g., John Wesley prayed for his horse). Furthermore, if praying for a chicken is out of bounds, then why is praying for our favorite NFL team to win on Sunday acceptable? Prayer is an ongoing discussion with God about *all* of life, not just our favorite parts of it.

In reflecting on my son's prayer, I am drawn to the Sabbath command. I am drawn to God's love of our chickens. I am almost certain that any Christian discomfort with praying for chickens arises mostly out of a hidden disconnect between our understanding of God and our understanding of what God has made—that kind of lopsided Christianity we spoke of at the beginning of the chapter. And this is a dangerous lopsidedness. We have become modern-day gnostics who wrongly believe the invisible alone is good and the visible is bad. But God loved the *kosmos*, the world, the whole thing (John 3:16). I am convinced that separating the life of faith and the gospel from the realm of creation is precisely why creation groans as it does in our current ecological disaster—this separation has caused us to think that we are *above* the world, when in reality we are in it. We are placed here by God. And by refusing to integrate our love of Jesus with a passionate care for the world his Father created, we have envisioned chickens as mere egg-laying, meat-making machines for us to do with as we please. But as my son would tell you, God is the maker of the chickens. God loves the chickens. And the Bible would agree: every creature God has made, God loves—so much so that God even has time to look after a sparrow.

The difference between humanity and the critters is that humans are moral beings. That is, we make decisions between right and wrong. The critters have no moral will. While animals do not have a responsibility to stand up to animal cruelties against humanity, humans *do* have a responsibility to stand up against cruelty toward animals.

Our chickens deserve our respect. I owe them my care and love. They need a day of rest just as much as I do. So on the Sabbath day, we do not bother our chickens. We do not collect any eggs on the Sabbath—we collect them the day before and the day after. We do not take any of their droppings for the garden. They get a day away from us. And I think they love it. I cannot say that they have ever verbally thanked us, but I can say that their eggs are always really, really tasty on the day *after* the Sabbath. I think they like giving us a little extra as a thank-you.

QUESTIONS
for Reflection

- Do you find that you lean toward caring about justice and activism or evangelism and doctrine? How might God be inviting you to care for all these interests?

- The gospel should change everything about the way we live. Are there areas of your life into which you have yet to invite God's Spirit?

- How might we come to a deeper realization of God's love for us by coming to understand how much he loves his critters?

- If you have animals under your care, what might it look like to extend Sabbath rest to them?

- How might God be leading you to stand up against cruelty toward animals?

- In what ways might you be able to provide rest to animals by means of your consumption practices?

PART 4

SABBATH FOR WORSHIP

10

Sabbath and Witness

Submission to God is eternal rest.

Irenaeus, *Against Heresies*

Witness

The good news of Jesus Christ—preached differently at different times—remains the same message today as it always was. The gospel announcement that God is ushering in a new kingdom through Christ's life, death, and resurrection never changes. The method of proclamation, however, *does* change. The church has had to learn the art of contextualizing its message to address the realities and situations of its particular time and place so that the gospel can be understood. For the gospel has to be good, and it also has to be news. If it ceases being good, it ceases being gospel. And if it ceases being news, it will not be heard. Any gospel ceasing to be good or news is not good news but fake good news. We each are invited to preach the ancient gospel in such a fresh way that a twenty-first-century audience can not only understand it but also experience it in a unique way at their unique time. In this chapter, we explore how the Sabbath command offers us a unique opportunity for witness in the twenty-first century, particularly in a world that is exhausted and tired and is searching for rest and peace.

Missionaries learn how to pay attention to the needs and questions of the people they seek to reach. I think of A. Paget Wilkes (1871–1934), who left

161

everything he owned to venture overseas as a missionary to the peoples of Japan.[1] As he began his ministry to the locals, he struggled to connect his message to the indigenous culture. Wilkes tried an experiment: he spent more time listening to the needs of the people he was ministering to. As he did, he discovered that the Japanese were particularly apprehensive about what lay after death. Wilkes decided to change his ministry approach, emphasizing those Scriptures dealing with resurrection and eternal life. What happened was nothing short of miraculous—countless Japanese people connected with his message and became Christians. A strong indigenous church is in Japan today as a testimony to Wilkes's ministry.

For Wilkes, it began with listening. Alongside Wilkes, I think of Charles Finney (1792–1875). History reminds us that amid the excitement of nineteenth-century revivalism, Finney played a particularly crucial role in the spread of the Christian faith in North America. Among other trademark distinctions, Finney's evangelistic method was made popular by the "anxious seat." His practice was a first of its kind. At the end of a tent prayer meeting, Finney invited those who felt anxious about their standing before God to the front of the tent. There the seeker would sit in a chair, the "anxious seat," and receive prayer and confess Jesus as Lord over their anxiety.[2] Finney's practice changed the Christian landscape. To this day, evangelicalism's practices of raising hands and praying the "sinner's prayer" locate their historical beginnings in Finney's "anxious seat." Finney molded his method around the anxiety people faced at the time.

Both Wilkes and Finney began with listening. This offers us a crucial lesson: our witness of the gospel must be set into a particular context and addressed to a particular people. We do not preach the gospel today in the same way Christians did in the second century. We do not preach the gospel today in the same way Christians did in the 1700s. The *way* we preach always changes, but the content of our message remains the same. The church of Jesus must speak to the real felt needs of the world in which the gospel is preached. Wilkes preached to Japanese people concerned with the afterlife, and Finney preached to those with great spiritual anxiety. Neither preached the message with the wrong method. The message, not the method, is eternal.

In my own experience, as our church community has sought to embody a gospel witness to inner-city Portland, I have become entirely convinced that in the twenty-first century the gospel of Jesus—again, particularly within the Western world—has great power to speak to the needs of an increasingly tired, exhausted, and boundaryless society that finds its value in doing. In short, the Sabbath is a unique witness to the gospel in the twenty-first century; the Sabbath will play a key role in the church's evangelism to the world in our day. The very rest that the world is yearning for is something we can offer.

When missionaries are sent to cross-cultural contexts, they are taught to look for local people whom they can partner with—what are called "people of peace." My friend Cam spent years serving in Tunisia and spent the first couple of months simply walking the streets and praying, asking God to bring him people of peace whom he could develop good relationships with. This strategy has great power. While sometimes our witness demands that we *find* people of peace, other times our ministry and evangelism to the world starts as we *become* people of peace—calm, hopeful, peaceful, not neurotic. There is a kind of quality to that person, to the person who has a deep, abiding sense of peace. I want to look for a few moments at how the Sabbath actually creates a church at peace, which can draw in the world.

Church as Contrast Society

In a very real way, the Sabbath puts the church at odds with the world because it reorients the church's relationship to time and even offers the world a prophetically different way of imagining *its* orientation toward time. Can you imagine a world in which Christians actually operated on a different time frame from the rest of the world? Can you imagine the church having its own calendar? Historically, this used to be the case. In 1370, King Charles V ordered all of Paris to orient its entire society around the newly invented mechanized clock. All private and industrial schedules were to be dictated by the mechanical clock, which rang every sixty minutes (like clockwork!) from the Royal Palace downtown. This created a big problem for the church: Should it conform to Charles's command? Or should it stand against this way of understanding time?

The church, in the end, moved from being oriented around liturgical hours primarily set by meals, gardening, and prayer times to the king's time. Soon, mechanized clocks ruled both society and church, and the liturgical time of the church was forced to assimilate to the world's time. In the arresting words of cultural prophet Neil Postman in his book *Technopoly*, the church began to give "material interests precedence over spiritual needs."[3]

The story continues today as the church has uncritically assimilated its life and sense of time into the life of the world. We learn about sexuality from our culture. We learn our leadership techniques from corporations. And we live according to the time of the world. We must recall that Scripture speaks of two kinds of time: *chronos* and *kairos*. The former speaks to chronological time—the time of clocks. Jesus, however, in inaugurating a new kingdom, discussed a new kind of time, which he called *kairos* time. "'The time [*kairos*] has come,' he said. 'The kingdom of God has come near. Repent and believe the good news!'" (Mark 1:15). *Kairos* time is not mediated through the ticking of the long and short hand; rather, it is the time of the kingdom of God. This is "discerned" time, the sacred and anointed time for something. The first (*chronos*) is the time of Earth and culture; the second (*kairos*) is the time of heaven. Too often, the church lives in *chronos* time and entirely ignores the *kairos* time.

The words of Scripture speak pointedly of how the church is to be different, to live a prophetically unworldly way of life:

"You are the light of the world." (Matt. 5:14)

"You are the salt of the earth." (Matt. 5:13)

"Do not conform to the pattern of this world." (Rom. 12:2)

These biblical vignettes are among countless texts calling the church to exist uniquely within the world. We are not to reflect the prevailing paradigms. We are to be *weird*. The church's witness is deeply connected to one thing: Jesus. And that means living differently from the rest of the world. But do we ever see ourselves as living in the world with a different orientation of time? Should "not conforming" also include refusing to conform to the world's notion of time? As it begins to live into this call, the church becomes what Gerhard Lohfink calls a "contrast society."[4] As such, the church becomes that one space where the ultimate and ideal expression of human life is embodied and where slavish obedience to the clock is absent. Here, Jesus is Lord. Not the clocks.

We Sabbath in the world in service of God for the world's sake. This is why the Sabbath has so often caused those who practice it, particularly the Jews, to be at odds with the world. In cultural terms, there have always been two ways for the Jewish communities to scream to the world that they are different from the world: circumcision and Sabbath-keeping. Of course, physical circumcision of the penis did not serve as an adequate visible sign to outsiders of one's covenant relationship with God. Circumcision, though physical, was a private sign unseen by the public eye. Sabbath-keeping, however, existed as a totally different kind of sign to the world. Sabbath has always been a way for Jews to identify themselves in the world. Circumcision was an inward sign. Sabbath was an outward sign. Sabbath was, for all intents and purposes, a visible sign to the outsider of one's identity within the covenant community of Israel, announcing to the world who Jews were and who their God was.

This is undoubtedly why rabbis during the time of Jesus exerted such great energy trying to determine what was rest and what was work. The Sabbath was not merely a day off each week when one ceased work. The Sabbath was a sign to the world that those who practiced it were, in fact, the people of God set apart from the rest of the world.

Sabbath-keeping was a circumcision of time.

The words of God to Moses underscore this reality: "You must observe my Sabbaths. This will be a *sign* between me and you for the generations to come, so you may know that I am the LORD, who makes you holy" (Exod. 31:12–13). The Sabbath was not merely a day. The Sabbath was a sign to everyone—for generations to come—a "perpetual witness of the covenant between God and Israel."[5]

The truth is that people's beliefs are revealed to outsiders more through their actions than their words. People's words are often the last thing we can rely on to discern their beliefs. The Jews believed that if you wanted to know who knew God, you could tell by looking at their schedules. Certainly, we can clarify people's doctrinal perspectives by discussing what they say they believe. But people's schedules and budgets often reveal their doctrines more than anything they might say. One Jewish scholar goes so far as to say that if Jews do not keep the Sabbath, they run the risk of going extinct.[6] It was *that* important for their witness to the world.

Christian Sabbath-keeping is a calendared sign, a confession that Christ is Lord and we are not. I think that the Sabbath very well could have the same effect in our world. As the world looks at the church and the way it rests, it would notice that Christians are a different kind of people who live according to a different set of commitments. But not only this: the church is to be that contrast society where the world learns what true rest is. I think of preindustrial farmers' use of "demonstration plots."[7] As farmers discovered new techniques, new tools, and better ways of deterring pests or bringing in a higher yield, they would take their idea to the demonstration plot for other farmers to see. These plots were incredibly important in pre-internet contexts in which face-to-face relationships were all people knew. Farmers would come from all over the region to gain wisdom and knowledge at plots like this, which were often situated in the middle of a number of farms.

The church is a demonstration plot where the world can enter in and learn about the principles of rest. The church, in other words, is a demonstration plot for the way humans *can* and *should* live in the community of the world. In this contrast community, people are empowered by the Holy Spirit to be not a fortress *against* the world, but a force *in* the world. This environment of grace makes room for all kinds of people who are desperately seeking rest.

The church is a place to learn how to rest. It is not the place we go to burn out. As I mentioned earlier, I used to get offended when someone fell asleep as I preached. Now that I am coming to appreciate the Sabbath, I have come to celebrate it. I love that someone could feel so at home, so safe, so welcome that they can take a break and close their eyes during my sermon. It's a jungle out there. The church is a refuge.

I am reminded that the Bible is chock-full of people who were asked by God to embody unique ways of living for the purposes of witness. I think, for example, of Daniel, Shadrach, Meshach, and Abednego in the book of Daniel. As they are taken off to exile, they are hired to be in the king's service because of their brilliance and physical well-being. The king offers them the food of the king's court. But as a witness to Yahweh, they choose to eat differently—they eat the food of the poor: vegetables and water (Dan. 1). We do not live differently for the sake of living differently. Rather, we know that these contrarian patterns become signs to the world of who we are. Christians, with our belief that the body is the temple of the Holy Spirit, should be the healthiest people in the world (1 Cor. 6:19–20). But we are time and again given over to forgetting who we are and slipping back to living according to the ways of the world. But the spirit of Daniel, Shadrach, Meshach, and Abednego is so important for our time: we eat differently to be a sign to the world.

As the church enters Sabbath, it is embodying the rest of God for the world. And it is God's rest that the world needs. In the fourth century, St. Ambrose said that the church is like the moon: it has no light of its own; it simply reflects it. The church at rest is a sign pointing toward the risen Christ; it is not an end in and of itself. We are a light shining the life of Christ in a dark, tired world. Sabbath is countercultural living. In a world where the overall sales of various energy drinks such as Monster Energy, Red Bull, and Rockstar have increased some 5,000 percent since 1999, embodying Sabbath will offer a witness and context for conversations of eternal importance with a broken, lost world.[8]

I remember one particular day our family was keeping a Sabbath. As we walked through the neighborhood, we bumped into a family down the street who does not identify as religious in any way, shape, or form. They asked us what we were up to for the day. Normally, we would be cautious to not shove religious language about our Sabbath down the throat of our nonreligious neighbors. But, thanks be to God, five-year-olds have no such complex. So my son told them that we were "Sabbathing because God wants us to." For the first time—even without intention—a conversation was opened up about our family commitments, about why we take a day of rest each week. These neighbors even said that the Sabbath sounded like something that *they* needed.

The Sabbath day, for a moment, opened an opportunity to witness to the good news of Jesus.

Keeping the Sabbath Weird

Sabbath-keeping often makes a unique impression on nonparticipants. In ancient cultures, in which people generally ate two meals a day (morning and evening), the Sabbath offered a diversion. On Jewish Sabbaths, meals played a heightened role, including *three* meals of fish, *kugel*, and pudding. Sometimes a fourth meal, called the *melaveh malkah*, would conclude a Sabbath.[9] For a people used to two meals a day, four meals screams "celebration!" The scent of these Sabbath meals caught the attention of Roman emperor Hadrian, who asked Rabbi Joshua ben Hannah, "Why is it that Sabbath foods have such a fragrant scent?" Joshua answered, "We put in a certain spice called Sabbath." The emperor reportedly responded, "Please give me some of that spice." Rabbi Joshua said, "It can only be tasted by those who keep the Sabbath."[10] Sabbath is never linked to fasting in either Jewish or Christian traditions. A fast suggests a demure, sad environment. But joy rules the Sabbath. Sabbath, in the words of one commentator, is "to be a day of consecrated happiness, not of religious gloom."[11]

For every person who has been attracted to the Sabbath, there are stories of those who have been repulsed by it. For example, the Jews continued to practice the Sabbath during the Maccabean revolt against the Greeks who overtaxed and abused the Jewish communities. Jewish communities continued to abstain from work on the Sabbath despite the harsh conditions and demands being placed on them. This severely hurt the Jews' reputation among the Greeks, who called them "lazy because [they] insisted on having a 'holiday' every seventh day."[12] Antiochus Epiphanes demanded that the Israelites profane the Sabbath day and turn to worship the false gods. Some did, turning to idolatry and false worship (1 Macc. 1:39–45). Seneca went so far as to call the Sabbath a "reprehensible Jewish superstition" that caused the Jews to "lose a seventh part of their lifetime, passing it in idleness." The Jews received more than an injury to their reputation; they were eventually widely persecuted for their practice of the Sabbath. It is believed that thousands of Jews were killed at this time because they were unwilling to work according to the slavish demands of the Greeks.[13]

After Israel's return from exile in Babylon, Ezra and Nehemiah rebuild the wall and the temple. Nehemiah stands and reads the law of Moses to the people. Along with a call to purity and repentance is a reestablishment of the Sabbath command among the non-Israelites who lived alongside them.

Nehemiah laments how the Jews there had neglected to observe the Sabbath: "I saw people in Judah treading winepresses on the Sabbath and bringing in grain and loading it on donkeys, together with wine, grapes, figs and all other kinds of loads. And they were bringing all this into Jerusalem on the Sabbath. Therefore I warned them against selling food on that day. . . . I rebuked the nobles of Judah and said to them, 'What is this wicked thing you are doing—desecrating the Sabbath day?'" (Neh. 13:15, 17). Nehemiah then commands that all the Jerusalem gates be shut before the Sabbath and not opened again until the Sabbath ends. He even sends some of his own men to protect against the clamor of consumerism; they are to "purify themselves . . . and guard the gates in order to keep the Sabbath day holy" (Neh. 13:22).

Nehemiah lamented that God's people did not consecrate themselves to Yahweh by obeying the Sabbath command. And he lamented hearing the clamor of consumerism, because it sent all the wrong messages to the peoples around them. That Israel was fraught with consumerism—running to and fro—was a sign to the world that Israel was conformed to the world. But Israel was not of the world. Israel belonged to God above all. Abraham Heschel speaks pointedly to this: "He who wants to enter the holiness of the day must first lay down the profanity of clattering commerce, of being yoked to toil. He must go away from the scratch of dissonant days, from the nervousness and fury of acquisitiveness and the betrayal in embezzling his own life."[14]

The Jewish Sabbath would have been welcome news to another group of people—those at war with Israel. History tells us that on the Sabbath the ancient Jews—who always seemed to be surrounded by violent, warmongering peoples drooling over their land and possessions—refused to go on the offensive when they were in war. On the Sabbath, they would only defend. Even the Mishnah forbade carrying a weapon on the Sabbath. No doubt, people felt some relief when warring with the Jews, because they knew one day a week everyone could stop and take a break. Later, during the Middle Ages, the church sought to influence leaders not to fight on Sunday, a day they called "the truce of God." On that day, people would literally lay down their weapons so that they could worship.[15]

This interplay between Sabbath observance and loving one's enemies is beautiful and painful at the same time. To Sabbath was to love your enemies, because it gave your enemies a day off from you. It was to give your worst nightmare a day off. What effect could this practice have on our relationships today? Imagine taking a break from the roommate battle over dishes that has been waging for weeks. Imagine putting down your arms one day a week with a boss who disrespects you. Imagine putting aside an argument over finances with your spouse for a day in order to enter into the rich provision of God. In his book *The Sabbath*, Samuel Dresner expresses how the Sabbath is a unique response to being at war with nature, with society, even with ourselves. In putting down our weapons and stepping away from our wars and battles one day each week—something that "seems strange, out of place, even absurd"[16]—we are invited into a deeper trust as we experience God as our protector.

What is unquestionable is that keeping a Sabbath will make us different from those around us no matter what time and place we live in. I remember the story of a young woman in our church who began to keep the Sabbath. She described two things about her experience. First, her family had no idea how to respond. Aside from actually changing the way she related to her family on a schedule level, it caused issues in how they coexisted, since the value of time was under a new sort of scrutiny. Second, her Sabbathing raised countless questions. She described how her family was intrigued more than anything. Had she joined a cult? Where had she learned about this? Why was she doing it?

Friends, to a world that worships at the altar of hyperactivity, Sabbath raises all kinds of questions. The Sabbath is weird. The Sabbath makes *us* weird. And we should keep it that way.

I remember back in the 1990s when my favorite basketball team, the Portland Trailblazers, was at the height of its success. With the likes of Clyde Drexler, Terry Porter, and—God rest their souls—Kevin Duckworth and Jerome Kersey, the Blazers stood tall against the NBA's best, nearly winning it all a couple of years. Every once in a while, the Blazers would play against the Denver Nuggets and one of the biggest centers in the NBA—Dikembe Mutombo. Mutombo, an African by descent, wreaked havoc on teams for years as one of the NBA's big men. But it was always great when the schedule-makers happened to schedule the Blazers to play Denver during the Muslim month of fasting, Ramadan. During Ramadan, a Muslim does not eat during the daytime. And because Mutombo was an observant Muslim—faithful to observe the rhythms of Ramadan—he would not eat during the day. This made playing against him much easier. I distinctly remember watching the Blazers and listening to the sportscaster talk at length about how Mutombo's religious observance affected his play.

Mutombo's actions sparked conversation. Now, I did not become a Muslim because of his actions. But I was provoked to think about what he believed and why he believed it. It is human nature—you always pay a little extra attention to the person who does not do what everyone does unthinkingly. You notice when people live by convictions, especially when it costs them.

Sabbath has that effect on people. It raises questions. My friend Tom Krattenmaker writes a lot about God. But he is not a Christian. He once told me that the one thing about Christians that he admires—and that even causes him to consider the truth of Christianity—is when people of faith do something that is deeply inconvenient and painful because they believe in it. "When someone does something inconvenient in a world that worships convenience," he told me over coffee, "it makes me do a double take."

Sabbath causes double takes. It is inconvenient. It creates problems. It is weird.

And that is good.

I appreciate the words of Erin Lane: "Sabbath freedom is not the freedom to spend our time wisely. Instead, Sabbath freedom is the freedom to live large."[17]

Sabbath Guests

In John 4:1–26, Jesus sits by a well. His disciples have run off to get some food. They have been doing lots of ministry and are tired. Apparently, so is Jesus. John tells us, "Jacob's well was there, and Jesus, tired as he was from the journey, sat down by the well. It was about noon" (John 4:6). Jesus gets tired. And sits. Does nothing. Then a woman comes to the well, and Jesus has a conversation with her about the kingdom of God. She experiences his message and eventually becomes the first missionary in John's Gospel. In this story, God's mission takes place as Jesus takes a rest and sits by a well.[18] He welcomes a woman into his rest, and she immediately experiences the grace of God's kingdom. While the church is a contrast society and should be a place where the world learns the art of rest, the Sabbath also provides space—like that in the life of Jesus—to encounter people. The Sabbath provides space in our schedules to waste time with others and, just like Jesus, minister out of our rest.

For quite some time, there was a young woman in our community who had a beautiful story. She grew up in a Jewish home. In her college years, she heard the message of Jesus and became a Christian. As she began to follow Jesus, she intentionally continued to practice the Jewish rhythms of her childhood and heritage. One of those rhythms was Passover. One year she celebrated a full Passover—with radishes, bitter herbs, and the lamb shank—in our living room with about ten other participants. Every minute of the entire evening dripped with symbol and beauty. As she walked us through the Passover, she shared points of contact between her Jewish ancestry and her Christian faith. She boiled over with excitement as she pointed out parts of the evening that pointed to Jesus as the Messiah.

One lesson I will never forget from the Passover experience was how important it was in the celebration for outsiders such as myself to have a chance to come in and learn. That young woman explained how, for many Jewish communities, welcoming outsiders and neighbors to the Passover celebration was one of the most meaningful ways to share their faith. There remained an open-door policy for the world to hear the story of God's people.

The Sabbath plays a similar role as a "sanctuary in time" where the alien, the nonbeliever, the outsider, the marginalized, the neighbor, and the friend can come and rest as well.[19] The church should embody that same spirit regarding the Sabbath—an open-door policy to share how we find God in this sacred practice. Doing so necessitates protecting margin to actually keep the Sabbath. Again, we must remember God's desire for margin. As the Levitical command says, "Do not reap to the very edges of your field or gather the gleanings of your harvest. Do not go over your vineyard a second time or pick up the grapes that have fallen. Leave them for the poor and the foreigner. I am the LORD your God" (Lev. 19:9–10). Isaiah speaks woe over those who have no such space: "Woe to you who add house to house, and join field to field till no space is left and you live alone in the land" (Isa. 5:8). The lesson signifies something very clear: margin is good. And Sabbath provides it. Sabbath creates margin, space, openings, room for the foreigners among us who themselves need to be blessed by Sabbath rest.

Margin is difficult to keep in a community. But without space, there cannot be community. To reflect this, our church has intentionally opted not to have a midweek worship gathering. We could have one. But we wanted to create space in people's week for them to be able to say yes to their neighbors and those around them. Christian community can easily become a place where we are so crammed with activities that we do not have time to do the things that Jesus cares most deeply about—such as loving the lost in our neighborhoods. The Sabbath, in our experience, creates a unique opportunity to share the gospel. For in that one day a week, we are unfettered with activity and can actually spend some time with those whom we live alongside. One ancient feature of the Sabbath is called the *oreah*, or the Sabbath "guest."[20] A Sabbath guest is a poor person, college student, widow, or refugee who is invited in for the Sabbath day. The Sabbath is not another flavor of individualism. It is a return to the communal roots of our faith, where we make room for the other. Again, in a tired society, keeping the Sabbath is a unique way to create space for others who are trapped by exhaustion.

There is nothing in Scripture that suggests that witness should not happen on the Sabbath day. In fact, quite the opposite. When Jesus died and lay in the tomb, he did so on the Jewish Sabbath. In what has been called "The Harrowing of Hell" and is alluded to in 1 Peter 3:18–20, Jesus went to Sheol and preached to the righteous dead of the coming of his kingdom. So what does Jesus do on the Sabbath of his death? Jesus saves. He redeems. He witnesses to his own power of death in the pits of Sheol.

Remember, Sabbath in the twenty-first century is not a day to hide God's light under a basket. In the twenty-first century, keeping a Sabbath *is* witness. I close with the breathtaking words of Wiel Logister: "At a feast there is something . . . brimming over. That is why guests are invited for a feast, why a chair stands ready for the stranger and why expansiveness predominates. Solipsism and individualism are not appropriate for a feast. This very sin is being overcome. And that gives joy, lightness, radiance."[21] The joy of the Sabbath, when we rest and feast in God's presence, is a powerful witness to the world.

QUESTIONS
for Reflection

- How might practicing the Sabbath be part of witnessing to your family, friends, or neighbors?
- What might keeping the Sabbath say to the world around you about the God you worship?
- What battle might God be inviting you to lay aside on the Sabbath?
- What questions might people ask you as they observe you keeping a Sabbath?
- How might those around you receive rest by your Sabbath practice?
- Who could you invite in as a Sabbath guest?

11

Sabbath and Worship

> A well-spent Sabbath we feel to be a day of heaven upon earth.
>
> Robert Murray M'Cheyne, "I Love the Lord's Day"

Sunday Best

In this chapter, we will explore Sabbath-keeping as an act of, and in relation to, Christian worship. How do Sabbath and worship relate to each other? Let us begin in our imaginations. It is Sunday morning, the Lord's Day. Imagine yourself entering a room of diverse, unfamiliar worshipers who have gathered to worship an unseen God. As the music begins, you observe those around you. The congregation's diversity almost shocks you. There, in the front rows, are some elderly individuals who have slowly risen to sing songs to God they have been singing for years. Throughout the sanctuary, married couples stand together to raise their voices as their children sit coloring, fidgeting in the seats beside them. A college student stands in the back, hoodie covering his head, hands in his pockets, directing his often-limited attention toward the musicians who begin to play a song. He puts his phone into his pocket. You see white people. Black people. Asian people. Young. Old. Men. Women. A woman in a wheelchair reclines at the side. The musicians begin their chorus. Slowly, everyone is caught up in the music.

What does imagining this worship gathering provoke within you?

Perhaps you are an ex-churchgoer for whom this image brings up feelings of anger, bitterness, or rejection. Or maybe you are a pastor who is brought to sudden nervousness—even now, your adrenaline has risen a few levels. Or perhaps you are a Christian who sees this gathering as a moment of intimacy with God before the workweek begins.

These are *our* perspectives of a worshiping church. From God's perspective, however, a worshiping church is a miracle. It is difficult to see as God sees, but this congregation is indeed a sign of the mercy of God that is being extended to a world of sinners. God has pursued each and every person in the room from the moment of their conception. Calling them. Disciplining them. Loving them. Chasing them. God knows all their stories. God sees no Democrats or Republicans, Calvinists or Arminians, Baptists or Pentecostals. God sees children whom he redeemed with the death and resurrection of Christ. He sees people who have at times hurt each other but who have also chosen to forgive one another and who continue to worship together. He sees people who would never spend time together in the world of the enemy but who now spend time together because of the work of grace.

Worship is a miracle. And this miracle has been taking place week in and week out as an act of Sabbath observance throughout church history. Of course, worship is not limited to merely what Christians do in church buildings. Nor must the Sabbath be observed on Sunday. But traditionally, corporate worship has been the way Christians have entered God's Sabbath rest. Sunday is the Lord's Day. It is as if Sabbath and worship always went hand in hand. This reality has forged a beautiful sense of identity in the life of the church. This act of gathering to worship is, in the words of Stanley Hauerwas and Samuel Wells, "the most regular way that most Christians remind themselves and others that they are Christians. It is the most significant way in which Christianity takes flesh, evolving from a set of ideas and convictions to a set of practices and a way of life."[1] Worship is the way the church reminds itself of who it is and who it worships. Christians cannot imagine their worship without understanding God's Sabbath rest.

Early in my Christian journey, the Sabbath was the day we put on our best clothes for worship with God's people. We called them our "Sunday best." Sabbath got our best clothing as a reflection of our deep sense of reverence and honor for God and his people. I have even learned that many Christians throughout history would take a Saturday bath in preparation for Sabbath worship. Putting on our Sunday best was our discipline of preparing our bodies, minds, and hearts for worship. It was like Sunday was unique, set apart, *qadosh*—a day set apart from all others in worship to God. That simple act of donning our Sunday best had a way of putting our hearts and minds in a posture of reverence and respect that this day was different from all the rest. That was the Sabbath spirit. The discipline of cleaning up, dressing up, and preparing yourselves was a reminder that this day was unlike any other.

Times have changed. A Sabbath worship day can no longer be assumed. People often work on Sundays. Christians go to church far less than they used to. And even the discipline of wearing one's Sunday best has largely been lost. Even in the community I shepherd, people opt for normal, everyday clothing in Sunday worship. Both Sabbath and worship have largely become individualized—a difficult reality we must be sensitive to when thinking through the Sabbath. Without being sentimental, I do wonder whether something critical is lost when we disconnect our corporate worship from our Sabbath. I even wonder whether something is lost when we stop donning our Sunday best.

Sabbath-keeping is like any discipline of the Christian tradition. A discipline is any repeated and intentional action that God uses to change our hearts and minds. Disciplines are critical to the Christian life. And there are many disciplines in the Christian tradition, such as prayer, Scripture reading, churchgoing, and confession.[2] Disciplines are external actions undertaken with the vision that God can use them to reform our internal affections. We must once again envision the Sabbath not in terms of a day that "just happens" but in terms of a discipline that transforms us inside. Sabbath is a proactive, intentional discipline, not an add-on that we get to when time makes space for it.

Let me illustrate how a discipline works. In my first year of seminary, I signed up for all the classes required of me, with little idea of what I should take first to graduate as early as possible. I had no idea what I was doing—neither did anyone else. My first term included a class on Christian history taught by Dr. Dan Brunner. I had never been too excited about history, until Dr. Brunner's class. I remember the first day, sitting with some twenty-five first-year seminary students who were beginning their seminary journey together. In walked Dr. Brunner—Oxford educated, plaid jacket, bow tie, and all. He embodied the iconic British academic nerd. For the next three hours, Dr. Brunner, a Lutheran, spoke eloquently about the nature of heresy in the early church and how we should continue to care about what is true and what is untrue in doctrine.

That was perhaps the best class I have ever taken. Nearly in entirety, my own teaching and academic pursuits are a reflection of that class and a reflection on Dr. Brunner. If you ask just about any teacher how they ended up teaching, they will tell you that they got into teaching because of some teacher they had at some point. I wanted to teach because I loved how Dr. Brunner taught. In the middle of that semester, I scheduled a meeting with Dr. Brunner to ask him what I needed to do to become a professor. He gave me the following advice: "Get a plaid jacket, a bow tie, and start dressing like a professor."

I would eventually have to get higher degrees. But he explained to me that if I dressed like a professor, I would start thinking like a professor. So I started. I bought my first tweed jacket and some ties (I could not stand bow ties). And I started to dress like a professor. Today I am a professor. End of story.

That is what a discipline is—it is something we do consistently that changes our hearts and minds over time. This is reflected in Paul's admonition to "clothe yourselves with the Lord Jesus Christ" (Rom. 13:14). What does it mean to put on Jesus Christ? The gist of what Paul commands is closely related to me dressing like a professor in order to become a professor. None of us are born into the world with the character of Jesus Christ. Character comes over time as we follow Christ. Disciplines are a way to "clothe ourselves with the Lord Jesus Christ." Disciplines, like worship, can include a variety of actions— prayer, fasting, contemplation, silence, service, reading Scripture. The hope is that by doing them our hearts are changed—that in dressing like Christ, we become like Christ. A discipline is putting on some attribute of Jesus in hopes that it changes the very makeup of our hearts and minds.

Sabbath is a discipline we put on. When we practice the Sabbath, it may feel a bit like we are putting on someone else's clothing. And indeed we are. Sabbath is foreign clothing—nay, heavenly clothing—and it may not fit for a while. But the hope is that, in doing it over a long period of time, it brings about real and substantive changes to our hearts, minds, and attitudes. In short, with a discipline, we dress for the character and virtue we *want*, not the character and virtue we *have*. Repetition has tremendous value for the formation of our hearts. For instance, one finds in Psalms 120–134 (also known as the Songs of Ascent, or *Shir Hama‘aloth*) songs that were sung the three times each year that faithful Jews would make their way to Jerusalem. One must wonder what it was like to come time and time again to the land of God's grace. Architecture and topography and repetition became spiritual formation. As people made these journeys over and over and over again, the songs would have transformed their hearts.

A Day to Worship Other Stuff

In her extraordinary book *Smoke on the Mountain*, Joy Davidman tells the tale of a student from Mars who comes to Earth to study the odd ways of human society. On one Sunday morning, the student examines the actions of the average resident in the United States. After careful observation, the Martian concludes that the inhabitants of Earth are, indeed, worshipers of the sun. For on the one day designated for worship, the people gather into large groups to undertake rather rowdy liturgies that draw people into big, open, green fields. Others, the Martian sees, go down to the water's edge and strip nearly naked, swimming frantically in the chilly saltwater. Then they lie, anointed with fine oils, on the sandy beach to glory in the sun they worship. But, the Martian discovers, there are the others who worship differently. Some, unlike the general populace, dress nicely and go indoors on the day of sun worship. There, they seem to worship something foreign to the rest of the world, a Being who cannot be seen. These different worshipers exude none of the "almost orgiastic religious frenzy with which the sun worshipers pursue their devotions."[3]

Davidman's book provokes an interesting question: If Martians came to Earth on our day of worship, what would they conclude we worship? Football? Youth sports? The great outdoors? Brunches with friends? Music festivals?

Of course, none of this is to suggest that these are bad. By no means. Sports, the outdoors, a good brunch, music—all of these are good in the right context. However, a survey of Sunday's activities raises the question of whether these pursuits have become dominant and take our ultimate attentions.

The difference between the church and the world is that the church worships the Creator God. The world worships *anything* else. In the end, it is impossible not to worship something. We all worship something. Some worship money. Some worship their jobs. Some worship their families. Others worship their churches. But the truth is we all worship something or someone. As was evidenced earlier, in the biblical story humans are prone to worship good things that God has made over God himself. However, we find that the biblical account consistently dethrones such "good" things that we tend to exalt in false worship. In Genesis 1:14–17, for example, the text explains *why* God makes the lights in the sky before God actually *makes* the lights of the sky. The explanation comes before the creation. "And God said, 'Let there be lights in the vault of the sky to separate the day from the night, and let them serve as signs to mark sacred times, and days and years, and let them be lights in the vault of the sky to give light on the earth.' And it was so" (Gen. 1:14–15). Why did the author of this narrative provide this explanation before the act of creation?

Gordon Wenham points out that in the ancient world, most of the pagan religions worshiped the lights in the sky. In fact, whole religions were based on worshiping celestial lights, which were given personal names. Wenham brilliantly articulates the context of the biblical author: "In neighboring cultures, the sun and the moon were some of the most important gods in the pantheon, and the stars were often credited with controlling human destiny."[4]

Sports, food, and fun have a purpose; God celebrates these things. But God's intention was never that we would replace him with these good things.

No wonder we struggle to find time to come together for a day of rest. The day of worship, when Christians gather in the name of Jesus, is stuffed to the brim with so many activities that we neglect to do the very thing that we are called to do on that day—worship God. We have become like Noah's ark. Noah sends out a dove, but it returns unable to find a place to rest. We are no different. We fly about in search of rest but find instead yet another day filled with chaos. We have no place to land and rest.

A day of worship is where Christians can return to find a much-needed place of rest. We need a day to rest and exalt God above all things. What can we do? In the seventeenth-century *Book of Sports*, King James I discussed how "no offensive weapons were to be carried or used during the time of recreation" on the Sabbath. He even barred "the meaner sort of people" from bowling on the Sabbath.[5] Of course, there are many contemporary examples of individuals who have gone to extreme measures to honor God with a Sabbath day of worship. Sandy Koufax, that famed pitcher for the Los Angeles Dodgers, refused to pitch the first game of the World Series because of his Sabbath obligation. There is also Eric Liddell, the famed runner depicted in *Chariots of Fire*, who refused to race on Sunday. Both of these are stories of people who took what they felt was a posture of worship to God on their day of rest. While we should not universalize their decisions, we should note them and ask ourselves some questions: What have we crowded our worship out with? What are those things we are willing to "make time for" by sacrificing something else? Watching football and eating good food and going outdoors are not bad things. These are tremendously good things. However, in making the day of worship all about these good experiences, we crowd out the encounter that once brought Christians together as a body.

The background of all this is that Sabbath has served as a weekly opportunity for the church to encounter Christ's story and his victory over death. Yet, again, what once drew people together in worship and rest has been replaced. And we pay a heavy price. I once heard of a Nigerian village that received its first electric light bulbs. Each family was given one for their home. Every night families would turn their lights on. A problem arose. Families would sit inside and stare at the light bulb rather than sit at the community fire, where they had for centuries told and listened to their tribe's stories. Nighttime had always been when their stories were passed along. Now, they stared at the light bulb.[6] The problem with the light bulb was not what it did (emit light); the problem was what the bulb didn't do (create meaningful connection). The light bulb took attention away from the time that was needed to pass along the cultural narratives of the people. The problem with a Sabbath as a mere day of activity is not that the activities are bad; it is that the activities replace the time-honored activity of passing along the story of Jesus to those around us.

Sunday used to be the day when we would hear the story of who we are as children of God. We would be reminded of who loves us and why we are here. Unfortunately, we have replaced those stories with stories of competition, luxury, and diversion. We make it a day about ourselves rather than a day about Someone else. In her iconic book *The Violent Bear It Away*, Flannery O'Connor's main character utters a prophetic idea: "No, no, no, the stranger said, there ain't no such thing as a devil. I can tell you that from my own self-experience. I know that for a fact. It ain't Jesus or the devil. It's Jesus or you."[7] We often think that the opposite of worshiping God is worshiping the devil. But that is not the problem. Often, our problem is that we worship ourselves. It ain't Jesus or the devil. It is Jesus or ourselves.

Sabbath as Trust

Sabbath is one of the ways that we learn to worship God through trust. When we sing songs of praise and worship, we are holding up words of promise that God is our provider, sustainer, and redeemer. As we look to the Psalms, which are the backdrop to our own worship of God, we find that time and again they ascribe trust and hope to God in a world of darkness and uncertainty. To sing worship is to lend trust to the goodness of God. We see this in Jesus as he utters some of his final words from the cross: "Father, into your hands I commit my spirit" (Luke 23:46). What does this mean? The weight of that text lies in the fact that Jesus is uttering a psalm that was memorized and uttered by Jewish boys and girls as they went to bed. It was the ancient version of "Now I lay me down to sleep . . ." As Jesus dies, he is worshiping and trusting his Father. It is as if Jesus is vocalizing his trust, "I am going to go to sleep right now—but I *know* you are going to wake me up, Father." The Psalms drip with this double ring of worship and trust of God.

Sabbath, then, is a form of trust. "Sabbath keeping is a publicly enacted sign of our trust," writes Will Willimon, "that God keeps the world, therefore we do not have to. God welcomes our labors, but our contributions to the world have their limits. If even God trusted creation enough to be confident that the world would continue while God rested, so should we."[8] Sabbath is stopping our work and announcing to all creation and everyone around us, "Jesus Christ is Lord." Sabbath helps us crucify our hidden desires to step into God's shoes and do his work, and it protects us from what Hilary of Poitiers called *irreligious solicitudo pro Deo*, "a blasphemous anxiety to do God's work for him."[9] Thus the Sabbath dissipates our desire to take ourselves too seriously and helps us rightly take God seriously in worship. It is the day that we are reminded that we are full of God's Spirit, not full of ourselves.

Rest in the Old Testament, particularly evidenced through the theme of sleep, has always implied a deep sense of trust in God. For the ancients, sleep was difficult to do and often hard to come by. When they slept, it was an implicit statement that they trusted that someone was watching over them. In the ancient world, sleep made a person vulnerable to attack from wild animals or violent robbers. Sleep was a scary venture. This is why the psalmists repeatedly connect safety with sleep for the follower of God. "In peace I will lie down and sleep, for you alone, LORD, make me dwell in safety" (Ps. 4:8). Time and again, the biblical witness connects trust with sleep. Although we may not be under physical threat while laying our heads down, it is often during sleep, and the stages just before, that we are most vulnerable to fears, even those that are subconscious. Sometimes to do nothing, to sleep, requires the most active trust in God. This is an important backdrop to the *shabbos schluf,* or the "Sabbath nap," which is celebrated in many Jewish communities. To nap on the Sabbath is to say that trust in God has taken its rightful place.

This emphasis on peace is why biblical scholar Matitiahu Tsevat insists that a Sabbath is, at its core, the "acceptance of the sovereignty of God."[10] Mark Buchanan stresses this very thing: "The Sabbath command, with its call to imitation, plays on a hidden irony: we mimic God in order to remember we're not God. In fact, that is a good definition of Sabbath: *imitating God so that we stop trying to be God.*"[11] When we rest, we are worshiping God. God is God. Not my work. Not our efforts. Only God is God. Therefore, we can trust with all of our being in his capacity to care for us.

I find it interesting that Jesus sleeps a good deal in the Gospels. But Jesus's rhythms of sleep are unlike anyone else's. Jesus is always sleeping when everyone else is awake and always seems to be awake when everyone else is sleeping. On the boat in the storm, Jesus sleeps as his disciples sweat with fear (Matt. 8:23–27; Mark 4:35–41). At Gethsemane, Jesus is awake, sweating blood in prayer, while his disciples cannot keep their eyes open (Luke 22:39–46). Indeed, Jesus's life was marked by a unique rhythm of rest that seemed disjointed from his own disciples' rhythm and was certainly different from the world's. But that sleep showed Jesus's deep sense of trust in his Father. Even storms did not unsettle his sleep rhythms.

Like rest in the ancient world, Sabbath-keeping in our present world is an embodied act of trusting God. When we worship and trust God, there is no one and nothing to fear. Fear, friend, is a disturbance in the force, a kind of invasive species in the garden of Eden. God never created humans to live with fear, other than a deep sense of fear and reverence toward God. The first encounter of "fear" in Scripture does not come until Genesis 3:10 and is clearly the result of sin, not God's original design. Instead, we were created to live in abundant trust in the Creator. Sabbathing is a way that we defy fear by actively trusting God.

To Sabbath, to rest, to step away from our work in the world, is typified in the moment Moses ascends Mount Sinai to receive the Ten Commandments from God for Israel waiting below. Moses descends the mountain only to find God's people worshiping a golden calf. The irony of the story lies in the fact that God's people have managed to break the law before they even receive it. A broken people God's people are!

My own discomfort with the Sabbath is connected to that Moses story. For me, if I go up the mountain and descend only to find God's people worshiping a golden calf, I feel like I have failed as a leader. The world has crumbled in my absence! But even worse than that feeling of failing everyone, if I descend the mountain to find the people worshiping God, I have to come face-to-face with my greatest fear: I am not as necessary as I once thought. We all get a Moses complex—we think that our absence will reveal either that we have failed others or that the world is better without us. Both are terror-inducing notions. But the Sabbath rescues us from our self-anointed Moses complex. The Sabbath simultaneously shows us our irrelevance and our dependence on God. It reminds us of our place in God's story. Sabbath reminds us that we never were necessary and that this world is, well, not ours.

Sabbath is a reminder that in our irrelevance we are still loved by the Maker of everything. It is only then that we can grasp how deeply we are loved—not because of our usefulness but because we are chosen.

Even now, as our world seems to be falling apart at the seams, consider where Jesus is presently. Jesus is in heaven. What is he doing there? "He was taken up into heaven and he sat at the right hand of God" (Mark 16:19). What a compelling and disturbing image. Right now our world is marred by sin and evil. The church is undergoing incredible difficulties. War seems to be at our doorstep. And what does Jesus do? He sits. This is not laziness or apathy. This is Jesus trusting his Father. Jesus trusts so deeply that he sits and rests at God's side. The world's brokenness does not make God neurotic. Jesus is at peace. He trusts his Father. He is not pacing back and forth in worry. Worship sometimes rests. "God gives himself," Karl Barth once wrote, "but he does not give himself away."[12] Jesus gives himself to care for and sustain the world. But in so doing he does not abandon any of the peace he has had with the Father from all eternity.

Sabbath declares that God's work is not ultimately dependent on ours and that God's rest is always more effective than human work. We often assume that God only works and acts when we are on the clock or have our act together. This is the worship of our own effort and the craftiness of our own works. Sabbath says no to that paradigm. God is constantly at work in his people even as we are resting in God on the mountain. Can you hear him calling? We are upheld, held together, continued, and sustained by the eternal grace of God. Our strength is not, in the end, our strength. God is our only strength. Sabbath-keeping beckons us to trust in him.

Entering Sabbath, Entering Heaven

One critical Sabbath text in the Old Testament is Numbers 10. Israel had been wandering through the desert on the way to the promised land: "So they set out from the mountain of the LORD and traveled for three days. The ark of the covenant of the LORD went before them during those three days to find them a place to rest. The cloud of the LORD was over them by day when they set out from the camp" (Num. 10:33–34). One might be tempted to move quickly beyond this little text. But Moses did not miss the power of what was going on. Moses caught a glimpse of God as *Yahweh Shabbat*, "Lord of the Sabbath." Pay close attention to what God did as his people wandered through the desert: "The LORD went before them . . . to *find them a place to rest*." God was going ahead of Israel to "find rest" on their behalf.

Time and again in the Bible, the language regarding the Sabbath is that we "enter" it. Sabbath is not self-created. Sabbath is not man-made. Sabbath is a day that God has gone in advance to prepare for us. The book of Hebrews stresses, "Make every effort to *enter* that rest" (Heb. 4:11). The lesson Moses learned was that he did not need to worry about when to find rest because God was more concerned with that than he would ever be. God was going ahead and preparing a place of rest for him. Our task, like Moses's, is to enter what God has already prepared for us.

Rest is, ultimately, the prevailing image of heaven throughout the New Testament. Heaven is eternal Sabbath. While Sabbath-keeping is not a condition for getting into heaven, we should remember that the condition of heaven is Sabbath before we get there. We will enter what is a present Sabbath in heaven. I remember one worship gathering in our church during a very painful cultural moment in our city. As I walked into the worship gathering to take my spot near the front, the musicians began to play. What was to be a normal worship gathering turned upside down. I have no way to describe it: the presence of God was so near, so close, so present that evening. Looking around at the congregation, I saw people on their knees, crying, repenting, worshiping, laughing. God came near. As I reflected on that evening, one thing stood out to me: no preparation, no liturgy, no sermon—nothing could prepare for what God did that evening. All we could do was *enter*. That was our task. Nothing more.

The book of Revelation is the picture John receives of heaven. What does he see? All the heavenly elders and angels worshiping God. Heaven is the eternal throne room where the Creator is worshiped. That means that anytime a church says "worship starts at 9:00 a.m.," we are lying through our teeth. Worship does not *start* at 9:00 a.m. We are merely *entering* at 9:00 a.m. Heaven is eternal worship that started before we ever did.

Sabbath is not something that begins when we begin it. Sabbath, like worship, is something we enter into and is always available to us. It is larger in scope than we could possibly imagine or ever create. When we enter Sabbath, we are entering God's eternal rest in the same way we join the angels in their forever worship of the Creator. The third time Noah released the dove from the ark, it found rest. The dove did not make its own tree to rest on. Rather, it found a tree that existed.

We have to be drawn to John's image of heaven—a feast. In fact, John describes the "wedding supper of the Lamb" (Rev. 19:6–9), which the saints will enjoy with Jesus forever. I wonder what that feast will be like. I have long had a theory. Remember that moment in Acts 9 when Saul, the persecutor of the church, became a Christian? "For three days he was blind, and did not eat or drink anything" (Acts 9:9). Many read this and simply think that Paul was a very observant fast-keeper. Although Paul may have been somewhat of a pro at fasting, he was not refraining from food here out of mere ritual. I think that he literally forgot to eat and drink anything for three days. Why? He had just seen Jesus. I think that when we enter glory—seated at the marriage supper of the Lamb—we will sit silently for about ten thousand years. We will not be able to eat. We, like Paul, will simply sit and look at the glory of the Lamb of God who was slain for the world.

That is worship: Awe. Wonder. The inability to eat.

That will be eternal Sabbath—our jaws eternally on the floor. We will be forever transfixed. Heaven will be like when God gave Israel the cloud in the desert. That is a powerful image. Clouds are all over the place in the Bible. When Jesus was on the mountain in the transfiguration, a cloud descended and made it hard to see. When the priests were in the tabernacle, the cloud of God's glory destroyed their church services, and the priests could not go about their normal duty. Time and time again, a cloud shows up. And that night of worship I learned: whenever God comes really, really close to his people, the visibility gets poor. The by-product of God's nearness is often that it seems like we cannot see more than a few feet from our noses.

A Sabbath day on earth is heaven's preseason. And heaven is an eternal Sabbath. When the Christians of the early church began to observe the Sabbath day on Sunday rather than Saturday, as their forebears did, the day of Sabbath then was not on the "first" day of the week but on the "eighth" day of the week. This came to resemble a picture of eternity. Dorothy Bass writes that Christians "came to believe . . . that Sabbath's meaning had changed within the new creation God began with Christ's death and resurrection. The holy day from now on, therefore, was not the seventh but the 'eighth'—an eschatological day on which the future bursts into the present."[13]

A weekly Sabbath is simply a preparation for the real thing. These Sabbath days are not the real thing. The Sabbath, a day of rest on earth, is a kind of foretaste of what is to come. "The Shabbat," writes Irving Greenberg, "is a foretaste of the messianic redemption."[14] Or as Marva Dawn puts it, "Sabbath rest is a foretaste of eternal life."[15] N. T. Wright stresses, "The Sabbath was the regular signpost pointing forward to God's promised future, *and Jesus was announcing that the future to which the signpost had been pointing had now arrived in the present.*"[16] Sabbath is that "tantalizing experience" that urges us to long for the new heaven and earth.[17] Abraham Heschel writes, "Unless one learns how to relish the taste of Sabbath while still in this world, unless one is initiated in the appreciation of eternal life, one will be unable to enjoy the taste of eternity in the world to come."[18] Heaven, Heschel says, will be an eternal Sabbath. Sabbath is not something that a world of decay is all that interested in. A Sabbathless world is a world that the devil takes pleasure in. Sabbath was created to be in place even in a world not ravaged by sin. Sabbath is not something foreign to the world. Rather, to not rest one day a week is foreign.

When we look back at the creation account, we find a pattern. When God makes each day, the text says there was "morning and evening." This happens on days one, two, three, four, five, and six. However, when the text depicts day seven, no such demarcation is mentioned. The seventh day has no evening. Why? It is like it never ends. John Andrews has considered this: "Could it be that here, at the beginning, the Lord of the Sabbath is giving us a huge nudge towards the truth that the rest enshrined on the seventh day was never meant to remain within the confines of the day, but was intended to be enjoyed every day?"[19]

To Sabbath is to enter into a different mode of time in which pressing matters do not become ultimate. Ephrem the Syrian writes, "For it was given to them in order to depict by a temporal rest, which He gave to a temporal people, the mystery of the true rest which will be given to the eternal people in the eternal world."[20] To be healthy is to learn how to be faithful to both kinds of time. There is time (*chronos*) for meetings, schedules, preaching, and evangelism. There is also time (*kairos*), which can only be discerned, for a word that must be spoken, a prophetic utterance, a confession, or an apology. Healthy rhythms in pastoral life are mindful of both kinds of time.

The beauty is that because Jesus has come, he is actively re-creating a world with Sabbath in it. His kingdom is one with rest and Sabbath built in. It has been said by Jewish rabbis that if everyone in the world kept a Sabbath at the same exact time, the Messiah would come.[21] Christians, I want to submit, have a different perspective. The Messiah, Jesus, has already come. And we have nothing to wait for. Messiah has come—that is why everyone can begin to Sabbath now.

Sabbath as Spiritual Warfare

"The devil never takes a Sabbath. That is why I don't."

A well-intended pastor who was seeking to legitimize overworking in ministry said that to me. For many, this has been a kind of cliché rationale for needing to be on the clock twenty-four hours a day. If the devil never rests, then why should we? As with any cliché, there is a sense of truth to the statement. The devil does not Sabbath. He does not have time for that because his days are numbered. In fact, the depiction that we have of Satan in the book of Job is as one who runs "to and fro" throughout the earth. He cannot rest. But that is no reason for us not to rest. At what point did we start basing our action and lifestyle on what the devil is doing? The devil never takes a rest. But that is why he is the devil. That should never be a framework for our lives.

But the notion that *we* cannot rest because the devil does not rest implies that the battle between God and Satan is somehow a battle of equals. It is not. Christ has already defeated evil even though evil continues to fight. The powers of the kingdom of God are both here and now. So is the kingdom of darkness. Evil has been defeated, but evil continues to fight. Because Christ followers walk in the authority and power of Christ, we are not on equal terms with the devil. Our battle has already been won. Therefore, even though the enemy continues to fight, we have the opportunity to rest. It is kind of unfair, actually.

If heaven is eternal Sabbath, can we say what hell will be like? The more I reflect on hell, the more inclined I am to see hell as a place that is *chosen* rather than forced. That is, hell is real. And hell is an option. But one must choose to go there. There is even a postexilic tradition among Jewish religious scholars that makes the case that Sabbath has such a sacredness to it that God extends his rest even to those in hell for a day a week despite the pain and toil of their damnation.[22] Some Jews would end the Sabbath day as late as possible because some believed it was then that the souls in damnation had to return to Gehenna.[23] While Scripture does not elaborate on any level whether there will be a Sabbath in hell, my gut tells me that even if there were, the people there would not be willing to enter into it. If one rejects the love and mercy of Christ at the cross, they will have no logical reason to receive a day of rest extended to them by God. It is not that it is not offered; it is that it is not taken.

I do not know whether there will be a Sabbath in hell, but I do know that the powers of hell do not like Sabbath here and now. It is fascinating to me the number of times in the Gospels that Jesus encounters a demon on the Sabbath. As Jesus entered the Sabbath as the "Lord of the Sabbath," we see him facing all sorts of things that are the works of the enemy. And I think that the enemy will always stand against the healing works of the Lord of the Sabbath.

In my experience, practicing a Sabbath opens one up to serious spiritual attack. I began to experience the dark side of work and adrenaline addiction when we started to Sabbath years ago. To this day, around 3:00 p.m. on the Sabbath, I bear what I call a "Sabbath depression." My brain starts craving stimulation, and my mind becomes sad as my body is not being pumped full of adrenaline. Again, the Jewish tradition holds that we must be deeply cautious of *muksteh*, things that tempt us to lose the spirit of rest and that we must put away.[24] For me, *muksteh* is the desire to open my email. How easy it is to be deceived into thinking that a full inbox means that I am important. This experience is not unique to me. Freud used to write about what he called "Sabbath neurosis," when people would get sick on the Sabbath.[25] Silence is hard. It is not uncommon to encounter a highly driven or a highly social person who often becomes depressed on the Sabbath day. When we are silent, our minds have time to examine problems that we have been suppressing all week long. Sabbath allows pain to come to the surface.

On the Sabbath day, I am incredibly susceptible to spiritual attacks and realities that on other days may not affect me as much. Many individuals have confessed to me that in their efforts at keeping a Sabbath day they experience a heightened sense of sexual temptation unlike other times during the week. Boredom can be fertile ground for the devil's best work. It is when we feel bored that we are most tempted to look at questionable materials or think about questionable things. I think our rest wakes the devil to action. He does not want us to rest in the presence of God. He wants to get us busy, up and at 'em. This is precisely why prayer needs to be an integral part of any Sabbath-keeping. We should not expect the Sabbath to be a day free from the devil's attacks.

Finally, the Sabbath allows space to detach from the influences and voices of the world. We often do not even know how attuned to these voices we have become. Before we know it, they reverberate in our spirits unthinkingly. For a couple of years of very intense ministry, my wife and I found it difficult to sleep at night. The combination of work, community, having a child, and financial pressures seemed to make closing our eyes at night difficult. It was around this time that we discovered Netflix. We found that Netflix was the easiest way in the world to fall asleep at night. Just turn on a show and fall asleep. But while it eventually caused us to go to sleep, our rest was not very good, and we would wake up almost sad in the morning. Plus we would stay up watching more shows than we should. After a few years of this habit, we decided that we needed to stop watching Netflix, an excruciating decision. Almost immediately upon canceling our subscription, our sleep became better, we woke up more rested, and our hearts and minds were more at peace. What was most surprising to me was how difficult the silence at night was at first. All these thoughts would come to my mind—disturbing thoughts that I would have normally crowded out by watching something. I can no longer binge-watch a program to help me feel better or laugh my way through a melancholy period. Yet there is consistent evidence suggesting that mild depression may come as a result of watching too much television or Netflix.[26]

John Climacus once drew a parallel between intentional detachment and spiritual warfare: "If you choose to go into exile, then be on the watch for the demon of wandering and of pleasure, since there is an opportunity here for him."[27] Detaching from normalcy opens us up to spiritual susceptibility. Intentional breaks from something—something a Sabbath provides—allows a kind of purification from dark voices that seek to pervade our thinking and our spirits. While Jesus did do a good deal of spiritual warfare on various Sabbath days in the Gospels, he was keenly aware that alongside doing battle with the devil he needed times of rest with the Father. To war against the devil without rest is something not even Jesus Christ modeled. When you begin to Sabbath and enter into a renewed relationship of worship toward the Father, you can expect the devil will take notice and fight back.

QUESTIONS
for Reflection

- If worship is living our entire lives in submission to God, can you identify areas of your life where you might be withholding worship from God?

- Like putting on your Sunday best, what are some ways in which you might make your Sabbath day special?
- If we develop Christlike character through practicing Christian disciplines, what areas of your character may God be wanting to conform to Christ's through the discipline of Sabbath?
- What might your schedule reveal that you worship?
- What do you sacrifice rest to make time for?
- What do you think might be lost culturally, or within your family or community, by not partaking in the Sabbath?
- How might entering into Sabbath be a reminder that we are living in God's story, not ours?

12

Sabbath and Discipleship

> There is perhaps no single thing that could better help us recover
> Jesus' lordship in our frantic, power-hungry world than to allow
> him to be Lord of our rest as well as our work.
>
> Andy Crouch, *Playing God*

The Vulnerability of Sabbath

It first dawned on me as I walked through the Metropolitan Museum of Art (MET) in New York City with my wife before we had to catch the subway to the Broadway show we had tickets for. Walking through the enormous museum, we passed by what seemed like the thousandth ancient Madonna and child. Over and over again. There were so many pictures of Jesus with his mother. And in nearly all of them, I pointed out to my wife, the baby Jesus was depicted as reaching for Mary's breast. So many of the ancient pictures of Jesus as a baby show him grabbing at his mother's bosom. Why? Even though I had been at home when my wife breastfed our child, it had never really set in why there were so many ancient paintings of the sovereign God of the universe reaching for his mother's breasts.

Jesus never tried to hide his humanness.

Like every human being, Jesus went through the true human experience: puberty, growth spurts, diaper changes, and, yes, breastfeeding. Despite his full humanity, he was not protected from experiencing any dimension of what it means to be a human being. At one point, I encountered a historian's take on why the early Christian artists were so infatuated with the image of Jesus reaching for his mother's breast: the artists believed the vulnerability of God was something noteworthy, something to draw, something for the world's attention to be drawn to.

Vulnerability is a scary thing to look at. We can even feel repulsed by it—perhaps you feel that way thinking about God breastfeeding. But the vulnerability of others (particularly in Jesus) has the capacity to awake us to our own vulnerabilities. Flannery O'Connor once wrote about how the poor—the most vulnerable among us—wake us up to our own needs by showing us a life that is not padded by material things and opulence. Most of us live with everything we need. We have food, shelter, and clothing. But the poor do not. They live, in O'Connor's words, with "less padding between them and the raw forces of life" such as hunger, sleeplessness, and the cold night.[1] The vulnerable do not have the padding most of us do to protect us from the difficult forces of this world.

I would imagine that someone hungry for power and prestige would be repulsed by Jesus. They would have no need for the suckling baby who is vulnerable. Nor the poor, rejected, marginalized Jesus who dies vulnerably on the cross for the world. Jesus is God being vulnerable.

While God *is* all-powerful, God still models a life of vulnerability by resting for a day during the week of creation. God does not simply demand vulnerability and humility. God becomes humble. He rests. He sends his Son, who embodied vulnerability and humility. God always does what he asks. God rests one out of seven days as an act of vulnerability for us. What an act of humility! When the God of the universe certainly could be running around doing more important things, God does what is needed by humanity and the rest of creation.

Why exactly *did* God rest on the seventh day in the creation story? Was the work too much for him? Did the six days simply take it out of him? Did he run out of energy? The question of why God rested on the Sabbath day is important. And it is a question that sparked no little theological and doctrinal argument among Jewish rabbis. For God resting on the seventh day seems to suggest that if God rested, he *needed* to rest. In the end the rabbis consistently made the case that God rested not out of necessity or exhaustion or losing all his energy but out of love. Even when we look at why God created the world, he did not do it because he was lonely or needed something. God created simply for one reason: love. Everything that was made is in existence because of the love of God. In the sixteenth-century, Jacob Boehme spoke of the creation story as the "concentration of desire."[2]

God created out of his own loving desire that he already had, not out of a need for love. In contrast to the creation stories of the other religions, the God of the Bible never *needs* food. God never *needs* drink. God does not *need* worshipers to exist. Nor does God *need* rest. God is God—he is not fulfilled by anything in creation.

Just as God created the world out of love, God enters into the Sabbath in love. In keeping a day of rest, God shows humanity the way life is supposed to be lived, even if he himself did not actually need it. God rests to be a good model. The debate about why God rested continued into the early church. Early church father Origen once wrote a scathing letter against Celsus, who argued that God rested on the seventh day because he was tired—suggesting that God was not all-powerful. Origen cuts it off at the head, saying that God rests in order to model rest, not because he was exhausted or fatigued from his work of creating.[3] When we see God resting in creation, we do not see someone who is exhausted from creating the universe—no, we see a God who does not tell us to rest without doing it first. God is no hypocrite.

Instead of simply telling us that we need to rest, what does God do? He rests. Jesus becomes God in human flesh so that we have a way of life to follow. Humans needed someone to follow, to copy, to imitate. When God invites humanity to live a certain way, we have an actual in-the-flesh person to look at and follow. God wants us to be patient. How does he develop patience in us? By coming as a carpenter who would wait until he was thirty years old to enter ministry. When God desires us to be long-suffering, what does he do? Jesus suffers for and loves his twelve disciples. God desires us to live Sabbath life, so what does God do when he creates the world? He keeps the Sabbath day. God does not demand what he will not model.

Obedience to this rhythm of life is our ultimate rationale for keeping a Sabbath. If there is anyone who has the capability to Sabbath the way God intends us to, it is the disabled and the underemployed. Why? One may not be able to work because of physical disability. The other may not be able to find work. But to be able to keep a Sabbath in both situations demands a kind of obedience to do something simply because God asks. I know a man who lost his ability to walk years ago. He does not have a job he goes to. He cannot help around his group home. He does not earn any money. But one day a week, he keeps a Sabbath. How Christlike. My friend keeps a Sabbath for one reason: out of obedience to following God's ways. God did not rest because he was tired. Neither does my friend rest because he is tired. One rests to model it for the world; the other rests out of obedience to the living God.

Riparian Buffers

As a preacher, it is my task to share the Scriptures with God's people. This often means I have what they call "preacher's deficit." In short, I am always a little behind in finding ways to illustrate what I am trying to say. In years past, I would tell endless stories about my son. Now I am much more careful about throwing him in the limelight. In speaking with those who grew up as pastors' kids, I have learned that the experience of having your story told in front of a congregation all the time can be very hard. Pastors' kids have told me how hard it is to be robbed of your obscurity when your mom or dad are the leaders of the church—you become famous whether you want it or not. And people know intimate details of your life that you never wanted them to know, especially if your parent never asked for your permission to share. Now when I preach, I will share a story about my son only if I have asked him, he agrees, and I pay him $20. He is getting quite rich. Now he can say whether he wants a story told about him or not. And he is making a killing off it.

There is a very healthy place for obscurity in the Christian walk. It is there—in obscurity, not in the lights—that our character is most formed. We need obscurity. Jesus lived in obscurity for nearly thirty years before entering public ministry. In fact, Mary gave enough material for only one chapter regarding Jesus's childhood, in Luke 2. I doubt Jesus got paid for that one!

Psalm 1 is about the beauty of obscurity in the life of faith. It speaks of the person who is "planted by streams of water," who "meditates . . . day and night" (Ps. 1:2–3). The psalm describes the person as one who is lush with life and full of the presence of God. Along a river or stream, there is often a space of grace for trees and flowers to grow. Unfortunately, in modern agriculture, crops are being planted right up to the very edge of the river. This can have disastrous effects on the river, causing soil erosion and dung to go into the water flow. In the natural world, that space next to a river has a name. Ecologists call it a "riparian buffer." What is the psalm speaking of but a plant that is growing in the riparian buffer of a stream or creek? It is a tree planted where there is space for it to grow and water to nourish its roots. It is difficult to grow by the stream of water if there is no space there. Like a riparian buffer, the Sabbath provides much-needed space for us to draw on the life source and grow.

Sabbath does that: it gives space to enter into obscurity for the purpose of Christian maturity with (much-needed) renewed vigor. For often, on the other six days a week, the life of the Spirit can go forgotten. There is a legend among the Jews that on the Sabbath, God gives us all an extra soul, or a *neshamah yetarah*.[4] Sabbath is the day with great soul. Other Jewish customs regard the

Sabbath as a day to contemplate and read works on ethics and morals. Many Jewish families will sit around and listen to a reading of the *Pirke Abot*, or the "Ethics of the Fathers." First-century historian Josephus writes in his book *Against Apion* about what Jews did on the Sabbath because of the leadership of Moses: "Permitting the people to leave off their other employments, and to assemble together for the hearing of the law, and learning it exactly; and this not once, or twice, or oftener; but every week. Which thing all the other legislators seem to have neglected."[5] Even 2 Kings 4:23 indicates that it was normal to visit the prophet on the Sabbath. The Sabbath was a day to focus on God's Spirit. What does Paul, in his journey to Philippi, do on the Sabbath day but go to the "place of prayer," as described in Acts 16:13. He was seeking a place to be with God in prayer and to connect with others who sought that same intimacy. The Sabbath creates much-needed time for quiet, silence, and intimacy with Jesus.

We desperately need obscurity. But our modern world is intent on keeping us from silence and solitude, scheming against moments of quietness and prayer. Silence is scary. Obscurity is difficult. Having a day of rest that may include silence can feel like a very long day. All of these thoughts and fears will run through our minds. But all we need to do with the things that arise from the silence is quietly bring them to Jesus as they come up. Doing so does not magically fix everything right away, but bringing them into the presence of Jesus generates a kind of lightness and transparency. With Jesus, we can hold the pain of the silence with his strong hands of grace.

We may unthinkingly assume that human beings have always gotten to sleep using something like Netflix. But of course the opposite is the case. One phenomenon of the last one hundred years has completely changed human history—we have light bulbs in our homes. During the time of Jesus, of course, when the sun went down, so did human heads. The lives of normal human beings were entirely mediated by the presence of sunlight. In fact, to have lights in one's house was incredibly costly. One estimate says that in the ancient world, fifteen minutes of light provided by a lantern or an oil lamp would have cost one entire day's wages. Can you imagine that? Fifteen minutes. So normal people would be up and at it when the sun was out. But when the sun went down, you had a lot of time to simply be by yourself. In silence. On your bed.

The Sabbath gives us silence, a kind of "revolutionary tranquility" that goes against everything it means to be an American.[6] The ancient Jewish rabbis tell a beautiful allegory: Angels sing songs to God their Creator on each of their six workdays. Yet on the seventh day the angels remain silent. Their silence becomes their Sabbath song, a hymn to God all by itself.[7]

We have developed an allergy to silence and obscurity. We have created within ourselves such a need to do and accomplish and make that effectiveness becomes the rudder of our entire existence. Silence terrifies us. After having been silent, we have nothing we can tell people we have done. We just were. Silence goes against what Henri Nouwen calls "the security of having something valuable to do."[8] Spending time in silence allows the things that crowd our existence to empty out. What effect does this have? Someone once described to me a lake that was being drained. When all the water was drained out, garbage and other debris were found at the bottom of the lake, which could then be cleaned up. Silence is giving space to see what is at the bottom of our souls.

As well as silence, Sabbath gives us time to simply be with God. The number of times that the Gospels describe Jesus as simply reclining at the table with his disciples has always been staggering to me. We may think that the Sabbath day is a waste of time and we are not getting anything out of it. But we can never be truly human without living in communion with God. Sabbath invites us to live with God as Adam and Eve did in Eden. But what about God? What if God gets something out of simply being with us? We forget that God really does enjoy being with his people. And while he desires to spend time with us, we consistently say no to his pursuit. We may condemn the Sabbath and write it off out of fear that we will get little to nothing out of it or that it is inefficient. Nevertheless, God just wants to be with us. He simply desires us, present, with him. That is what intimacy—certainly intimacy between two who call themselves friends—is truly all about. Friends do not enter into time together for the purposes of productivity or what we get out of it. Friends simply love to *be* with one another.

The biblical creation story tells us nothing about what God did on that first Sabbath day. But I can only imagine that on that day God walked with Adam and Eve and the animals among the lush garden in which he had made a home for them. God did not do *nothing* on the Sabbath. Rather, he enjoyed his creation with his creation. Tilden Edwards writes, "God alone rests, not because he is idle, but because he works with absolute ease."[9]

Sabbath as Renunciation

Long ago, William Temple wrote that when we frame our entire lives on the love of God, we will be able to enter into rest. Before that, we will always struggle to rest. Temple writes, "That is the assurance that we need: that He with whom we know we have dealings is none other than the eternal God. If my soul can hear that word, then it can rest. . . . I need divine assurances of the divine love."[10] True rest cannot be fully realized outside the context of the abiding and unshakable love of God. If God is a tyrant, then we cannot rest. If God is demanding, then we cannot rest. If God is the Lord of the harvest alone, then we can never fully rest. But he is the Lord of the harvest *and* the Lord of the Sabbath. This God orders our work and our rest through his love and mercy. Not only can we Sabbath because of the love of God, but the Sabbath actually helps concretize our lives around the love of God week in and week out. Sabbath offers us a weekly return to the loving grace of God from the frenetic, works-based ways of living we have grown accustomed to. The Sabbath is part of the process of becoming holy, sanctified, transformed. It returns us to God and sanctifies us from those forceful realities that ultimately seek to take us away from the love of God.

But this return to the love of God on the Sabbath can be a painful journey. Silence and presence often are painful. On the Sabbath, God helps us sort out our intentions and desires that lie in the foundations of our lives. Sabbath, for me, is God's creative way of entirely undermining my overdeveloped drive to work, which is closely connected to my idolatrous desire to become famous. We all have inner drives, those things that get us out of bed in the morning. I am no different. All of the writers and thinkers I have admired have one thing in common. For me it all started with Donald Miller (who wrote *Blue Like Jazz*), then moved to Dietrich Bonhoeffer, then to Henri Nouwen, then finally to Eugene Peterson. All of these people are different, but all of them have one thing in common. All of them are famous Christian authors who were surprised by their fame. None of them really tried to become famous. Fame just came upon them. And for years I have struggled with a deep desire to make any fame I receive look so effortless that it is like I cannot help but be famous. The Sabbath helps orient me back to the love of God by causing me to denunciate all my false desires. On the Sabbath, I cannot pretend to be anyone else before the living God. I have to be me.

Our false desires and motivations often come to the surface on the Sabbath. You may find that as you enter into the Sabbath, all sorts of odd and even disgusting desires float to the surface of your mind. It is okay. Offer those false motivations to Jesus and invite him to help you understand them and live more contentedly. Sabbath, in fact, is contentment. It is a day that we sit in contentment and gratitude for God and for what we already have. We cannot attain and accumulate more on the Sabbath, so we have to come to terms with what we already have. The Sabbath reminds us that the opposite of less is not more; it is *enough*. This is the eternal connection between two of the Ten Commandments: the commandment to rest and the commandment to not be jealous. For to enter into the first invites us to be free of the want of more, and particularly of wanting what someone else has.

Sabbath is renunciation. It is self-restraint. It is a day of radical self-inquiry to repent and turn from the ways of destruction that we have been doing unthinkingly all week long, so that we might heal in God's rest. Sabbath invokes us to be skeptical of all our desires. Not every one of our wants is what we need. Is it wrong to use the day of rest to turn to the living God in repentance? Of course not! Repentance is not work. Sin is work. Sin is the productivity of seeking that which God does not desire. Sin is also seeking productivity at a time when God does not desire. This connection between jealousy and rest is seen in Thomas à Kempis's *The Imitation of Christ*: "When a man desires a thing too much, he at once becomes ill at ease." Our unencumbered and uncontrolled desires to possess more and more and more will eventually lead to a place of complete restlessness. Thomas concludes, "A proud and avaricious man never rests."[11]

Many of you who read this may be at a place in your life where a need for rest runs so deep that you are burning out. Perhaps boundaries have been broken for so long that the fringes of your life have become burned. The need for a Sabbath, and even perhaps a sabbatical, is intruding on you. Do not resist this moment. There are moments in all of our lives when God, by his sovereign and good grace, almost seems to force us to enter into Sabbath rhythms whether we want to or not. David reflects on the heart of God for his own life: "He *makes me* lie down" (Ps. 23:2). Sometimes our wills are open to the Sabbath. Sometimes the Sabbath is forced on us. Richard Wurmbrand, a Romanian pastor who spent fourteen years—three of which were in solitary confinement—in a communist prison for his Christian faith, reflects on that kind of journey—the journey of a forced Sabbath: "Things seem to be getting worse and worse. It is a Sabbath day. This time I am not only in a strait-jacket and gagged but I have heavy chains at my feet which prevent me from walking. A Sabbath day. The fullest Sabbath I have ever enjoyed in my life. I cannot disturb my rest even by a movement of my hands, feet or lips."[12] There are times God makes us lie down. Embrace it. God is getting his loving way. One of God's greatest gifts is leading us into a scenario in which we are unable to resolve everything on our own. Unfixable situations are God's gift, for they force us to rest.

In his well-known book on fasting, *God's Chosen Fast*, Arthur Wallis writes that there is always the chance of pride for the person who does one of the Christian disciplines.[13] When we do well, we often look down on others. There is always a possibility of this in Sabbath-keeping—that we become "good" at Sabbath-keeping. But our worship of God keeps us from that kind of pride.

It protects us from the kind of arrogance that the religious are known for. Sabbath humbles us.

Beginning the Sabbath Journey

We end this chapter on a practical note, asking a few crucial questions. For one, how do we start? The truth is, every river starts somewhere. Be it a small tributary, it must begin somewhere. Every river begins with a drop of water. Remember that we are not interested in mere reflection on the Sabbath. One must be willing to start to *do* it in order to experience its joys. As Augustine said, a picture of food does not nourish. Only eating food nourishes. We do the Sabbath before we understand the Sabbath, before it makes sense. We should remember that in the Old Testament we are invited to "do" before we "hear."[14]

Second, it is helpful in our Sabbath journeys to imitate someone who has been walking down the Sabbath path longer than we have. We often need to follow someone who knows how to do it. It turns out a cat does not know how to kill a mouse until it has watched another cat do it, which is called "imprinting." This is why Paul, on so many occasions, speaks of "imitating" his faith—there are just so many elements of faith that cannot be ironed out by a Google search. We need a relationship in order to do it. Again, resources and books can be helpful. But you will most likely find that following someone's experience of the Sabbath can help you enter into yours more prepared.

Third, what day should one keep a Sabbath? This is a very practical and important question. Preachers have, at times, spent too much energy on putting unnecessary boundaries around the Sabbath. In Christian history, there have been admonitions against a Donkey's Sabbath (lying about and doing nothing), a Golden Calf Sabbath (filled with indulgence and pleasure), a Devil's Sabbath (a day filled with silliness, idolatry, and dancing), a Joshua Sabbath (longing for the day to end, when it seems as though the sun has stood still), a Pleasure Sabbath (when we play around and sail on the lake), a Sensual Sabbath (when we do anything that feels good), and the Outward Sabbath (observing the Sabbath without a fleck of enthusiasm).[15] There are more. We can easily spend all our time describing the Sabbath day in terms of what it is *not* rather than what it *is*.

Lamentably, the issue of which day one Sabbaths often becomes a question about rules and laws. And this question is anything but new. For example, the rabbis discuss it at length. In the Talmud there is a story of a man who gets lost in the desert. In the desert, he loses track of time. "On which day should a good Jew, lost in the desert, observe the Sabbath?" the rabbis asked. The Talmud presents a fiery debate on the topic. Some argue he should keep the

Sabbath on the first day he is lost. Others, that he should wait for six days and then keep a Sabbath.[16] Such questions still frequently arise in conversations about the Sabbath: Which day do we keep a Sabbath? Must it be Saturday, as it was for Jewish communities? Or Sunday, like it was for the earliest Christians? What about some other day?

I believe that God's ideal picture for Sabbath rest is that everyone would get to enter in together on the same day. Imagine what that ideal would look like. The land would get rest and would not be disturbed by anyone. Families could spend time together. Parents could have a day of rest as they share with others the responsibilities of caring for the young. God's design was that we would rest together on the same day. But God's ideal is not always a possibility. In one conversation, Jesus is asked whether divorce is to be permitted. His response is interesting: it is permitted, but it is not God's design (Matt. 19:1–8). Here we see God giving an ideal and then meeting people where they are. The approach we should take toward the Sabbath is to aim for God's intent. It most certainly would be ideal for everyone to Sabbath on the same day together, but this is not a realistic possibility for everyone.

So what do we do? There is endless debate on the topic.[17] Willard Swartley's insightful book *Slavery, Sabbath, War and Women* identifies three main approaches to answering the question: the Saturday Sabbath, the Sunday Sabbath, and the Lord's Day position, in which every day is a holy day.[18] All three positions have precedent in the life of the church. For me, what is more important than where we land is how we land there. I think this gets at the heart of the Sabbath for the contemporary follower of Jesus.

There are two propensities in the life of the church that must be guarded against: what I call the "legalizing" and "spiritualizing" tendencies toward the Sabbath. To rigidly argue that everyone *must* observe one particular day is approaching legalism.[19] Martin Luther strongly stood against any such legalistic practices: "If anywhere the day is made holy for the mere day's sake, then I order you to work on it, to ride on it, to feast on it, to do anything to remove this reproach from Christian liberty."[20] To universalize our own Sabbath preferences by saying the day of rest must be Saturday, or Sunday, or Friday puts on others' backs a heavy religious burden that may not even be possible to actually do. The Seventh-day Adventist approach, for example, unnecessarily interprets the Sabbath day as only Saturday. Although well-intended, this approach is excessive and unrealistic. By contrast, our approach toward the Sabbath must walk along a path of grace and empathy for real people in a real world. For the narrow road of legalism quietly meanders to an end in shame. If we do the Sabbath without the spirit of generosity, we have not kept a Sabbath.

Mark 4 tells the story of Jesus healing a man on the Sabbath. The religious leaders' response is cold and calculated: they begin their plans to murder Jesus. This is the first report in Mark's Gospel of Jesus's death being plotted. Consider the irony: these religious leaders are willing to break the seventh command ("Thou shalt not murder") to punish a person they perceive to have broken the fourth command ("Keep the Sabbath"). That is what religious rigidity does—it trades the mercy of God for the justice of humankind. In her essay "Christian Morality," Dorothy Sayers argues that Jesus was murdered for two rationales: he was a "gluttonous man and a winebibber, a friend of publicans and sinners," and he was a Sabbath-breaker.[21] The way Jesus embodied the Sabbath did not fit neatly into the rigid religious systems of his time. Nor will Sabbath fit neatly into the systems of today.

Furthermore, a legalistic Sabbath fails to account for the fact that followers of Jesus are not bound by Jewish law. If we were to return to Jewish law, we would need to quickly recognize that anyone who fails to keep a Sabbath day is to be stoned to death (Num. 15:35). But as Paul argues in Galatians 3, the law "was added because of transgressions until the Seed to whom the promise referred had come" (Gal. 3:19). We do not walk according to the law; we walk in God's Spirit. A rule-based spirituality is the very thing Jesus came to frustrate. The Sabbath is by grace or it ceases to exist. Mark Buchanan has aptly written, "This is maybe the primary mistake we make when we try to figure out the Sabbath: we go straight to the rules."[22] We must orient ourselves toward grace instead of rule-based rest.

Legalism is never the answer. Quite frankly, the very people who say they do not like the Sabbath because they do not support legalism are often the first to be legalistic about working too much. Legalism regarding work *or* rest is dangerous. We must remember that Jesus did not descend to humanity and die on a cross that we might worship the law. We worship him. Jesus "fulfills" the law, inviting us to embody the original intentions of God's commandments. Marva Dawn articulates it brilliantly: "We lose the freedom of the gospel if we become too legalistic about [the Sabbath]. What God wants from us is a whole day that we set apart to honor him by gathering with a sacred assembly and by ceasing from work."[23]

The other extreme is to spiritualize the Sabbath, turning it into some kind of abstract, nonrooted idea—not something actually to be practiced but rather something that symbolizes a deeper reality. Jesus, of course, did not come to abolish the law, as spiritualists would perhaps believe. Yet, sadly, the idea of a spiritualized Sabbath has a long history in the church. St. Augustine, for one, spiritualized the Sabbath principle by arguing that it had faded away with the rest of the Jewish laws in the new Christian community. Throughout

Augustine's writings, he describes what he calls the "perpetual Sabbath."[24] Similarly, St. Ignatius, in arguing against "Judaizing" the Sabbath day, writes, "Let us therefore no longer keep the Sabbath after the Jewish manner, and rejoice in the days of idleness." Ignatius implores the Christians to "keep the Sabbath after a spiritual manner."[25] Both approaches reconceive the Sabbath as a mere spiritual reality rather than something to actually be done.

More often than not, and to their detriment, many Protestants, evangelicals, and Pentecostals and charismatics have held to the idea of a kind of spiritualized Sabbath and have failed to actually practice it. A fundamental problem resides in this approach. If we spiritualize the Sabbath, it becomes the only one of the Ten Commandments that we are brash enough to do so with. Nobody spiritualizes murder, or lying, or adultery, saying these are merely spiritual practices rather than actions that take place in space and time. If we spiritualize Sabbath, we must be ready to do so with all aspects of the Old Testament; out of consistency, we would need to spiritualize tithing as well. The principle of tithing prescribes that we are to give one-tenth of our income to God; this is a great place to start! And as a principle, tithing transcends the Jewish law. It is a framework for life, not just for money. I dare any pastor who spiritualizes the Sabbath to extend the same hermeneutical approach toward the practice of tithing.

It is important that we take an actual day a week to rest. A parallel may help: I love my wife dearly. Our weekly date night is a special, scheduled opportunity to nurture our relationship. While I love my wife every second, a weekly date night embeds that love into both of our lives. The same applies to tithing. All of my money is the Lord's; still, I give him a portion of it. The same goes for the Sabbath. Every day is God's day, but I actualize that reality by setting aside one day to pray and play with God. When Scripture invites us to "keep" a Sabbath—when we Sabbath-*keep*—we must remember that the word *keep* in Scripture never means hiding it away. Rather, it entails continuing in something, keeping it active, putting it into constant use. Just as love must be kept, so must the rest of God. The spirit of this is found in the words of Dietrich Bonhoeffer as he reflects on the Sabbath: "Jesus broke through the Jewish laws about Sabbath rest. He did it so that the Sabbath could truly be hallowed. The Sabbath is hallowed not by means of what human beings do or do not do, but by means of the action of Jesus Christ for human salvation. . . . Our Sunday is the day on which we allow Jesus Christ to act toward us and all people. To be sure, this ought to occur every day; but on Sunday we rest from our work so that it might take place in a special way."[26] Our rest should complement our belief in a God who desires peace in our bodies, minds, hearts, and world. Whether or not we are entering into that rest matters far more than the day we practice Sabbath.

There is the danger of a legalistic or spiritualized Sabbath. And as Tilden Edwards shows, the church has historically gone back and forth between legalistic and spiritualizing approaches toward the Sabbath.[27] The earliest Christians were mostly Jews. Until the split of the church from the synagogue in about 70 CE, Christians kept the Sabbath with the Jewish community on Saturday. After this the church would gather in each other's homes and worship with other Christians on Sunday evening, a day they called the "Lord's Day" (Rev. 1:10). They began to call Sunday a "little Easter," during which they would celebrate Christ's resurrection, the resurrection of the dead, and the new creation. Thus waned Saturday observance for the church. Again, the church did not chuck the practice of keeping the Sabbath. "The Christians had moved on. Yet they still lugged the Sabbath around with them."[28] Eventually, Constantine ended Saturday Sabbath observance by ensuring Sundays would be a day of rest by mandating it as a day off work.[29] In essence, this struck a middle ground. Writes Jürgen Moltmann, "The Christian Sunday neither abolishes Israel's Sabbath, nor supplants it. . . . The Christian feast-day must rather be seen as the messianic extension of Israel's Sabbath."[30]

We do not need to live in the extreme of strictly observing the Sabbath on a particular day. There is a middle ground that stays its course, cautiously avoiding the extremes. I believe a third approach exists between legalism and spiritualizing. My approach to our commitment is what I call the *one-in-seven principle*. That is, I do not believe that the Sabbath must be observed on one specific day. I do not think Saturday *or* Sunday has to be the day of worship. Rather, we must find one day out of seven as a day of rest.

To illustrate, our family Sabbaths on Wednesdays. That is a reflection of our vocation as pastors. The truth is, this rhythm was not realized overnight; this pattern took nearly a decade to discover. Yet it has worked so well that we have not moved away from it since. In a short time, our son will be going to school, and we will need to revisit this conversation. Again, the principle is *one-in-seven*. Days may change when you have children who are in school all week long or changes happen in one's work schedule. There are changes in many of life's rhythms. The goal should be *one-in-seven*.

Most importantly, Jesus himself, not only the day, is our Sabbath. As the Lord of the Sabbath, he gives us a day to rest. But he is the source of our Sabbath rest, not the day itself. We should be centering on *who* our Sabbath is rather than *when* we Sabbath. Intricate debates about specific days often only detract from this matter. The apostle Paul recognized that "one person considers one day more sacred than another; another considers every day alike." What is significant is that we are settled in our own consciences and hearts. Paul continues, "Each of them should be fully convinced in their own mind. Whoever regards one day as special *does so to the Lord*" (Rom. 14:5–6). As Paul writes elsewhere, "Therefore do not let anyone judge you by what you eat or drink, or with regard to a religious festival, a New Moon celebration or a Sabbath day" (Col. 2:16).

If you are going to Sabbath on Saturday, do it "to the Lord." Sunday? Do it "to the Lord." Wednesday? Monday? To the Lord! Norman Wirzba offers solid words on the heart of the Sabbath day: "Sunday, far from being the obliteration of Sabbath teaching, represents a profound rearticulation of God's overarching purpose and plan for creation. Sunday is our day of joy, for here we remember our memberships one with another and commit ourselves to the health and wholeness—the salvation—of physical and social bodies, of communities and creation, made possible by Christ's resurrection power and redeeming love."[31]

Above all, Sabbath must be undertaken with great grace. Rigidity is not the solution. Whenever we see rigidity in the created realm, it is often a sign of death. As Gordon MacDonald writes, "There is no legalism here—rather a freedom to accept a gift. Frankly, I think some have destroyed the joy of Sabbath . . . by surrounding it with prescriptive laws and precedents. That is not our Sabbath. Our Sabbath was made for us, given to us by God. Its purpose is worship and restoration, and whatever it takes to make that happen, we will do."[32] When rigidity rules, we become like the religious leaders in Matthew 12:9–14, who, when seeing the man with the withered hand healed, were so concerned that Jesus had audaciously healed on the Sabbath day that they were crippled from being able to experience the joy of the miracle. But Jesus does not obey the wishes of legalistic and hostile religious leaders. Despite Jesus's knowledge of their hearts, his desire is to bring healing.

Graceless Sabbath is legalism. That is why it is better to do the Sabbath poorly than never try. Make Sabbath mistakes. Learn from them. Then enter the next Sabbath with your lesson in hand. Learning how to fail at the Sabbath is a critical part of learning how to Sabbath. Let us have grace for ourselves and for others. Yes, questions about which day to Sabbath are important, but they are never ultimate. "I begin to think," says Brian Doyle, "that it does not matter how or when or how long we observe the Sabbath; it matters only that we do."[33]

QUESTIONS
for Reflection

- How might keeping a Sabbath be part of Christian discipleship even when we may not feel that we require rest?

- Like a riparian buffer, how might Sabbath provide the space needed for us to draw on the life source and grow?
- What garbage may God want to clean out of your life in times of silence?
- What things may God be asking you to hand over to him in times of solitude?
- What do you think of the idea that God orders both our work and our rest? That he is God of the harvest and of the Sabbath?
- By not entering into Sabbath, what aspects of God's character might we miss?
- How may God be using the Sabbath in your life to rightly order your drives and desires?
- What masks might God be leading you to remove on the Sabbath?
- Practically, what can you do to receive Sabbath as the gift that it is?

Notes

Prologue

1. Brennan Manning, *Ruthless Trust: The Ragamuffin's Path to God* (New York: Harper-Collins, 2000), 6.

2. Marva J. Dawn, *Being Well When We're Ill: Wholeness and Hope in Spite of Infirmity* (Minneapolis: Augsburg Fortress, 2008), 8.

3. The title *Subversive Sabbath* reflects a tone similar to Walter Brueggemann's little volume *Sabbath as Resistance: Saying No to the Culture of Now* (Louisville: Westminster John Knox, 2014).

4. Flannery O'Connor, *Habit of Being: Letters of Flannery O'Connor*, ed. Sally Fitzgerald (New York: Farrar, Straus & Giroux, 1979), 65.

5. Madeleine L'Engle, *Two-Part Invention: The Story of a Marriage* (New York: Harper-Collins, 1988), 32.

6. Wendell Berry, *Citizenship Papers* (Washington, DC: Shoemaker & Hoard, 2003), 39.

Chapter 1: Sabbath and Time

1. Rita Reif, "Declaration of Independence Found in a $4 Picture Frame," *New York Times*, April 3, 1991, http://www.nytimes.com/1991/04/03/arts/declaration-of-independence-found-in-a-4-picture-frame.html.

2. Damon Sims, "Whatever Happened to . . . the Fight over Money Found in Wall of West Side Home?," *Northeast Ohio Media Group*, December 28, 2008, http://blog.cleveland.com/metro/2008/12/whatever_happened_to_the_fight.html.

3. Georgia McCafferty, "Bought for $3 at Yard Sale, Bowl Sells for $2.2 million," *CNN*, March 21, 2013, http://www.cnn.com/2013/03/20/business/sothebys-china-bowl/.

4. Dina Abou Salem, "California Couple Finds $10M Buried Treasure in Back Yard," *ABC News*, February 25, 2014, http://abcnews.go.com/blogs/headlines/2014/02/california-couple-finds-10m-buried-treasure-in-back-yard/.

5. Bill Waterson, *There's Treasure Everywhere: A Calvin and Hobbes Collection* (Kansas City, MO: Andrews McNeel, 1996), 3.

6. The title of Michel Foucault's iconic *The Archeology of Knowledge* provokes this imagery of discovery—ours is a world of ideas waiting to be discovered. Foucault, *The Archeology of Knowledge: And the Discourse on Language* (Abingdon, UK: Routledge Classics, 2002), 23.

7. Howard Zinn, *Passionate Declarations: Essays on War and Justice* (New York: Harper-Collins, 2003), 1–2.

8. Dallas Willard, *Hearing God: Developing a Conversational Relationship with God* (Downers Grove, IL: InterVarsity, 1999), 10.

9. The church's best ideas are its oldest. And the church is constantly going through the process of forgetfulness and retrieval. For example, not a single book on fasting was published in America between 1861 and 1954. Now there is a plethora of books on the topic. On this, see throughout Arthur Wallis, *God's Chosen Fast: A Spiritual and Practical Guide to Fasting* (Fort Washington, PA: Christian Literature Crusade, 1975). On the theme of "theology as retrieval" and its importance for the church's vitality, see David Buschart and Kent Eilers, *Theology as Retrieval: Receiving the Past, Renewing the Church* (Downers Grove, IL: IVP Academic, 2015).

10. There is no better examination of this 24/7 world than Matthew Sleeth, *24/6: A Prescription for a Healthier, Happier Life* (Carol Stream, IL: Tyndale, 2012). Some even speak of a 25/8 culture, where boundaries are completely undone. On this, and seeing the Sabbath as a lost artifact that we must rediscover, see Rob Muthiah, *The Sabbath Experiment* (Eugene, OR: Cascade, 2015), 1–9.

11. There remain various traditions in both Christianity and Judaism pertaining to the candle-lighting aspect of the Sabbath. For an expansive discussion on the candle traditions, see Tilden Edwards, *Sabbath Time* (Nashville: Upper Room Books, 1992), 126–29. Simply remembering is critical though difficult. Remembering can be even more difficult after having forgot for a long time. As David Shepherd has keenly written regarding our forgetfulness of the Sabbath, "The longer something has been lost, the harder it seems to be to find." Shepherd, *Seeking Sabbath: A Personal Journey* (Oxford: Bible Reading Fellowship, 2007), 5.

12. See more on this in Abraham E. Milligram, *Sabbath: The Day of Delight* (Philadelphia: Jewish Publication Society of America, 1944), 2–3. The word *kiddush* means "sanctification" and represents the ceremonial welcoming of the Sabbath, including prayers and thanksgiving that set the Sabbath mood. Heschel furthers this, pointing out that in Hebrew "sanctification" is the same word for "marriage." Abraham Joshua Heschel, *The Sabbath* (New York: Farrar, Straus & Giroux, 1951), 43.

13. It is important for the reader to note that there are two lists of the Ten Commandments. In the first list, the Sabbath command is fourth. In the second list, the Sabbath command is third. For the purposes of this book, I will refer to the Sabbath as the fourth commandment. For a great examination of the two lists of commands, see Muthiah, *Sabbath Experiment*, 26.

14. Judith Shulevitz, *Sabbath World: Glimpses of a Different Order of Time* (New York: Random House, 2011), 154 (emphasis added). Also see her article "Bring Back the Sabbath," *New York Times Magazine*, March 2, 2003, http://www.nytimes.com/2003/03/02/magazine /bring-back-the-sabbath.html. Billy Graham was once asked about the fourth commandment and responded, "I'm afraid we are in danger of forgetting the commandment today—but when we do, we pay a price both physically and spiritually. Instead, God loves us, and he wants to bless us by giving us rest and restoring our souls." In remembering the Sabbath, we are reminded, Graham argues, of the love of God. See "Billy Graham's Answer: What Is the Sabbath Really For?," Billy Graham Evangelistic Association, June 22, 2015, https://billygraham.org/story /billy-grahams-answer-what-is-the-sabbath-really-for/.

15. Diana Butler Bass, *Receiving the Day: Christian Practices for Opening the Gift of Time* (San Francisco: Jossey-Bass, 2000), 48.

16. Janine Willis and Alexander Todorov, "First Impressions: Making Up Your Mind after a 100-Ms Exposure to a Face," *Psychological Science* 17, no. 7 (July 2006): 592–98.

17. Karl Barth, *Church Dogmatics*, III/1, ed. G. W. Bromiley and T. F. Torrance (New York: Charles Scribner's Sons, 1957), 216, 219. Barth actually had a good deal to say about the

Sabbath. For a thorough examination of Barth's theology of the Sabbath, see A. J. Cocksworth, "Attending to the Sabbath: An Alternative Direction in Karl Barth's Theology of Prayer," *International Journal of Systematic Theology* 13, no. 3 (July 2011): 251–71. Notice as well that even the structure of the days reflects this restful quality that precedes work. In each of the days of creation, the night happens before the day. Thus, creation would get sleep before work each day. Rest, not work, begins the day in the creation narrative.

18. C. S. Lewis, *The Silver Chair*, The Chronicles of Narnia (New York: HarperCollins, 1981), 24.

19. Eric O. Jacobsen, *The Space Between: A Christian Engagement with the Built Environment* (Grand Rapids: Baker Academic, 2012), 31.

20. Thorkild Jacobsen contrasts Genesis with the Mesopotamian creation myth Eridu Genesis, in which "things were not nearly as good to begin with as they have become since." In the Genesis creation narrative, however, "things began as perfect from God's hand." Jacobsen, "The Eridu Genesis," *Journal of Biblical Literature* 100, no. 4 (1981): 529.

21. James M. McKeown, *Genesis* (Grand Rapids: Eerdmans, 2008), 279.

22. Claus Westermann, *Creation* (Philadelphia: Fortress, 1974), 50–51.

23. Al Baylis, *From Creation to the Cross: Understanding the First Half of the Bible* (Grand Rapids: Zondervan, 1996), 30. And yes, other religious traditions had something similar to the Sabbath. For example, the Akkadians had something called the *shappatu*, which appears to have some similarity to the Hebrew *shabbat*. But this kind of rest was understood as a day when the gods, not humans, were finally appeased and would enjoy divine rest.

24. Alan Padgett, *God, Eternity, and the Nature of Time* (Eugene, OR: Wipf and Stock, 1992). Padgett offers a comprehensive vision of the Bible's theology of time. From a thousand feet, he suggests that the Bible offers little to no idea of eternity without reference to time. That is, even eternity will have some form and rhythm of time as it did in the garden of Eden.

25. Henri Blocher, *In the Beginning: The Opening Chapters of Genesis*, trans. David G. Preston (Downers Grove, IL: InterVarsity, 1984), 39.

26. Colin E. Gunton, *The Christian Faith: An Introduction to Christian Doctrine* (Malden, MA: Blackwell, 2002), 6–7.

27. Heschel, *Sabbath*, 55.

28. Chaim Nahman Bialik, as quoted in Shulevitz, *Sabbath World*, xviii.

29. Dietrich Bonhoeffer, *Creation and Fall: A Theological Exposition of Genesis 1–3* (Minneapolis: Fortress, 2004), 42. Or as Jürgen Moltmann writes, "The promised life . . . is the life commanded." Moltmann, *Theology of Hope: On the Ground and the Implications of a Christian Eschatology* (Minneapolis: Augsburg Fortress, 1993), 121.

30. H. H. Farmer, quoted in Eugene Peterson, *A Long Obedience in the Same Direction: Discipleship in an Instant Society*, 2nd ed. (Downers Grove, IL: InterVarsity, 2000), 109.

31. Skye Jethani, "Work Is the New Sex (Part 2)," *Skye Jethani* (blog), September 25, 2015, https://skyejethani.com/work-is-the-new-sex-part-2/.

32. Heschel, *Sabbath*, 9.

33. Unlike other religions, the Judeo-Christian worldview primarily views time as *qadosh*—sanctified, holy—yet no place is holy in the creation story. One wonders whether Jesus was alluding to this in his dialogue with the Samaritan woman: "A *time* is coming when you will worship the Father neither on this mountain nor in Jerusalem. . . . Yet a *time* is coming and has now come when the true worshipers will worship the Father in the Spirit and in truth" (John 4:21, 23).

34. Some have theorized that it was the destruction of the temple in 586 BCE that caused the writers of Genesis to depict the Sabbath in terms of its holiness. The assumption is that the holiness of the Sabbath replaced the holiness of the temple. The sacredness of space was

subsumed by the sacredness of time. The Sabbath became a replacement temple wherein Jews could worship—it was a kind of "temple in time." See Craig Harline, *Sunday: A History of the First Day from Babylonia to the Super Bowl* (New Haven: Yale University Press, 2011), 3–5. A Jewish essayist, Achad Haam, writes about this: "We can affirm without any exaggeration that the Sabbath has preserved the Jews more than the Jews have preserved the Sabbath. If the Sabbath had not restored to them the soul, renewing every week their spiritual life, they would have become so degraded by the depressing experiences of the workdays, that they would have descended to the last step of materialism and of moral and intellectual decadence." Quoted in Karen Burton Mains, *Making Sunday Special* (Dallas: Word, 1987), 25.

35. Jacques Ellul, *The Subversion of Christianity*, trans. and ed. G. W. Bromiley (Grand Rapids: Eerdmans, 1986), 63.

36. Quoted in Mrs. Andrew Charles, "Hearth and Home," in *The Lutheran Witness*, ed. Martin J. Heinicke (St. Louis: Concordia, 1917).

37. For this reported quotation, I'm indebted to Timothy Keller in his sermon "How to Change—Part III," *The Timothy Keller Sermon Archive* (New York: Redeemer Presbyterian Church, 2013). I have taken liberties to paraphrase the quotation.

38. I am indebted to Colin Gunton's work on the Trinity in his groundbreaking *The One, the Three, and the Many: God, Creation and the Culture of Modernity* (Cambridge: Cambridge University Press, 1993).

39. Interestingly enough, God's creative work through sleep in itself is presented consistently through Scripture. For example, in Genesis 15, Abraham "deep sleeps," as did Adam, before God passes between the halved animal carcass and the firepot, thus establishing a new covenant with him. Matthew's Gospel tells us that it was while Joseph slept that he received word from God that his young family was in danger from Herod (Matt. 1:20). Sleep is a unique state where God meets human beings and meets their needs.

40. Thomas Williams, introduction to Augustine, *On Free Choice of the Will*, trans. Thomas Williams (Indianapolis: Hackett, 1993), xiv.

41. Lesslie Newbigin, *The Open Secret: An Introduction to the Theology of Mission* (Grand Rapids: Eerdmans, 1995), 30–31.

42. Samuele Bacchiocchi, *Divine Rest for Human Restlessness: A Theological Study of the Good News of the Sabbath for Today* (Rome: Pontifical Gregorian University Press, 1980), 17–76. Marva Dawn points this out in *Keeping the Sabbath Wholly: Ceasing, Resting, Embracing, Feasting* (Grand Rapids: Eerdmans, 1989), 139.

43. Marilyn Gardner, "The Ascent of Hours on the Job," *Christian Science Monitor* 97, no. 110 (2005): 14.

44. Sandra Block, "Working, Even after Retirement Age," *USA Today*, August 31, 2007, http://usatoday30.usatoday.com/money/workplace/2007-08-30-not-retired_N.htm.

45. Jürgen Moltmann, *The Passion for Life: A Messianic Lifestyle* (Philadelphia: Augsburg Fortress, 1978), 70–71. Similarly, Dan Allender describes this vacation mindset like eating sugar: "Many modern-day 'vacations' have the allure of cotton candy—a brightly colored candy puff on a paper stick that promises a feast of fullness and is nearly impossible to eat without sticky compromise. Once we tear into the sugary diversion, it disappears in a flash and offers no substance. It is not enough, and it doesn't satisfy, even for a minute." Allender, *Sabbath* (Nashville: Thomas Nelson, 2009), 11.

46. Benoit Hamon, quoted in David Z. Morris, "New French Law Bars Work Email After Hours," January 1, 2017, http://fortune.com/2017/01/01/french-right-to-disconnect-law.

47. Eugene H. Peterson, "The Good-for-Nothing Sabbath," *Christianity Today*, April 4, 1994, 34.

48. Peterson, "Good-for-Nothing Sabbath."

49. I appreciate Dan Allender's words: "Sabbath is not about time off or a break in routine. It is not a mini-vacation to give us a respite so we are better prepared to go back to work. The Sabbath is far more than a diversion; it is meant to be an encounter with God's delight." Allender does a marvelous job unpacking the theme of Sabbath as delight, for which I am greatly indebted. Allender, *Sabbath*, 12.

50. Jean-Jacques Suurmond, "The Uselessness of God," in *Word and Spirit at Play: Towards a Charismatic Theology*, trans. John Bowden (Grand Rapids: Eerdmans, 1995), 29.

51. Colin E. Gunton, *Act and Being: Towards a Theology of the Divine Attributes* (London: SCM, 2002), 7.

52. Karl Barth, *Church Dogmatics*, II/1, ed. G. W. Bromiley and T. F. Torrance (Edinburgh: T&T Clark, 1957), 257.

53. Gerald G. May, *The Awakened Heart: Opening Yourself to the Love You Need* (New York: HarperCollins, 1991), 94–95.

54. Dorothy Sayers, *The Whimsical Christian: 18 Essays* (New York: Collier Books, 1978), 152. For a further examination of play and the Sabbath, see Edwards, *Sabbath Time*, 74–76.

55. This is the argument throughout Harvey Cox, *Feast of Fools: A Theological Essay on Festivity and Fantasy* (New York: Harper & Row, 1969). In her classic text *The Overworked American*, Juliet Schor examines why, with increased productivity, people are working more and more. The answer? They have to pay for their equally increased consumerism, which has led to fewer and fewer hours devoted to play and leisure. See Juliet B. Schor, *The Overworked American: The Unexpected Decline of Leisure* (New York: Basic Books, 1991). For another helpful discussion of the role of play for the Sabbath, see David and Karen Burton Mains, "The Sacred Rhythm of Work and Play," *Moody Monthly*, June 1985, 18–21.

56. Christopher Lasch, *The Culture of Narcissism* (New York: W. W. Norton, 1979), 7.

57. Soong-Chan Rah, *The Next Evangelicalism: Freeing the Church from Western Captivity* (Downers Grove, IL: InterVarsity, 2009), chap. 1.

58. Philip Rieff, *The Triumph of the Therapeutic: Uses of Faith after Freud* (Chicago: University of Chicago Press, 1966), 24–26. Pleasure, we should remember, is not the goal of a Sabbath. There are always dangers of hedonism and asceticism. As hedonists, we will worship the pleasures and celebrations as our ultimate gods. In so doing, we become like Sodom and Gomorrah, whose biblical description sounds like much of Western culture: "She and her daughters were arrogant, overfed and unconcerned; they did not help the poor and needy" (Ezek. 16:49). Sodomites were overfed and unwilling to care for others. They were hedonists. As ascetics, however, we will reject all forms of celebration and joy and assume God can only be worshiped with a straight face. These extremes undermine the Sabbath joy God desires. Joy is permitted. We delight not because we worship pleasure or our own desires but because we are faithful to God and he honors our intentionality.

59. The overall theme of Dawn, *Keeping the Sabbath Wholly*.

60. Eugene H. Peterson, *Working the Angles: The Shape of Pastoral Integrity* (Grand Rapids: Eerdmans, 1987), 75–77.

61. Donna Schaper, *Sabbath Keeping* (Boston: Cowley, 1999), xii.

62. "Whether I see it scattered down among tangled woods, or beaming broad across the fields, or hemmed in between brick buildings, or tracing out the figure of the casement on my chamber floor, still I recognize the Sabbath sunshine. And ever let me recognize it! Some illusions—and this among them—are the shadows of great truths." Nathaniel Hawthorne, "Sunday at Home," in *Twice-Told Tales* (n.p.: Renaissance Classics, 2012), 10.

Chapter 2: Sabbath and Work

1. Richard J. Mouw, *When the Kings Come Marching In: Isaiah and the New Jerusalem* (Grand Rapids: Eerdmans, 2002), 20.

2. Mouw argues that these ships will make it to heaven, but they will be stripped of their old purposes to the other gods. He writes, "It is not, then, the ships *as such* that will be destroyed; it is their former *function* that will perish. It is worth noting that it was a ship from Tarshish that Jonah boarded to flee from the call of the Lord (Jon. 1:3). This incident aptly suggests the ships' pagan function, because they are means of rebellion against God. They are vessels used to flee from his presence, instruments designed to thwart his will. God's judgment is meant to destroy this paganness" (Mouw, *When the Kings Come Marching In*, 30). This is precisely how he interprets the text of Revelation 21:26: "The glory and honor of the nations will be brought into [the transformed city]."

3. Mouw, *When the Kings Come Marching In*, 20.

4. Miroslav Volf, "On Loving with Hope: Eschatology and Social Responsibility," *Transformation* 7, no. 3 (July–September 1990): 31. I'm grateful to Peter Althouse for his discussion on Volf's theology in *Spirit of the Last Days: Pentecostal Eschatology in Conversation with Jürgen Moltmann* (New York: T&T Clark, 2003), 72–75.

5. Douglas Moo, "Nature in the New Creation: New Testament Eschatology and the Environment," *Journal of the Evangelical Theological Society* 49, no. 3 (September 2006): 468.

6. Abraham Joshua Heschel, *The Sabbath* (New York: Farrar, Straus & Giroux, 1951), 15.

7. For more on this, see John Andrews, *First Day: Discovering the Freedom of Sabbathcentric Living* (Kent, UK: River Publishing, 2011), 27.

8. Quoted in Timothy Keller, *Counterfeit Gods: The Empty Promises of Money, Sex, and Power, and the Only Hope That Matters* (New York: Dutton, 2009), 74.

9. *Batman Begins*, directed by Christopher Nolan (Burbank, CA: Warner Home Video, 2005).

10. Philipp W. Rosemann, *Peter Lombard* (New York: Oxford University Press, 2004), 107.

11. Matthew Henry, "Genesis 2 Commentary—Matthew Henry Commentary on the Whole Bible (complete)," in *Matthew Henry Commentary on the Whole Bible* (n.p.: Bible Study Tools, 2016).

12. Daniel Fleming, "By the Sweat of Your Brow: Adam, Anat, Athirat and Ashurbanipal," in *Ugarit and the Bible: Proceedings of the International Symposium on Ugarit and the Bible, Manchester, September 1992* (Munster: Ugarit-Verlag, 1994), 93–100.

13. Sandra L. Richter, *The Epic of Eden: A Christian Entry into the Old Testament* (Downers Grove, IL: InterVarsity, 2008), 111.

14. Evangelical John Stott once wrote of the Sabbath as the "protection" against this kind of enslavement: "The end point is not our toil (subduing the earth) but the laying aside of our toil on the sabbath day. For the sabbath puts the importance of work into perspective. It protects us from the total absorption in our work as if it were to be the be-all and end-all of our existence. It is not. We human beings find our humanness . . . in relation to the Creator." Stott, *The Radical Disciple: Some Neglected Aspects of Our Calling* (Downers Grove, IL: InterVarsity, 2010), 54.

15. David R. Montgomery, *Dirt: The Erosion of Civilizations* (Berkeley: University of California Press, 2012), 3.

16. This happens all the time—people start thinking of ways that they *can* burn out to break out of their cycle of insanity. An example of this is the story of Senator Mark Sanford, whose national-headline-making affair rocked the Republican Party. He writes at length about when he thought about ways he could "fall from grace" so that he no longer had to keep the insane pace he kept. Read his fascinating reflections on the whole ordeal in Tim Alberta, "I'm A Dead Man Walking," *Politico*, February 17, 2017, http://www.politico.com/magazine/story/2017/02/mark-sanford-profile-214791.

17. Flannery O'Connor, *Flannery O'Connor: Spiritual Writings*, ed. Robert Ellsberg (Maryknoll, NY: Orbis, 2003), 86.

18. A classic phrase by the ever-witty Stanley Hauerwas, quoted in William H. Willimon, *Pastor: The Theology and Practice of Ordained Ministry* (Nashville: Abingdon, 2002), 60. The willingness to become, as it were, unavailable to everybody is at the heart of the Sabbath. "Keeping Sabbath—a day of studied and vowed resistance to doing anything so they could be free to see and respond to who God is and what he is doing," writes Eugene Peterson in *Living the Resurrection: The Risen Christ in Everyday Life* (Colorado Springs: NavPress, 2006), 44.

19. Yosef Hayim Yerushalmi, *Zakhor: Jewish History and Jewish Memory* (Seattle: University of Washington Press for Jewish Publication Society of America, 1982), 42–43.

20. Jacques Ellul, *The Ethics of Freedom*, trans. and ed. Geoffrey W. Bromiley (Grand Rapids: Eerdmans, 1976), 496. I am thankful to Marva Dawn for this reference; she remains a helpful interpreter of Ellul's lasting theological legacy. Dawn, *Keeping the Sabbath Wholly: Ceasing, Resting, Embracing, Feasting* (Grand Rapids: Eerdmans, 1989), 15.

21. See Paul Vitello, Robin Swift, and Tony Cox, "Clergy Members Suffer from Burnout, Poor Health," *Talk of the Nation*, NPR, August 3, 2010, http://www.npr.org/templates/story/story.php?storyId=128957149; Paul Vitello, "Taking a Break From the Lord's Work," *New York Times*, August 1, 2010, http://www.nytimes.com/2010/08/02/nyregion/02burnout.html; and Anne Dilenschneider, "Soul Care and the Roots of Clergy Burnout," *Huffington Post*, August 12, 2010, http://www.huffingtonpost.com/anne-dilenschneider/soul-care-and-the-roots-o_b_680925.html.

22. This is a question Eugene Peterson asks. I too write with pastors in mind. For the pastor desiring to responsibly respond to the demands of those we care for and the demands of God, note Peterson's words: "The single act of keeping a Sabbath does more than anything else to train pastors in the rhythm of action and response so that the two sets of demands are experienced synchronically instead of violently." Peterson, *Working the Angles: The Shape of Pastoral Integrity* (Grand Rapids: Eerdmans, 1987), 66.

23. Barbara Brown Taylor, "Divine Subtraction," *Christian Century* 116, no. 30 (November 3, 1999).

24. Henri Blocher, *In the Beginning: The Opening Chapters of Genesis*, trans. David G. Preston (Downers Grove, IL: InterVarsity, 1984), 57. I'm thankful to Sandra Richter for pointing this quote out to me in her book *Epic of Eden*.

25. Heschel, *Sabbath*, 32. And that sense of incompleteness is quite alright. The following sentence, of course, harks back to that famous line by Reinhold Niebuhr: "Nothing that is worth doing can be achieved in our lifetime; therefore we must be saved by hope." Niebuhr, *The Irony of American History* (Chicago: University of Chicago Press, 2008), 63.

26. Mark Buchanan, *The Rest of God: Restoring Your Soul by Restoring Sabbath* (Nashville: Thomas Nelson, 2006), 93.

27. Heschel, *Sabbath*, 22.

28. Nathan T. Stucky, "A More Excellent Way: The Promise of Integrating Theological Education and Agrarianism," in *Rooted and Grounded*, ed. Ryan Dallas Harker and Janeen Bertsche Johnson (Eugene, OR: Pickwick, 2016), 106–7. Norman Wirzba writes:

> Quoting from a midrash, the medieval rabbi Rashi claimed that after the six days of divine work creation was not yet complete. What it lacked, and thus what remained to be created, was *menuha*, the rest, tranquility, serenity, and peace of God. In the biblically informed mind, *menuha* suggests the sort of happiness and harmony that come from things being as they ought to be; we hear in *menuha* resonances with the deep word *shalom*. It is this capacity for happiness and delight, rather than humanity, which sits as the crowning achievement of God's creative work. It is as though by creating *menuha* on the seventh day God gathered up all previous delight and gave it to creation as its indelible stamp. *Menuha*, not humanity, completes creation. God's rest or *shabbat*, especially when understood within a *menuha* context, is not simply a cessation from activity but rather

the lifting up and celebration of everything. (Wirzba, *Living the Sabbath: Discovering the Rhythms of Rest and Delight* [Grand Rapids: Brazos, 2006], 33)

29. Research has been done on the importance of "doing nothing." What has been discovered is that, in the long run, "doing nothing" actually helps productivity. See, e.g., Ray Williams, "Why 'Doing Nothing' Improves Productivity and Well Being," *Psychology Today*, November 9, 2016, https://www.psychologytoday.com/blog/wired-success/201611/why-doing -nothing-improves-productivity-and-well-being.

30. Dawn, *Keeping the Sabbath Wholly*, 65.

31. Writes Jürgen Moltmann, "All Creation moves towards Sabbath (it crowns Creation as its final act). It is not an interruption of Creation, but the hallmark of every doctrine thereof— Christian and Jewish. Sabbath is the celebration that identifies Creation as such, rather than simply nature. Western tradition misses this nuance by speaking of God as Creator and understanding Sabbath as Him stepping away from Creation. However, Sabbath is part and parcel of Creation where it exults in His glory and has the opportunity to simply be. Not only this, but each Sabbath points towards the sabbatical year where human relationships are restored. Therefore, Sabbath anticipates redeemed Creation." Moltmann also speaks of the messianic Sabbath inaugurated by the resurrection which sheds its light on transient Creation both past, present, and future. Christians begin their week with Sabbath as an interpretative lens for reality. Moltmann, *God in Creation: A New Theology of Creation and the Spirit of God* (Minneapolis: Fortress, 1993), 5–7.

32. Martin Luther, "Treatise on Good Works," in *The Christian in Society I*, trans. W. A. Lambert, rev. James Atkinson, vol. 44 of *Luther's Works*, ed. Helmut T. Lehmann (Philadelphia: Fortress, 1966), 72.

33. As Gordon MacDonald writes, "We do not rest because our work is done; we rest because God commanded it and created us to have a need for it." MacDonald, *Ordering Your Private World* (Nashville: Thomas Nelson, 2003), 174.

34. These come from the Mishnah, Tractate Shabbat, chap. 7, and other rabbinic sources. This collection of commentaries and oral opinions was put down on paper in the second century CE. The second section offers Sabbath-observance guidelines. I am thankful for the helpful discussion and illumination of these in Rob Muthiah, *The Sabbath Experiment* (Eugene, OR: Cascade, 2015), 20–22; also Samuel H. Dresner, *The Sabbath* (New York: Burning Bush, 1987), 80–84. In the Roman Catholic tradition, work that is not to be done on the Sabbath is called "servile work."

35. John Murray, *Principles of Conduct: Aspects of Biblical Ethics* (Grand Rapids: Eerdmans, 1957), 33.

36. Tilden Edwards, *Sabbath Time* (Nashville: Upper Room Books, 1992), 24.

37. Craig Harline, *Sunday: A History of the First Day from Babylonia to the Super Bowl* (New Haven: Yale University Press, 2011), 30–31. Diogenes Allen picks up on this in the Sabbath healings of Jesus: "That is why some of the scribes and Pharisees attacked Jesus for some of his teachings and actions, such as healing a man on the Sabbath. Jesus did not deny the importance of observance of the Sabbath, but he pointed out that to heal on the Sabbath did not violate it, since the Sabbath was made for the benefit of people, not people for the Sabbath." Allen, *Spiritual Theology: The Theology of Yesterday for Spiritual Help Today* (Cambridge, MA: Cowley, 1997), 85.

38. Wirzba, *Living the Sabbath*, 21.

Chapter 3: Sabbath and Health

1. There is no better section on the word *no* than chapter 4 of Marva J. Dawn, *The Sense of the Call: A Sabbath Way of Life for Those Who Serve God, the Church, and the World* (Grand Rapids: Eerdmans, 2006).

2. "All you need to say is simply 'Yes' or 'No'; anything beyond this comes from the evil one" (Matt. 5:37).

3. "Corrie ten Boom: 10 Quotes from the Author of *The Hiding Place*," *Christian Today*, April 15, 2016, http://www.christiantoday.com/article/corrie.ten.boom.10.quotes.from.the .author.of.the.hiding.place/84034.htm.

4. Carl Gustav Jung, *Psychology and Religion* (New Haven: Yale University Press, 1938), 92.

5. Eugene Peterson, "Confessions of a Former Sabbath Breaker," *Christianity Today*, September 1988, 25. Peterson argues that the root sin of Sabbath-breaking is sloth.

6. Tony Horsfall, *Working from a Place of Rest: Jesus and the Key to Sustaining Ministry* (Abingdon, UK: Bible Reading Fellowship, 2010), 118.

7. "Study Finds Unique Positive Mental Health Factors for Clergy," Duke Global Health Institute, April 19, 2016, https://globalhealth.duke.edu/media/news/study-finds-unique-positive -mental-health-factors-clergy.

8. Barbara Brown Taylor, "Sabbath: A Practice in Death," video interview, 2:15, The Work of the People, http://www.theworkofthepeople.com/sabbath-a-practice-in-death.

9. Bruce Waltke has called these rhythms in the creation story the "libretto for all of Israel's life." Waltke, "The Creation Account in Genesis 1:1–3; Part IV: The Theology of Genesis 1," *Bibliotheca Sacra* 132, no. 528 (October 1975), 339.

10. Nikos Kazantzakis, *The Table of Inwardness: Nurturing Our Inner Life in Christ* (Downers Grove, IL: InterVarsity, 1984), 78.

11. "The Spirit gives life; the flesh counts for nothing. The words I have spoken to you—they are full of the Spirit and life" (John 6:63).

12. Cornelius Plantinga, *Not the Way It's Supposed to Be: A Breviary of Sin* (Grand Rapids: Eerdmans, 2010), 10.

13. Lorna Green, *Earth Age: A New Vision of God, the Human, and the Earth* (New York: Paulist Press, 1994), 17.

14. Gary D. Badcock, *Light of Truth and Fire of Love: A Theology of the Holy Spirit* (Grand Rapids: Eerdmans, 1997), 140.

15. Randy Woodley, *Shalom and the Community of Creation: An Indigenous Vision* (Grand Rapids: Eerdmans, 2012), 14–15.

16. This material is from Daniel L. Brunner, Jennifer L. Butler, and A. J. Swoboda, *Introducing Evangelical Ecotheology: Foundations in Scripture, Theology, History, and Praxis* (Grand Rapids: Baker Academic, 2014), 241. For further discussion of the Sabbath as ceasing mastery over the world, with particular attention to the theme of *tikkun olam*, see Arthur Waskow, "*Tikkun Olam*: The Adornment of the Mystery," *Religion and the Intellectual Life* 2 (Spring 1985): 111. Marva Dawn suggests that to keep a Sabbath is to initiate what the early church called "recapitulation." The early church believed that there would be a time in the future when everything would be put together the way it was supposed to be—that Christ would be "re-headed" over creation. Right now, the world is under the control of the dark one, and so it reflects Satan's rule. Dawn writes, "Recapitulation . . . means literally to put the Head back on. All creation will one day be put into subjection to Christ, our Head, and then there will be Joy for aeons upon aeons!" Dawn, *Being Well When We're Ill: Wholeness and Hope in Spite of Infirmity* (Minneapolis: Augsburg Fortress, 2008), 20.

17. Robert Ellis, "Creation, Vocation, Crisis and Rest: A Creational Model for Spirituality," *Review and Expositor* 103 (Spring 2006): 319.

18. Joel Salatin, *The Marvelous Pigness of Pigs: Respecting and Caring for All God's Creation* (New York: Faith Words, 2016), 29.

19. I am thankful for Tony Horsfall's biblical narration of exhaustion in his *Working from a Place of Rest*, 48.

20. Brian W. Ward, Jeannine S. Schiller, and Richard A. Goodman, "Multiple Chronic Conditions among US Adults: A 2012 Update," *Preventing Chronic Disease* 11 (2014), https://www.cdc.gov/pcd/issues/2014/13_0389.htm.

21. Norman Wirzba, *Living the Sabbath: Discovering the Rhythms of Rest and Delight* (Grand Rapids: Brazos, 2006), 45.

22. Gregory of Nyssa, "Sermon on the Sixth Beatitude," in *Theological Anthropology: Sources of Early Christian Thought*, ed. J. Patout Burns, trans. Joseph W. Trigg (Philadelphia: Fortress, 1981), 31.

23. Sholem Asch, *Salvation*, 2nd ed. (New York: Schocken Books, 2000).

24. Margaret Diddams, Lisa Klein Surdyk, and Denise Daniels, "Rediscovering Models of Sabbath Keeping: Implications for Psychological Well-Being," *Journal of Psychology and Theology* 32, no. 1 (March 22, 2004): 3–11. Also, for a helpful overview of pastoral health and stress, see C. A. Darling, E. W. Hill, and L. M. McWey, "Understanding Stress and Quality of Life for Clergy and Clergy Spouses," *Stress & Health: Journal of the International Society for the Investigation of Stress* 20, no. 5 (2004): 261–77.

25. On how thinking about work actually affects us, see Mark Cropley and Lynne Millward Purvis, "Job Strain and Rumination about Work Issues during Leisure Time: A Diary Study," *European Journal of Work and Organizational Psychology* 12, no. 3 (September 2003).

26. Archibald Hart, *Thrilled to Death: How the Endless Pursuit of Pleasure Is Leaving Us Numb* (Nashville: Thomas Nelson, 2007), 7–8.

27. Arthur Agatston, "6 Surprising Heart Attack Triggers," NBCNews.com, December 3, 2009, http://www.nbcnews.com/id/34092793/ns/health-heart_health/t/surprising-heart-attack-triggers/.

28. C. S. Lewis, *Out of the Silent Planet* (New York: Simon and Schuster, 1996), 73–74.

29. Abraham Joshua Heschel, *The Sabbath* (New York: Farrar, Straus & Giroux, 1951), 6.

30. John Webster, "What Makes Theology Theological?," *Journal of Analytic Theology* 3 (May 2015): 26.

31. Hartmut Esser, "Social Modernization and the Increase in the Divorce Rate," *Journal of Institutional and Theoretical Economics / Zeitschrift für die gesamte Staatswissenschaft* 149, no. 1 (March 1993): 252–77. As my assistant Madalyn Salz has pointed out, this has greatly shifted the human family. For centuries, people stayed at home to work. Now, we *leave* home to work. Undoubtedly, this has changed the institution of the family at its very core. "We are strangers in an urban landscape," Salz brilliantly writes, "which does not lend itself to accountability" (Salz, personal communication).

32. Marva J. Dawn, *Keeping the Sabbath Wholly: Ceasing, Resting, Embracing, Feasting* (Grand Rapids: Eerdmans, 1989), 69.

33. Kate Rugani, "Lowering Blood Pressure, One Day Off at a Time," *Faith & Leadership*, December 5, 2011, https://www.faithandleadership.com/lowering-blood-pressure-one-day-time.

34. J. Martin Bailey, ed., *Meet Your Neighbors: Interfaith FACTs* (Hartford, CT: Faith Communities Today, Hartford Institute for Religion Research, 2003), 7, https://faithcommunitiestoday.org/sites/all/themes/factzen4/files/MeetNgbors1.pdf.

35. Carl S. Dudley and David A. Roozen, *Faith Communities Today: A Report on Religion in the United States Today* (Hartford, CT: Faith Communities Today, Hartford Institute for Religion Research, 2001), 42.

36. Ryan Buxton, "What Seventh-Day Adventists Get Right That Lengthens Their Life Expectancy," *Huffington Post*, July 31, 2014, http://www.huffingtonpost.com/2014/07/31/seventh-day-adventists-life-expectancy_n_5638098.html.

37. One study by Karl Bailey indicates that the least-healthy people are those religious people who have little practical commitment to actually living out their religious convictions. In the

long run, it is the people who are committed to living out their religious convictions who live the longest. Karl G. D. Bailey and Arian C. B. Timoti, "Delight or Distraction: An Exploratory Analysis of Sabbath-Keeping Internalization," *Journal of Psychology and Theology* 43, no. 3 (Fall 2015): 193.

38. Lesslie Newbigin, *The Good Shepherd: Meditations on Christian Ministry in Today's World* (Grand Rapids: Eerdmans, 1977), 111.

39. Lin Taylor, "Compassion Fatigue: How Much Is Too Much Bad News?," *SBS*, August 1, 2014, http://www.sbs.com.au/news/article/2014/08/01/compassion-fatigue-how-much -too-much-bad-news.

40. Gordon MacDonald, *Ordering Your Private World* (Nashville: Thomas Nelson, 2003), 175.

41. J. R. R. Tolkien, "On Fairy-Stories," in *The Monsters and the Critics: The Essays of J. R. R. Tolkien*, ed. Christopher Tolkien (London: George Allen and Unwin, 1983), 148.

42. For more on this connection between Sabbath and escapism, see N. T. Wright, *For All God's Worth: True Worship and the Calling of the Church* (Grand Rapids: Eerdmans, 1997), 69.

43. Samuel H. Dresner, *The Sabbath* (New York: Burning Bush, 1987), 19.

Chapter 4: Sabbath and Relationships

1. On this, see Pinchas H. Peli, *Shabbat Shalom: A Renewed Encounter with the Sabbath* (Washington, DC: B'nai B'rith Books, 1989), 77–78.

2. Anne Chamberlain, "Israel on Rush," *Vogue*, July 1969, 11.

3. See Christopher D. Ringwald, *A Day Apart: How Jews, Christians, and Muslims Find Faith, Freedom, and Joy on the Sabbath* (New York: Oxford University Press, 2006), 23.

4. Robert D. Putnam, *Bowling Alone: The Collapse and Revival of American Community* (New York: Simon & Schuster, 2000).

5. David O. Jacobson, *The Space Between: A Christian Engagement with the Built Environment* (Grand Rapids: Baker Academic, 2012), 184.

6. Jacobson, *Space Between*, 184–85.

7. As discussed throughout Zygmunt Bauman, *Community: Seeking Safety in an Insecure World* (Cambridge: Polity Press, 2000), esp. 71.

8. John G. Gager, *Kingdom and Community: The Social World of Early Christianity* (Englewood Cliffs, NJ: Prentice Hall, 1975), 114–48.

9. Dietrich Bonhoeffer, *Life Together: A Discussion of Christian Fellowship* (New York: Harper & Row, 1954), 27.

10. Emmanuel Levinas, *Difficult Freedom: Essays on Judaism* (Baltimore: Johns Hopkins University Press, 1990), 10 (emphasis added).

11. This is the overall thesis of Roland Allen's revelatory text, *Missionary Methods: St. Paul's or Ours?* (Grand Rapids: Eerdmans, 1959).

12. Tom A. Steffen, *Passing the Baton: Church Planting That Empowers* (La Habra, CA: Center for Organizational & Ministry Development, 1997), 16.

13. It is interesting to consider that all of the Abrahamic traditions, with all of their differences, share one thing—a day of rest. For a helpful discussion about these three days, see an elongated discussion on this throughout Ringwald, *Day Apart*.

14. Willard M. Swartley, *Slavery, Sabbath, War and Women: Case Issues in Biblical Interpretation* (Harrisonburg, VA: Herald Press, 1983), 65.

15. Richard A. Swenson, *Margin: Restoring Emotional, Physical, Financial, and Time Reserves to Overloaded Lives* (Colorado Springs: NavPress, 2004), 77.

16. American Society of Landscape Architects, "ASLA 2006 Student Awards: Residential Design Award of Honor," accessed June 20, 2017, https://www.asla.org/awards/2006/student awards/282.html.

17. Winston Solberg, *Redeem the Time: The Puritan Sabbath in Early America* (Cambridge, MA: Harvard University Press, 1977), 114. I am thankful to David Shepherd for these comical historical insights on sex and Sabbath in his *Seeking Sabbath: A Personal Journey* (Oxford: Bible Reading Fellowship, 2007), 65.

18. Craig Harline, *Sunday: A History of the First Day from Babylonia to the Super Bowl* (New Haven: Yale University Press, 2011), 22.

19. In the Talmud, scholars debated the relationship of sex to Sabbath. The rabbis wrote, "Rab Judah in the name of Samuel replied: Every Friday night. 'That bringeth forth its fruit in its season' (Ps. 1:3), Rab Judah . . . stated: 'This [refers to the man] who performs his marital duty every Friday night.'" Babylonian Talmud: Ketubot 62b.

20. In personal conversation—used with permission.

21. Nancy Shute, "Is Sex Once a Week Enough for a Happy Relationship?," NPR, November 18, 2015, http://www.npr.org/sections/health-shots/2015/11/18/456482701/is-sex-once-a-week-enough-for-a-happy-relationship.

22. Abraham E. Milligram, *Sabbath: The Day of Delight* (Philadelphia: Jewish Publication Society of America, 1944), 8.

23. Milligram, *Sabbath*, 10–11.

24. Rob Muthiah, *The Sabbath Experiment* (Eugene, OR: Cascade, 2015), 3.

25. Charles Dickens, *Sunday under Three Heads* (London: J. W. Jarvis & Son, 1884), 29.

26. Lyn Cryderman, *Glory Land: A Memoir of a Lifetime in Church* (Grand Rapids: Zondervan, 1999), 12.

27. Marva J. Dawn, *Keeping the Sabbath Wholly: Ceasing, Resting, Embracing, Feasting* (Grand Rapids: Eerdmans, 1989), 12–14.

28. Eugene Peterson, *The Contemplative Pastor: Returning to the Art of Spiritual Direction* (Grand Rapids: Eerdmans, 1989), 21–23.

Chapter 5: Sabbath, Economy, and Technology

1. Karen Burton Mains, *Making Sunday Special* (Dallas: Word, 1987), 21 (emphasis added).

2. I borrow this witty phrase from John Andrews, *First Day: Discovering the Freedom of Sabbathcentric Living* (Kent, UK: River Publishing, 2011), 13.

3. Quoted in Craig Harline, *Sunday: A History of the First Day from Babylonia to the Super Bowl* (New Haven: Yale University Press, 2011), vii.

4. Abraham Joshua Heschel, *The Sabbath* (New York: Farrar, Straus & Giroux, 1951), 51–52. This is why the *havdalah* braided candles are lit at the end of the Sabbath and mark the distinction between the Sabbath and the other days. As they are lit, a blessing is read: "Blessed are you, God, because you separate the holy from the everyday, the light from the darkness, the people of Israel from everyone else, and the seventh day from the six days of creation." The intent of this is to remind us that the Sabbath day is set aside from the others. It is holy, separate. See Marva J. Dawn, *Keeping the Sabbath Wholly: Ceasing, Resting, Embracing, Feasting* (Grand Rapids: Eerdmans, 1989), 34–35.

5. Abraham E. Milligram, *Sabbath: The Day of Delight* (Philadelphia: Jewish Publication Society of America, 1944), 1–2.

6. Nancy Sleeth, *Almost Amish: One Woman's Quest for a Slower, Simpler, More Sustainable Life* (Carol Stream, IL: Tyndale, 2012).

7. Walter Brueggemann, *Sabbath as Resistance: Saying No to the Culture of Now* (Louisville: Westminster John Knox, 2014), 37. Brueggemann locates the amnesia of Israel, which

forgot the Sabbath day, in Moses's language to the people of God in Deuteronomy 6:12 and 8:14.

8. Discussed at length in Brueggemann, *Sabbath as Resistance*, 3.

9. Rob Muthiah, *The Sabbath Experiment* (Eugene, OR: Cascade, 2015), 65.

10. Laura Hartman offers an excellent overview of much of the Sabbath Economics Collaborative in *The Christian Consumer: Living Faithfully in a Fragile World* (New York: Oxford University Press, 2011), chap. 5.

11. Jim Forest, *Love Is the Measure: A Biography of Dorothy Day* (New York: Paulist Press, 1986), 92, quoted in Hartman, *Christian Consumer*, 100.

12. Hartman offers a phenomenal discussion of Woolman's consumer habits in *Christian Consumer*, chap. 1.

13. Marva Dawn has done excellent work connecting social justice and Sabbath practices. She writes, "The more we imitate God in Sabbath keeping, the more our reforming and renewing work on the other six days will contribute to the rebuilding of the cosmos according to God's purposes. How urgent is the mandate in the first version of the Sabbath commandment: imitate God!" Dawn, "Sabbath Keeping and Social Justice," in *Sunday, Sabbath, and the Weekend: Managing Time in a Global Culture*, ed. Edward O'Flaherty, Rodney L. Petersen, and Timothy A. Norton (Grand Rapids: Eerdmans, 2010), 35.

14. Quoted in Milligram, *Sabbath*, 3.

15. Kenneth E. Bailey, *Jesus through Middle Eastern Eyes: Cultural Studies in the Gospels* (Downers Grove, IL: InterVarsity, 2008), 381–82.

16. Lane Anderson, "Do the Poor Give More Than the Rich?," *Deseret News*, March 31, 2015, http://www.deseretnews.com/article/865625341/Do-the-poor-give-more-than-the-rich.html.

17. Miroslav Volf, *Work in the Spirit: Toward a Theology of Work* (New York: Oxford University Press, 1991), 189.

18. Thanks to Craig Harline for pointing this out in *Sunday*, 44–45.

19. For a thorough examination of a Puritan Sabbath, see Winton Solberg, *Redeem the Time: The Puritan Sabbath in Early America* (Cambridge, MA: Harvard University Press, 1977).

20. Tilden Edwards, *Sabbath Time* (Nashville: Upper Room Books, 1992), 19.

21. Edwards, *Sabbath Time*, 15.

22. On the dangers of forcing Sabbath legislation on a society, see the very helpful Samuele Bacchiocchi, *Divine Rest for Human Restlessness: A Theological Study of the Good News of the Sabbath for Today* (Rome: Pontifical Gregorian University Press, 1980), 10n3.

23. Milligram, *Sabbath*, 161.

24. Judith Shulevitz, *Sabbath World: Glimpses of a Different Order of Time* (New York: Random House, 2011), xxix.

25. Daniel Harris, *Cute, Quaint, Hungry, and Romantic: The Aesthetics of Consumerism* (New York: Basic Books, 2000), 75–76.

26. Jesuit theologian Gerard W. Hughes in *God in All Things* (London: Hodder & Stoughton, 2004).

27. Jarrod Longbons, "Rowan Williams and Ecological Rationality," in *Being-in-Creation*, ed. Brian Treanor, Bruce Ellis Benson, and Norman Wirzba (New York: Fordham University Press, 2016), 46–47.

28. Louis Jacobs, *Jewish Preaching: Homilies and Sermons* (London: Mitchell Vallentine, 2004), 129–30.

29. Peter Scazzero, *The Emotionally Healthy Leader: How Transforming Your Inner Life Will Deeply Transform Your Church, Team, and the World* (Grand Rapids: Zondervan, 2015), 159–60.

30. For a helpful discussion of the relationship of Sabbath to consumerism, see Hartman, *Christian Consumer*, 130–52.

31. Wendell Berry, *Sex, Economy, Freedom and Community: Eight Essays* (New York: Pantheon Books, 1993), 14.

32. Tristan Harris, "How Technology Hijacks People's Minds—from a Magician and Google's Design Ethicist," *Thrive Global*, May 18, 2016, https://journal.thriveglobal.com/how-technology-hijacks-peoples-minds-from-a-magician-and-google-s-design-ethicist-56d62ef5edf3. This fascinating article suggests that the constant checking of our iPhones actually has the same kind of effect on our minds that a slot machine does.

33. I am thankful to my friend Ken Wytsma for providing me with some of this information in his book *The Grand Paradox: The Messiness of Life, the Mystery of God, and the Necessity of Faith* (Nashville: Word, 2015), chap. 10. See also David Daniels, *The ROI of Video in Email Marketing* (n.p.: Relevancy Group, 2013), 2, https://www.streamsend.com/pdf/The_ROI_of_Video_in_Email_Marketing-StreamSend-The%20RelevancyGroup.pdf.

34. Jimmy Daly, "18 Incredible Internet-Usage Statistics," *FedTech*, June 12, 2013, http://www.fedtechmagazine.com/article/2013/06/18-incredible-internet-usage-statistics.

35. Harris, "How Technology Hijacks People's Minds."

36. Joseph Ratzinger, *"In the Beginning . . .": A Catholic Understanding of the Story of Creation and the Fall* (Grand Rapids: Eerdmans, 1995), 30–39.

37. Marilyn Gardner, "The Ascent of Hours on the Job," *Christian Science Monitor* 97, no. 110 (2005): 14.

38. Dan Allender, *Sabbath* (Nashville: Thomas Nelson, 2009), 50.

39. Wayne Muller, *Sabbath: Finding Rest, Renewal, and Delight in Our Busy Lives* (New York: Random House, 2000), 160.

40. Richard A. Swenson, *The Overload Syndrome: Learning to Live within Your Limits* (Colorado Springs: NavPress, 1998), 36.

41. "The danger of multitasking," stresses Norman Wirzba, is that "the frantic, fragmenting, multitasking character of contemporary living has made it likely that many of us will simply evade, or fail to consider with much seriousness or depth, life's most basic and profound questions: What is all our living finally for?" Wirzba, *Living the Sabbath: Discovering the Rhythms of Rest and Delight* (Grand Rapids: Brazos, 2006), 20.

42. "Doctors Diagnose 'Hurry Sickness,'" *Preaching Today*, 2015, http://www.preachingtoday.com/illustrations/2015/november/7111615.html. See also David W. Henderson, *Tranquility* (Grand Rapids: Baker Books, 2015), 131.

43. Shulevitz, *Sabbath World*, 5. The first clock was invented by monks in an effort to guide monastic time. Because of this and the invention of the light bulb, the role of artificial light has exponentially grown. Before the clock, human society generally lived according to the rhythms of the sun. But now, time has become abstract and entirely disconnected from the rhythms of the sun's light. See Mattie Glenhaber, "The Invention of the Mechanical Clock and Perceptions of Time in the 13th–15th Centuries," *Concord Review* 24, no. 2 (2013), available at http://modelsofexcellence.eleducation.org/file/3970/download?token=3xnY9JBB.

44. John Ortberg, *The Life You've Always Wanted* (Grand Rapids: Zondervan, 1997), 81, 84.

45. Kelly Wallace, "Teens Spend a 'Mind-Boggling' 9 Hours a Day Using Media, Report Says," CNN, November 3, 2015, http://www.cnn.com/2015/11/03/health/teens-tweens-media-screen-use-report/.

46. "Nature-Deficit Disorder," Children and Nature Network, accessed April 27, 2017, https://www.childrenandnature.org/about/nature-deficit-disorder.

Chapter 6: Sabbath and the Marginalized

1. Jürgen Moltmann, *Man: Christian Anthropology in the Conflicts of the Present* (Minneapolis: Fortress, 1974), 8.

2. McDonald's, "Balance Work & Life," accessed June 21, 2017, http://corporate.mcdonalds.com /mcd/corporate_careers/benefits/highlights_of_what_we_offer/balance_work_and_life.html.

3. Sam Stier, "Seeing the Devastation of Climate Change in the Ruins of Aleppo," *Los Angeles Times*, January 6, 2017, http://www.latimes.com/opinion/op-ed/la-oe-stier-climate-change -and-syrian-civil-war-20170106-story.html.

4. Amy Westervelt, "Does Climate Change Really Cause Conflict?," *Guardian*, March 11, 2015, https://www.theguardian.com/vital-signs/2015/mar/09/climate-change-conflict-syria -global-warming.

5. Susanne Posel, "Military Study: Climate Change Will Cause Civil Unrest," Susanne Posel: Investigative Headline News, July 13, 2013, https://www.occupycorporatism.com/military -study-climate-change-will-cause-civil-unrest/.

6. Richard A. Swenson, *Margin: Restoring Emotional, Physical, Financial, and Time Reserves to Overloaded Lives* (Colorado Springs: NavPress, 2004), chap. 5.

7. Norman Wirzba, *Living the Sabbath: Discovering the Rhythms of Rest and Delight* (Grand Rapids: Brazos, 2006), 148.

8. Samuel H. Dresner, *The Sabbath* (New York: Burning Bush, 1987), 44.

9. Thomas Shepard, *The Works of Thomas Shepard*, ed. John A. Albro (Boston: n.p., 1853), 3:7–271. For this quotation, I am indebted to the brilliant examination of Puritan Sabbath practices, Winton Solberg, *Redeem the Time: The Puritan Sabbath in Early America* (Cambridge, MA: Harvard University Press, 1977).

10. George Wolfgang Forell, *Faith Active in Love* (Eugene, OR: Wipf & Stock, 1999), 101 (emphasis added).

11. Walter Brueggemann, *Sabbath as Resistance: Saying No to the Culture of Now* (Louisville: Westminster John Knox, 2014), 40.

12. This material is drawn from Dresner, *Sabbath*, 65–70.

13. Again, with great wisdom, Wirzba writes:

By proclaiming that everyone should rest together, we begin to see some of the revolutionary potential latent within a Sabbath sensibility. Put simply, the rest of one person should not be at the expense of another's exhaustion or toil. Having just come from the experience of slavery in Egypt, where the wealth and success of a minority clearly depended on the systematic abuse and oppression of the majority, the Israelites would have readily seen that Sabbath teaching is about the liberation of all to share in the goodness of God. God's grace is not reserved for the select, powerful few. It extends to the whole community of life." (Wirzba, *Living the Sabbath*, 39)

14. A fascinating study reveals that "when religious practices are controlled by guilt, social pressure, fear, or shame, believers generally report lower levels of well-being." Karl G. D. Bailey and Arian C. B. Timoti, "Delight or Distraction: An Exploratory Analysis of Sabbath-Keeping Internalization," *Journal of Psychology and Theology* 43, no. 3 (Fall 2015): 193.

15. "Nelson Mandela Quotes: A Collection of Memorable Words from Former South African President," *CBS News*, December 5, 2013, http://www.cbsnews.com/news/nelson -mandela-quotes-a-collection-of-memorable-words-from-former-south-african-president/.

16. For an excellent article applying the Sabbath principle to those in prison and torture situations, see Edward Feld, "Developing a Jewish Theology Regarding Torture," *Theology Today* 63 (2006): 324–29.

17. John Goldingay, *Approaches to Old Testament Interpretation* (Toronto: Clements, 2002), 59–62.

18. Anja Kollmuss and Jullian Agyeman, "Mind the Gap: Why Do People Act Environmentally and What Are the Barriers to Pro-Environmental Behavior?," *Environmental Education Research* 8, no. 3 (2002): 239–60.

19. Laura Ruth Yordy, *Green Witness: Ecology Ethics and the Kingdom of God* (Cambridge: Lutterworth, 2008), 10. See Romans 7:14–20; Augustine, *Confessions* 4.4; Aristotle, *Nicomachean Ethics*, book 7.

20. Yordy, *Green Witness*, 9–10.

Chapter 7: Sabbath and Creation

1. Paige Bierma and Chris Woolston, "Phantom Limb Pain," last updated January 20, 2017, https://consumer.healthday.com/encyclopedia/pain-management-30/pain-health-news-520/phantom-limb-pain-646208.html.

2. Matthew Sleeth, *24/6: A Prescription for a Healthier, Happier Life* (Carol Stream, IL: Tyndale, 2012), 3–6. For another excellent treatment on God's love for the whole planet, see Sleeth, *Serve God, Save the Planet: A Christian Call to Action* (Grand Rapids: Zondervan, 2007).

3. It should be pointed out that the Hebrew text uses the causative verb "to grow," implying that God is not passively making the grass grow—God himself actually makes it sprout and grow so that the cattle can survive.

4. I am deeply thankful to Leah Kostamo for her description of the "Four Pests Campaign" in *Planted: A Story of Creation, Community, and Calling* (Eugene, OR: Cascade, 2013), 6.

5. John Muir, *My First Summer in the Sierra* (Boston: Houghton Mifflin, 1911), 110.

6. In fact, the term *ecology* is believed to have been coined in 1886 by German biologist and naturalist Ernst Haeckel. He derived the concept itself from the Greek notion of a household (*oikos*). The household (*oikos*) of the universe is where everything (animate or inanimate) is understood to be related to everything else.

7. This is a theme found throughout G. Tyler Miller, *Living in the Environment* (Belmont, CA: Wadsworth, 1992).

8. *Grand Canyon*, directed by Lawrence Kasdan, written by Lawrence Kasdan and Meg Kasdan (Beverly Hills, CA: Twentieth Century Fox, 1991), DVD.

9. Cornelius Plantinga, *Not the Way It's Supposed to Be: A Breviary of Sin* (Grand Rapids: Eerdmans, 2010), 7–8.

10. Fred Bahnson and Norman Wirzba, *Making Peace with the Land: God's Call to Reconcile with Creation* (Downers Grove, IL: InterVarsity, 2012), 38–39.

11. Bahnson and Wirzba, *Making Peace with the Land*, 39.

12. Jonathan Sacks, *The Persistence of Faith: Religion, Morality and Society in a Secular Age*, 2nd ed. (London: Weidenfeld and Nicolson, 1992), 26–27.

13. Thomas Merton, *Disputed Questions* (San Diego: Harcourt Brace, 1960), 98.

14. "The Russell-Einstein Manifesto," Pugwash Conferences on Science and World Affairs, July 9, 1955, https://pugwash.org/1955/07/09/statement-manifesto.

15. Diogenes Allen and Eric O. Springsted, *Spirit, Nature and Community: Issues in the Thought of Simone Weil* (Albany: State University of New York Press, 1994), 55.

16. Wendell Berry, *Sex, Economy, Freedom and Community: Eight Essays* (New York: Pantheon Books, 1993), 97 (emphasis added).

17. Chris Sugden, "Christians, Environment and Society: A Response to Michael Northcott," *Transformation* 16, no. 3 (July 1999): 110, http://www.jstor.org/stable/43053909.

18. For a critical response to the guilt and shame trip that we "ought to care," see Peter William Metcalf, "Fertile Ground: Reflections on Christian Faith Practices as Care for the Earth" (master's thesis, University of Montana, 2009), http://scholarworks.umt.edu/etd/442.

19. Douglas John Hall, *The Stewardship of Life in the Kingdom of Death* (Grand Rapids: Eerdmans, 1988), 37.

20. Chris Huntington, "Learning to Measure Time in Love and Loss," *New York Times*, December 26, 2013, http://www.nytimes.com/2013/12/29/fashion/learning-to-measure-time -in-love-and-loss.html.

Chapter 8: Sabbath and the Land

1. Alan Weisman, *The World without Us* (New York: Picador, 2008).

2. One cannot underscore the importance of this triadic relationship between God, humanity, and creation. On this "triad," see Jarrod Longbons, "Rowan Williams and Ecological Rationality," in *Being-in-Creation*, ed. Brian Treanor, Bruce Ellis Benson, and Norman Wirzba (New York: Fordham University Press, 2016), 37.

3. Daniel Stiegerwald and Kelly Crull, eds., *Grow Where You're Planted: Collected Stories on the Hallmarks of Maturing Church* (Portland, OR: Christian Associates Press, 2013), 12.

4. Quoted in Wayne Muller, *Legacy of the Heart: The Spiritual Advantages of a Painful Childhood* (New York: Simon & Schuster, 1992), 106.

5. These magazine covers in *Time* are documented in the final chapter of Jon C. Teaford, *The Rough Road to Renaissance* (Baltimore: Johns Hopkins University Press, 1990).

6. Edward L. Glasser, "Are Cities Dying?," *Journal of Economic Perspectives* 12, no. 2 (1998): 139–60.

7. Glasser, "Are Cities Dying?," 141.

8. Philip Langdon, *A Better Place to Live: Reshaping the American Suburb* (Boston: University of Massachusetts Press, 1994), 1.

9. "Ethics and the Environment: The Spotted Owl Controversy," Markkula Center for Applied Ethics, Santa Clara University, November 13, 2015, https://www.scu.edu/ethics/focus-areas /more/environmental-ethics/resources/ethics-and-the-environment-the-spotted-owl/.

10. Steven Bouma-Prediger and Brian J. Walsh, *Beyond Homelessness: Christian Faith in a Culture of Displacement* (Grand Rapids: Eerdmans, 2008).

11. "Flipping" is the process of buying a house, fixing it up with lower-quality items, and putting it back on the market to make, at times, a big profit. I also tell this story in Daniel L. Brunner, Jennifer L. Butler, and A. J. Swoboda, *Introducing Evangelical Ecotheology: Foundations in Scripture, Theology, History, and Praxis* (Grand Rapids: Baker Academic, 2014).

12. Paul Brooks, *The Pursuit of Wilderness* (Boston: Houghton Mifflin, 1971), 13.

13. Norman Wirzba, *Living the Sabbath: Discovering the Rhythms of Rest and Delight* (Grand Rapids: Brazos, 2006), 38.

14. Jürgen Moltmann et al., *Theology of Play* (New York: Harper & Row, 1972), 5.

15. This is pointed out in Tilden Edwards, *Sabbath Time* (Nashville: Upper Room Books, 1992), 70.

16. I'm indebted to the late Chuck Colson for pointing these stories out to me in *Burden of Truth: Defending Truth in an Age of Unbelief* (Wheaton: Tyndale, 1997), 203–4.

17. Augustine, "Sermon 242A," in *Sermons*, trans. Edmund Hill, ed. John E. Rotelle, The Works of Saint Augustine III/7 (New York: New City Press, 1993), 85.

18. Elizabeth A. Johnson, "The Banquet of Faith" (paper delivered at the Leadership Conference of Women Religious and Conference of Major Superiors of Men Assembly, 2008), 2.

19. Wendell Berry, *The Art of the Commonplace: The Agrarian Essays of Wendell Berry*, ed. Norman Wirzba (Berkeley: Counterpoint, 2002), 298.

20. John O'Donohue, *Anam Ċara: A Book of Celtic Wisdom* (New York: HarperCollins, 1997), 151.

Chapter 9: Sabbath and Critters

1. Josh Harkinson, "Turns Out Your 'Hormone Free' Milk Is Full of Sex Hormones," *Mother Jones*, April 20, 2014, http://www.motherjones.com/media/2014/04/milk-hormones -cancer-pregnant-cows-estrogen.

2. "Steroid Hormone Implants Used for Growth in Food-Producing Animals," US Food and Drug Administration, last updated October 20, 2015, https://www.fda.gov/AnimalVeterinary /SafetyHealth/ProductSafetyInformation/ucm055436.htm.

3. Holly Grigg-Spall, *Sweetening the Pill, or How We Got Hooked on Hormonal Birth Control* (Alresford, UK: Zero Books, 2013), 46.

4. Darryl Fears, "As More Male Bass Switch Sex, a Strange Fish Story Expands," *Washington Post*, August 3, 2014, https://www.washingtonpost.com/national/health-science/as-more-male-bass -switch-sex-a-strange-fish-story-expands/2014/08/03/89799b08-11ad-11e4-8936-26932bcfd6ed _story.html.

5. Jessie Black, "Hunting Ways to Keep Synthetic Estrogens Out of Rivers and Seas," *NPR*, June 19, 2015, http://www.npr.org/sections/health-shots/2015/06/19/415336306/hunting -ways-to-keep-synthetic-estrogens-out-of-rivers-and-seas.

6. Fears, "As More Male Bass." It should also be noted that several other endocrine disruptors are at play here, such as the pollutant BPA.

7. Lindsey Konkel, "Why Are These Male Fish Growing Eggs?," *National Geographic*, February 3, 2016, http://news.nationalgeographic.com/2016/02/160203-feminized-fish-endocrine -disruption-hormones-wildlife-refuges.

8. I wish to thank Madalyn Salz and Alec Eagon for bringing these issues to my attention.

9. The story is retold in Ronald J. Sider, *Good News and Good Works: A Theology for the Whole Gospel* (Grand Rapids: Baker, 1993), 15–17.

10. Nicholas Wolterstorff, *Until Justice and Peace Embrace* (Grand Rapids: Eerdmans, 1983), 146.

11. Sider, *Good News and Good Works*, 26.

12. A. J. Swoboda, *The Dusty Ones: Why Wandering Deepens Your Faith* (Grand Rapids: Baker Books, 2016).

13. Craig L. Blomberg writes, "To reassure the disciples of God's fatherly love, Jesus contrasts their great worth with the comparatively insignificant value of sparrows, a cheap marketplace item sold for 1/32 of the minimum daily wage ('penny' is literally an *assarion*, which equaled 1/16 of a denarius). So, too, God knows the very number of our hairs. If he is aware and in control of such minor details, 'how much more' will he not care for his own people and vindicate them despite their present suffering?" Blomberg, *Matthew*, New American Commentary 22 (Nashville: Broadman & Holman, 1992), 178.

14. For an interesting discussion on God's love for the sparrows, see Denis Edwards, *Ecology at the Heart of Faith: The Change of Heart That Leads to a New Way of Living on Earth* (Columbia, SC: Orbis, 2006), 92–98; also Edwards, "Every Sparrow That Falls to the Ground: The Cost of Evolution and the Christ-Event," *Ecotheology* 11, no. 1 (March 2006): 103–23.

15. "Why the Forest Needs the Salmon: An Interview with Dr. Thomas Reimchen," *Cascade Bioregion*, accessed April 27, 2017, http://cascadia-bioregion.tripod.com/forestneedsalmon.html. I am thankful to Randy Woodley for pointing this out in his *Shalom and the Community of Creation: An Indigenous Vision* (Grand Rapids: Eerdmans, 2012), 121–22.

16. Dietrich Bonhoeffer, *Creation and Fall; Temptation: Two Biblical Studies* (New York: Touchstone, 1997), 19.

17. Quoted in Brennan Manning, *Ruthless Trust: The Ragamuffin's Path to God* (New York: HarperCollins, 2000), 8.

18. Norman Wirzba, *Living the Sabbath: Discovering the Rhythms of Rest and Delight* (Grand Rapids: Brazos, 2006), 40.

19. E.g., Arctic ground squirrels hibernate for up to eight months of the year. Samantha J. Wojda et al., "Arctic Ground Squirrels Limit Bone Loss during the Prolonged Physical Inactivity Associated with Hibernation," *Physiological & Biochemical Zoology* 89, no. 1 (January 2016): 72–80.

20. "Hibernating Animals Suffer Dangerous Wakeup Calls Due to Warming," *National Geographic*, February 2, 2007, http://news.nationalgeographic.com/news/2007/02/070202-ground hog.html.

21. Barrett Duke, "10 Biblical Truths about Animals," The Ethics and Religious Liberty Commission, January 5, 2015, http://erlc.com/resource-library/articles/10-biblical-truths-about -animals.

22. "Treatment of Animals," *Judaism 101*, accessed June 23, 2017, http://www.jewfaq.org /animals.htm.

23. This is a fascinating story from a Sabbatarian denomination that illustrates how one person has attempted to keep the Sabbath holy in relation to the animals under her care. Lynn Marshall, "Horses That Keep the Sabbath," *Beyond Today*, April 10, 2005, https://www.ucg .org/the-good-news/horses-that-keep-the-sabbath.

24. These are listed at Menachem Posner, "How Does Shabbat Observance Affect Pet Owners?," *Chabad.org*, accessed June 23, 2017, http://www.chabad.org/library/article_cdo/aid /522415/jewish/How-does-Shabbat-observance-affect-pet-owners.htm.

25. Menuchat Ahavah 3:18:3. For a concise yet in-depth look at various Sabbath exhortations from the Jewish tradition, see Gersion Appel, *Concise Code of Jewish Law: A Guide to the Observance of Shabbat* (New York: Orthodox Union, 2016).

26. Both stories are told in Gerald Root, *C. S. Lewis as an Advocate for Animals* (Washington, DC: The Humane Society of the United States, n.d.), 3, http://www.humanesociety.org/assets /pdfs/faith/cs_lewis_advocate_animals_gerald_root.pdf.

27. Stanley Hauerwas, *Prayers Plainly Spoken* (Downers Grove, IL: InterVarsity, 1999), 57.

Chapter 10: Sabbath and Witness

1. I was introduced to the ministry of this man in Walter L. Liefeld, *1 & 2 Timothy, Titus*, NIV Application Commentary (Grand Rapids: Zondervan, 1999), 319.

2. It should be noted that Finney was of such passionate political persuasion that he would, following the "anxious seat" experience, go to the back of the tent to sign a petition to end slavery. For Finney, conversion and political action were inseparable.

3. Neil Postman, *Technopoly: The Surrender of Culture to Technology* (New York: Vintage Books, 1993), 27.

4. Described throughout Gerhard Lohfink, trans. John P. Galvin, *Jesus and Community: The Social Dimensions of Christian Faith* (Minneapolis: Fortress, 1982).

5. Abraham E. Milligram, *Sabbath: The Day of Delight* (Philadelphia: Jewish Publication Society of America, 1944), 4.

6. Milligram, *Sabbath*, 7.

7. Demonstration plots were utilized by a community of Christian farmers in the 1940s. Clarence and Florence Jordan and Martin and Mabel England started Koinonia Farm in Sumter County, Georgia, as a demonstration plot for the kingdom of God. As Christ followers, the Jordans and the Englands set out to create a farm in which the principles of the kingdom of God as found in the book of Acts could be demonstrated for the world to see. The families lived there in mutuality and love; they shared goods and lived a simple life. People from all over the world flocked to the farm and experienced the gospel in a profound way.

8. Roberto O. Ferdman, "The American Energy Drink Craze in Two Highly Caffeinated Charts," *Quartz*, March 26, 2014, https://qz.com/192038/the-american-energy-drink-craze -in-two-highly-caffeinated-charts/.

9. These three Sabbath meals, one scholar explains, are to honor Abraham, Isaac, and Jacob, who apparently kept the Sabbath even *before* the Torah was given to Moses. See Milligram, *Sabbath*, 19–22. David Shepherd contends that this is connected to Exodus 16:25, where the word *day* is mentioned three times. Therefore, "Jews are to eat three square meals on the sabbath even when . . . they would normally only eat two." Shepherd, *Seeking Sabbath: A Personal Journey* (Oxford: Bible Reading Fellowship, 2007), 18.

10. Samuel H. Dresner, *The Sabbath* (New York: Burning Bush, 1987), 21–22. I am thankful to Rob Muthiah for mentioning this in his *The Sabbath Experiment* (Eugene, OR: Cascade, 2015), 2.

11. Charles Gore, Henry Leighton Goudge, and Alfred Guillaume, eds., *A New Commentary on Holy Scriptures* (New York: Macmillan, 1928), 477.

12. "Shabbat," *Judaism 101*, accessed June 24, 2017, http://www.jewfaq.org/shabbat.htm.

13. Dresner, *Sabbath*, 42.

14. Abraham Joshua Heschel, *The Sabbath* (New York: Farrar, Straus & Giroux, 1951), 13.

15. On both Jewish and Christian perspectives on war and the Sabbath, see Marva J. Dawn, *Keeping the Sabbath Wholly: Ceasing, Resting, Embracing, Feasting* (Grand Rapids: Eerdmans, 1989), 90–91.

16. Dresner articulates the kind of violent world that a Sabbath-keeper will always encounter. Dresner, *Sabbath*, 11–13.

17. Erin S. Lane, *Lessons in Belonging from a Church-Going Commitment Phobe* (Downers Grove, IL: InterVarsity, 2015), 93.

18. Tony Horsfall writes powerfully about this and identifies the same theme in the story. Jesus rests and does nothing. And with such a posture, he is available for ministry. Horsfall writes, "Everything that happens in this story happens because Jesus was doing nothing. . . . We can learn to work and minister as Jesus did, from a place of rest." Horsfall, *Working from a Place of Rest: Jesus and the Key to Sustaining Ministry* (Abingdon, UK: Bible Reading Fellowship, 2010), 9–11.

19. Kendra Haloviak, "The Sabbath Song: An Alternative Vision," *Living Pulpit* 7, no. 2 (1998): 41.

20. Milligram, *Sabbath*, 12.

21. Wiel Logister, "A Small Theology of Feasting," in *Christian Feast and Festival: The Dynamics of Western Liturgy and Culture*, ed. Paulus G. F. Post (Sterling, VA: Peeters, 2001), 162–63.

Chapter 11: Sabbath and Worship

1. Stanley Hauerwas and Samuel Wells, "Christian Ethics as Informed Prayer," in *The Blackwell Companion to Christian Ethics*, ed. Nicholas Adams, Scott Bader-Saye, and Frederick Christian Bauerschmidt (Malden, MA: Blackwell, 2006), 7.

2. I can think of no better book that deals with Christian disciplines than Richard Foster's *The Celebration of Discipline: Paths to Spiritual Growth* (San Francisco: Harper & Row, 1978).

3. Joy Davidman, *Smoke on the Mountain: An Interpretation of the Ten Commandments*, 2nd ed. (Philadelphia: Westminster Press, 1954), 49–51. I am thankful to George H. Guthrie for pointing out this text to me in his *Hebrews*, NIV Application Commentary (Grand Rapids: Zondervan, 1998), loc. 8861–65, Kindle.

4. Gordon Wenham, *Genesis 1–15*, Word Biblical Commentary (Dallas: Word, 1987), 21.

5. Cited in David Shepherd, *Seeking Sabbath: A Personal Journey* (Oxford: Bible Reading Fellowship, 2007), 32.

6. Max De Pree, *Leadership Is an Art* (New York: Currency, 2004), 81–82.

7. Flannery O'Connor, *The Violent Bear It Away* (New York: Farrar, Straus & Giroux, 2007), 39.

8. William H. Willimon, *Pastor: The Theology and Practice of Ordained Ministry* (Nashville: Abingdon, 2002), 329.

9. As defined in Eugene Peterson, *A Long Obedience in the Same Direction: Discipleship in an Instant Society*, 2nd ed. (Downers Grove, IL: InterVarsity, 2000), 109. I appreciate the words of Walter Brueggemann, who connects God's Sabbath with his own confidence: "The celebration of a day of rest was, then, the announcement of trust in this God who is confident enough to rest. It was then and is now an assertion that life does not depend upon our feverish activity of self-security, but that there can be a pause in which life is given to us simply as a gift." Brueggemann, *Genesis: A Bible Commentary for Teaching and Preaching* (Louisville: Westminster John Knox, 2010), 35.

10. Matitiahu Tsevat, "The Basic Meaning of the Biblical Sabbath," in *The Meaning of the Book of Job and Other Biblical Studies: Essays on the Literature and Religion of the Hebrew Bible* (New York: Ktav, 1980), 48–49. Marva Dawn points this out in her book *Keeping the Sabbath Wholly: Ceasing, Resting, Embracing, Feasting* (Grand Rapids: Eerdmans, 1989), 57.

11. Mark Buchanan, *The Rest of God: Restoring Your Soul by Restoring Sabbath* (Nashville: Thomas Nelson, 2006), 87.

12. Karl Barth, *Church Dogmatics*, IV/1, ed. G. W. Bromiley and T. F. Torrance (Edinburgh: T&T Clark, 1956), 185.

13. Dorothy C. Bass, "The Practice of Keeping Sabbath: A Gift for Our Time," *Living Pulpit* 7, no. 2 (1998): 30.

14. Irving Greenberg, *The Jewish Way: Living the Holidays* (New York: Touchstone, 1993), 129.

15. Dawn, *Keeping the Sabbath Wholly*, 62.

16. N. T. Wright, *Simply Jesus: A New Vision of Who He Was, What He Did, and Why He Matters* (New York: HarperCollins, 2011), 137 (emphasis added).

17. "Tantalizing experience" is the language of Jon Levenson in his *Creation and the Persistence of Evil: The Jewish Drama of Divine Omnipotence* (San Francisco: Harper & Row, 1988), 123.

18. Abraham Joshua Heschel, *The Sabbath* (New York: Farrar, Straus & Giroux, 1951), 74.

19. John Andrews, *First Day: Discovering the Freedom of Sabbathcentric Living* (Kent, UK: River Publishing, 2011), 13.

20. Ephrem the Syrian, "Commentary on Genesis," in *The Patristic Understanding of Creation*, ed. William A. Dembski, Wayne J. Downs, and Justin B. A. Frederick (Riesel, TX: Erasmus Press, 2008), 239.

21. Larry Hurtado, *Mark*, New International Biblical Commentary (Peabody, MA: Hendrickson, 1995), 47.

22. G. van der Leeuw, *Religion in Essence and Manifestation: A Study in Phenomenology* (Gloucester, MA: Peter Smith, 1967), 389.

23. "It is the custom to delay the recital of the evening prayers at the close of the Sabbath, because the souls of sinners do not return to the punishments of Gehenna until after the congregations on earth have concluded the final prayers. . . . When Israel begins the Sabbath, the sinners may leave the fire and cool themselves in a stream of water. From this arises the custom that one whose father and mother have died may not drink water on the Sabbath between the afternoon and evening prayers, for they may at that very time be cooling themselves in the water." Chaim Grade, *My Mother's Sabbath Days: A Memoir* (Northvale, NJ: Aronson, 1997), 9–10.

24. Described in Samuel H. Dresner, *The Sabbath* (New York: Burning Bush, 1987), 23.

25. Judith Shulevitz, *Sabbath World: Glimpses of a Different Order of Time* (New York: Random House, 2011), 10–12.

26. Martin E. P. Seligman, *Authentic Happiness: Using the New Positive Psychology to Realize Your Potential for Lasting Fulfillment* (New York: Free Press, 2004), 117.

27. John Climacus, *The Ladder of Divine Ascent* (New York: Paulist Press, 1982), 86.

Chapter 12: Sabbath and Discipleship

1. Flannery O'Connor, *Mystery and Manners: Occasional Prose*, ed. Sally and Robert Fitzgerald (New York: Farrar, Straus & Giroux, 1969), 132.

2. Quoted in Erin S. Lane, *Lessons in Belonging from a Church-Going Commitment Phobe* (Downers Grove, IL: InterVarsity, 2015), 43.

3. William A. Dembski, Wayne J. Downs, and Justin B. A. Frederick, eds., *The Patristic Understanding of Creation* (Diesel, TX: Erasmus Press, 2008), 148–49.

4. See Samuel H. Dresner, *The Sabbath* (New York: Burning Bush, 1987), 43.

5. Flavius Josephus, *Against Apion* 2.18, trans. William Whiston, available at http://penelope.uchicago.edu/josephus/apion-2.html.

6. This word is from Arthur Waskow, cited by Gabe Huck in *Keeping Sunday Holy*, a cassette of the *National Catholic Reporter*, Kansas City, MO. Quoted in Tilden Edwards, *Sabbath Time* (Nashville: Upper Room Books, 1992), 101.

7. Abraham Joshua Heschel, *The Sabbath* (New York: Farrar, Straus & Giroux, 1951), 24.

8. Henri Nouwen, *Spiritual Direction* (San Francisco: HarperSanFrancisco, 2006), 18.

9. Edwards, *Sabbath Time*, 64.

10. William Temple, *Readings in St. John's Gospel: First and Second Series* (New York: Morehouse Barlow, 1986), 67.

11. Thomas à Kempis, *The Imitation of Christ*, ed. Susan L. Rattiner, trans. Aloysius Croft and Harold Bolton (New York: Dover, 2003), 5.

12. Richard Wurmbrand, *Sermons in Solitary Confinement* (Basingstoke, UK: Marshall Morgan & Scott, 1984), 121.

13. Arthur Wallis, *God's Chosen Fast: A Spiritual and Practical Guide to Fasting* (Fort Washington, PA: Christian Literature Crusade, 1975), 8.

14. Judith Shulevitz, *Sabbath World: Glimpses of a Different Order of Time* (New York: Random House, 2011), 201.

15. These are discussed and described at length in Craig Harline, *Sunday: A History of the First Day from Babylonia to the Super Bowl* (New Haven: Yale University Press, 2011), 87–88.

16. Shulevitz, *Sabbath World*, 8.

17. One should read Samuele Bacchiocchi, *From Sabbath to Sunday: A Historical Investigation of the Rise of Sunday Observance in Early Christianity* (Berrien Springs, MI: Biblical Perspectives, 1999). Also see the exhaustive and extremely helpful book edited by D. A. Carson, *From Sabbath to the Lord's Day: A Biblical, Historical, and Theological Investigation* (Eugene, OR: Wipf & Stock, 1999).

18. Willard M. Swartley, *Slavery, Sabbath, War and Women: Case Issues in Biblical Interpretation* (Harrisonburg, VA: Herald Press, 1983), chap. 2.

19. I appreciate the words of Timothy Keller, who writes that Jesus "affirms, even celebrates, the original principle of the Sabbath—the need for rest. Yet he squashes the legalism around its observance. He dismantles the whole religious paradigm." Keller, *Jesus the King: Understanding the Life and Death of the Son of God* (New York: Penguin, 2016), 44.

20. Quoted in Dorothy C. Bass, "Keeping Sabbath," in *Practicing Our Faith: A Way of Life for a Searching People*, ed. Dorothy C. Bass, 2nd ed. (San Francisco: John Wiley & Sons, 2010), 83.

21. Dorothy Sayers, *The Whimsical Christian: 18 Essays* (New York: Collier Books, 1978), 151–56.

22. Mark Buchanan, *The Holy Wild: Trusting in the Character of God* (Sisters, OR: Multnomah, 2003), 219.

23. Marva J. Dawn, *Keeping the Sabbath Wholly: Ceasing, Resting, Embracing, Feasting* (Grand Rapids: Eerdmans, 1989), 7.

24. See, e.g., Augustine's *Sermon* 362. He even named one of the chapters in *The City of God* "The Eternal Felicity of the City of God in Its Perpetual Sabbath."

25. Ignatius of Antioch, *St. Ignatius of Antioch: The Epistles* (Pantianos Classics, 2016), 34.

26. Dietrich Bonhoeffer, *Conspiracy and Imprisonment: 1940–1945*, ed. Mark S. Brocker, trans. Lisa E. Dahill, vol. 16 of *Dietrich Bonhoeffer Works* (Minneapolis: Augsburg Fortress, 2004), 644. I am indebted to my friend Dr. Chris Green for pointing out this reference to me.

27. Edwards, *Sabbath Time*, 38.

28. Shulevitz, *Sabbath World*, xxviii.

29. According to Henning Graf Reventlow, the early Christians did not regard Sunday as the Sabbath. They regarded the Sabbath as something that gentile Christians were not required to observe, and while they observed the first day of the week to commemorate Jesus's resurrection, they did not associate the first day of the week with the Sabbath commandment in the Decalogue. The first ruler to do that was Constantine in the fourth century, who used the Sabbath command to declare Sunday as a day of rest (which later was extended to slaves), and the day was designated for Christian worship services. According to Reventlow, Germanic kings followed this practice as well. Reventlow, "The Ten Commandments in Luther's Catechism," in *The Decalogue in Jewish and Christian Tradition*, ed. Henning Graf Reventlow and Yair Hoffman (New York: T&T Clark, 2011), 142–43.

30. Jürgen Moltmann, *God in Creation: A New Theology of Creation and the Spirit of God* (Minneapolis: Fortress, 1993), 294.

31. Norman Wirzba, *Living the Sabbath: Discovering the Rhythms of Rest and Delight* (Grand Rapids: Brazos, 2006).

32. Gordon MacDonald, *Ordering Your Private World* (Nashville: Thomas Nelson, 2003), 204.

33. Brian Doyle, "Give It a Rest," *U.S. Catholic*, September 2001, 27, https://www.questia.com/magazine/1G1-77660024/give-it-a-rest.

Index

achievement, 28
activism, 148
Adam and Eve, 7–8, 12, 25, 28–30
adrenaline, 53, 186
airplane mode, 99–100
Aldrin, Buzz, 139
Allen, Diogenes, 212n37
Allen, Roland, 73
Allender, Dan, 209n49
Ambrose, 166
amnesia, 8. *See also* Sabbath: forgetfulness
Amos, 94–95
ancient Near Eastern creation myths, 9
anhedonia, 53
animals
  in the Bible, 149–52
  covenant with, 150
  diversity of, 152
  flourishing of, 146
  joy of, 153–54
  and the Sabbath, 148, 152–57
annuals (plants), 30–31
anticipatory brain, 54
Antiochus Epiphanes, 167
anxiety, 72, 162
"anxious seat," 162
Armstrong, Neil, 139
artificial light, 218n43
asceticism, 209n58
Asch, Sholem, 52
Augustine, 15, 141, 197, 199–200

baby boomers, 34
Badcock, Gary, 48
Bahnson, Fred, 125–26
Bailey, Karl, 214n37
Bailey, Kenneth, 91
Barth, Karl, 7, 19, 181, 206n17
Basil of Caesarea, 10
Bass, Diana Butler, 7
Bass, Dorothy, 184
"bastard Sabbaths," 19
Bauman, Zygmunt, 68
Baylis, Al, 9
"beauty exhaustion," 141
Bell, Mary, 28
Berry, Wendell, xiii, 96, 128, 142
Black Friday, 93, 94–95
blessing, 103–4
Blocher, Henri, 10, 36
Blomberg, Craig, 222n13
blue laws, 92
body, and the Sabbath, 55–57
Boehme, Jacob, 190
Bonaventure, 142
Bonhoeffer, Dietrich, 11, 69, 152, 195, 200
boredom, 79–80
Borman, Frank, 139–40
"borrowed compassion," 129
Bouma-Prediger, Steven, 137
boundaries, of the Sabbath, 74–77
Bradford, John, 13
Brooks, Paul, 138

Brueggemann, Walter, 87, 111, 216n7, 225n9
Brunner, Dan, 175–76
Buchanan, Mark, 36, 180, 199
burdens, rest from, 58–60
burnout, 31–34
busyness, 34, 45, 141

candle-lighting on the Sabbath, 6, 206n11,
    216n4
care and compassion toward others, 40–41
celebration, 20–21
Celsus, 191
chickens, 155–57
Cho, David Yonggi, 73
chronic health conditions, 50
chronos, 163–64, 185
church
    assimilated to the world, 163
    as contrast society, 163–65
    as safe place to resist the world, 72
church growth, built on no rest, 71
circumcision, 164
Climacus, John, 187
clocks, 163–64, 218n43
"Coca-Cola philosophy," 18
cockfighting, 155
Columbus, Christopher, 103
community
    margin in, 171
    and Sabbath, 67–70, 72
compulsivity, 59
Constantine, 201
consumerism, 43, 83, 93–94, 168, 209n55
contemplation, 148
contentment, 195–96
Council of Rouen (650 CE), 78
covenant, with animals, 150. *See also* animals
cows, 145
Cox, Harvey, 20, 139
creatio continua, 140
creation
    beauty of, 140–43
    flourishing of, 132–33
    goodness of, 12–13
    interconnectedness of, 124, 131
creation care, 121, 128–29, 135–38
creation narrative, 9, 12, 16, 132
critters. *See* animals
Crouch, Andy, 189

crown of thorns, 31
curse (of the fall), 29–31, 37, 90

Daniel, 166
Davidman, Joy, 176–77
Dawn, Marva, xi, 21, 56, 184, 199, 213n16,
    217n13
Day, Dorothy, 89
day of preparation, 83–87
days off, 17–19
deists, 140
demilitarized zone (between North and
    South Korea), 133
demonstration plots, 165, 223n7
devil, does not Sabbath, 105, 185–86
Dickens, Charles, 80
distress, 58
doing nothing, 212n29
downward mobility, 91
Doyle, Brian, 202
Dresner, Samuel, 109, 169

earth, rhythms of productivity and rest, 122
ecology, 123, 125–26, 220n6
economic justice, 87–95
economy, as Sabbathcentric, 84
ecopsychology, 115
Eden, as state of shalom, 48
Eden Reforestation Project, 125, 129
Edwards, Dennis, 151
Edwards, Tilden, 40, 92, 93, 194, 201
Einstein, Albert, 127
Ellis, Robert, 49
Ellul, Jacques, 12, 33
emergencies, on the Sabbath, 40–41
emotional Sabbath, 58–60
England, Martin and Mabel, 223n7
environmental movement, 134
escapism, 58–60
estradiol, 145–46
eternal Sabbath, 182–85
ethical communities, 68–70
eugenics, 4
eustress, 58
evangelism, 147–48
exhaustion, 50, 106–7
exile and rest, 132
exodus, the, 95
extroverts, 77

false freedoms, 97
fame, 195
Farmer, H. H., 11
fear, 30, 181
finitude, 33
Finney, Charles, 162, 223n2
Fitch, Steve, 125
Fleming, Daniel, 30
flipping houses, 137–38, 221n11 (chap. 8)
FOMO (fear of missing out), 43–44
Four Pests Campaign (China), 124, 126
fourth commandment, 34, 146, 153,
    206nn13–14
France, and the ten-day week, 10–11
Frankl, Victor, 4
freedom
    through boundaries, 76
    false freedoms, 97
    versus license, 114
Freud, Sigmund, 186
fundamentalism, 43

Gager, John, 69
gentiles, in the Old Testament, 112
God
    blessing to whole world, 104
    care for creation, 128, 150–52
    compassion of, 129
    creates intentionally, 123
    as Lord of time, 10
    love of, 190–91
    rest of, 7, 9–10, 45, 126
    sovereignty of, 180
    sustains creation, 140–41
Goldingay, John, 114
good Samaritan, parable of, 40–41
gospel, the, 147, 161, 171
Graham, Billy, 206n14
Grand Canyon (film), 125
gratitude, 48, 195
Greenberg, Irving, 184
Gregory of Nyssa, 51–52
Gunton, Colin, 10, 19

Haam, Achad, 207n34
Hadrian, 167
Haeckel, Ernst, 220n6
Hagel, Chuck, 106
Hall, Douglas John, 129

Harris, David, 93
Hart, Archibald, 53
Hauerwas, Stanley, 156, 174
Hawthorne, Nathaniel, 22
health, and Sabbath, 123
heaven, as eternal Sabbath, 182–85
hedonism, 209n58
hell, 185–86
Henderson, Linda, 154
Heschel, Abraham, 10, 12, 28, 36, 37, 54,
    85, 184
hesed, 111
hibernation, 122, 153
Hilary of Poitiers, 179
hoarding, 84
Holmes, Oliver Wendell, 103
Holocaust, 4, 112
holy days, 10, 12
holy indifference, 58–59
homelessness, 137
Horsfall, Tony, 46, 224n18
hospitality, 89
hostility toward the Sabbath, x, 71, 112
house flipping, 137–38, 221n11 (chap. 8)
household pets, 154. *See also* animals
Hughes, Gerard, 93
humanity
    enslaved to work, 30
    flourishing of, 84, 88, 114, 123
    limits and boundaries of, 74
    made to rest, 6–7
    parasitic relationship with land, 139
    as part of creation, 127
humility, 14, 150
Hummel, Charles, 83
hurrying, 100
"hurry sickness," 98
husbandry, 133, 137
hyperactivity, 98–100

Ignatius, 200
image of God, 15
imitating God, 180
individualism, 20–21, 66–67
Industrial Revolution, 127
intentional detachment, 187
intentional Sabbath community, 79, 89
intimacy with God, 194
introverts, 77

Irenaeus, 161
Irwin, James, 139–40
Israel
    amnesia of, 216n7
    slavery in Egypt, 35–36, 87–88, 95, 104

Jacobson, David, 67
James I (king of England), 178
jealousy, and rest, 196
Jerusalem Sabbath, 65–66
Jesus Christ
    on "being connected," 99
    death and resurrection of, 47
    and debates about Sabbath-keeping, 38
    healing on the Sabbath, 50–51, 67, 77, 199
    humanness of, 189, 190, 191
    as Lord of the harvest, 35, 195
    as Lord of the Sabbath, 16, 35, 186, 195,
        201
    rhythms of sleep of, 180
    saying no, 45–46
    on work and rest, 39
Jewish Sabbaths, 57, 66–67, 92–93, 154, 167,
    192–93
Jordan, Clarence and Florence, 223n7
Josephus, 193
Joshua ben Hannah, 167
Josiah (king), 4
Jubilee, 107–8, 135
Jung, Carl, 45
justice, 147–48
Justin Martyr, x

kairos, 163–64, 185
kavod habriyot, 113
Kazantzakis, Nikos, 47
Keller, Timothy, 226n19
Koufax, Sandy, 178

land Sabbaths, 131–38
Lane, Eric, 170
Lao-tzu, 135
Lasch, Christopher, 20
laziness, 35, 45
legalism on the Sabbath, 40, 56, 198–200,
    202, 226n19
L'Engle, Madeleine, xii
Lerman, Juan-Carlos, 56
Leviathan, 153

Levinas, Emmanuel, 70
Lewis, C. S., 8, 54, 155
Liddell, Eric, 178
light bulbs, 193
listening, 162
livestock, 123, 146
Logister, Wiel, 172
Lohfink, Gerhard, 164
Lombard, Peter, 29
Longbons, Jarrod, 94
lopsided Christianity, 148, 156
Lord's Day, 174, 201
love
    for enemies, 168
    for God, 109–11
    for neighbor, 109–11
Luther, Martin, 13, 38, 198

Maccabean revolt, 167
MacDonald, Gordon, 202, 212n33
Mains, Karen Burton, 84
Mandela, Nelson, 113
mangoes, 13
manna, 84–85
Mao (Chinese ruler), 124, 126
margin, in life of community, 171
marginalized, the, 103–16
marital health, and the Sabbath, 78–81
marriage, 16, 133
May, Gerald, 20
M'Cheyne, Robert Murray, 173
mechanical clock, 163
melachah (categories of work), 38–40
menukhah, 39
Merton, Thomas, 127
millennials, 34, 55, 98
Miller, Donald, 195
Miller, G. Tyler, 125
mind, and the Sabbath, 52–55
Mishnah, 49
mobility, 137
Moltmann, Jürgen, 18, 139, 201, 212n31
Montgomery, David, 31
Moo, Douglas, 27
Moses complex, 181
Mouw, Richard, 25–27, 210n2
Muir, John, 124
muksteh, 186
Muller, Wayne, 98

multitasking, 98, 141
Murray, John, 39–40
Muslims, 57
Muthiah, Rob, 79
Mutombo, Dikembe, 169
mutuality, of Adam and Eve, 29

Nature-Deficit Disorder, 100
near occasion of sin, 53
necessary works of the Sabbath, 40
Nehemiah, 167–68
Netflix, 187, 193
Newbigin, Lesslie, 17, 59
new creation, 27
new Jerusalem, 26–27
Niebuhr, Reinhold, 211n25
Noah, 150, 178
Nouwen, Henri, 48, 194, 195

obedience, 44
obscurity, 194
observing the Sabbath, 6
O'Connor, Flannery, xi, 32, 179, 190
O'Donahue, John, 142
one-in-seven principle, 201
Origen, 191
Ortberg, John, 100

Padgett, Alan, 207n24
Palen, Ernest R., 65
parable of the good Samaritan, 40–41
parable of the rich man and Lazarus, 90
Passover celebration, 170–71
Paul, the apostle
   on creation being liberated from bondage,
      129
   on imitating his faith, 197
   responsible disengagement of, 73
   on the Sabbath, 115, 193
Paul III (pope), 103
peace. See shalom
peg communities, 68–69
people of peace, 163
perennials (plants), 30–31
PETA (People for the Ethical Treatment of
   Animals), 149
Peterson, Eugene, 19, 32, 34, 81, 195, 211n22
Pharisees and Sadducees, 8, 38
Philo, 90

physical Sabbath, 55–57
Plantinga, Cornelius, 48, 125
play, on Sabbath, 20, 153–54
pleasure, 53, 209n58
Pogue, William, 11
Postman, Neil, 163
pragmatism, 19–20
preparation, 85–87
pride, 196
progress, 96, 127
Puritans, 78, 92, 110
Putnam, Robert, 67

qadosh, 12, 35, 174, 207n33

Rah, Soong-Chan, 20–21
Ramadan, 169
Ratzinger, Joseph, 96
recapitulation, 213n16
recycling, 129
Reiff, Philip, 21
Reimchen, Thomas, 151
relational strife and unrest, 107
remembering, 6
renewal of all things, 26
repetition, 176
rest
   for introverts and extroverts, 77
   need for, 15–16
   and work, 35–41, 52
restlessness, 48, 126, 196
Reventlow, Henning Graf, 227n29
rich man and Lazarus, parable of, 90
Richter, Sandra, 30
riparian buffer, 192
Root, Jerry, 155
Russell, Bertrand, 127

Sabbath
   and animals, 148, 152–57
   as any day of the week, 201
   "bastard Sabbaths," 19
   and the body, 55–57
   boundaries of, 74–77
   as bridge commandment, 110
   as buffer, 192
   candle-lighting, 6, 206n11, 216n4
   and children, 79–80
   as commandment, 33

and community, 67–70, 72
as complete reorientation of lives, 9
as counterrhythm to workdays, 57
as delight, 19
depression, 186
devil does not, 105, 185–86
as discipline that transforms us inside, 175–76
as ecological, 126, 139
as economic justice, 87–95
emergencies on, 40–41
emotional, 58–60
entering, 182–83
eternal Sabbath, 182–85
before the fall, 31
forgetfulness, 5–6, 71, 206n11
as gift, x, 36, 202
as goal of creation, 17
guest, 171
health and, 123
as holy, 12, 35, 207n34
as homecoming, 66
hostility toward, x, 71, 112
intentional Sabbath community, 79, 89
land Sabbaths, 131–38
and legalism, 40, 56, 198–200, 202, 226n19
marital health and, 78–81
mind and, 52–55
nap, 180
necessary works of, 40
as obedience, 115–16, 132
observing, 6
Paul on, 115, 193
play on, 20, 153–54
provides silence, 193
and relationships, 65–82
as renunciation, 194–97
and restoration, 16
rhythms, 33, 47, 113
as sanctification of time, 12
and sex, 78
single persons and, 81
spiritualizing, 199–200
as subversive, xi, 112
and technology, 95–100
as "temple in time," 207n34
as weird, 169–70
as witness to the world, 162–65

Sabbath-breaking, not sustainable in ministry, 72
Sabbath Economics Collaborative, 88–89
Sabbath-keeping, 12
    as communal, 72
    as earth-keeping, 128–30
    as Sabbath-giving, 89
    as trump card, 75–76
    as trusting God, 179–82
Sabbath manna, 84–85
"Sabbath neurosis" (Freud), 186
Sacks, Jonathan, 126
Salatin, Joel, 50
Salz, Madalyn, 214n31
Sanford, Mark, 210n16
Satan. See devil, does not Sabbath
Sayers, Dorothy, 20, 199
saying no, 46, 76
Schaper, Donna, 21
Schor, Juliet, 209n55
sedentary living, 55–56
selah, 35
selfless, 32
Seneca, 167
seven-day rhythm, 11
Seventh-Day Adventists, 51, 56–57, 198
Shadrach, Meshach, and Abednego, 166
shalom, 48–52
shame, 113, 134
Shepherd, David, 206n11, 224n9
ships of Tarshish, 26–27
shomer shabbos ("protectors" of the Sabbath), 76
Shulevitz, Judith, 6, 93
Sider, Ronald, 147–48
silence, 54, 55, 193–94
Silesius, Angelus, 152
simplicity, 86
sin, near occasion of, 53
single persons, and the Sabbath, 81
slavery, 4
"slavery of activity," 96
sleep, 15, 180, 208n39
Sleeth, Matthew, 122
Sleeth, Nancy, 78, 86
sloth, 45
smartphones, 96, 98
social gospel, 147

social justice, 217n13
social media, 96
solitude, 193–94
Solzhenitsyn, Aleksandr, 97
"sovereignty of the body," 123
spiritualizing the Sabbath, 199–200
spiritual warfare, 185–87
spotted owl controversy, 136
Steffen, Tom, 73
Stiegerwald, Dan, 134
storage facilities, 88
Stott, John, 210n14
stress, 58
Stucky, Nathan, 37
Sunday, as "little Easter," 201
Sunday best, 174–75
Suurmond, Jean-Jacques, 19, 209n50
Swartley, Willard, 198
Swenson, Richard, 74, 98, 107

Taylor, Barbara Brown, 34, 47
technology, and the Sabbath, 95–100
temple, Sabbath as, 207n34
Temple, William, 194–95
temptations, 53
ten Boom, Corrie, 44
Ten Commandments, 11, 109–10
"theology of ideal and condescension"
    (Goldingay), 114
therapeutic individualism, 20–21
Thomas à Kempis, 196
tikkun olam, 49
time, 163–64, 185
  and eternity, 10
  as holy, 207n33
  oriented around Sabbath, 130
  worshiping of, 70
Tolkien, J. R. R., 60
trust, 179–82
Tsevat, Matitiahu, 180
turtle population, 149
24/7 world, 5, 33, 85, 93, 106

urban migration, 135–36

vacations, 17–19
vocation, 28, 30
Volf, Miroslav, 27, 91
vulnerability, 190

Wallis, Arthur, 196
Walsh, Brian, 137
Waltke, Bruce, 213n9
Webster, John, 55
Weil, Simone, 128
Weisman, Alan, 133
Wells, Samuel, 174
Wenham, Gordon, 177
Wilberforce, William, 60, 155
Wilkes, A. Paget, 161–62
Willard, Dallas, 4
Williams, Thomas, 15
Willimon, Will, 179
Wirzba, Norman, 41, 125–26, 139, 153, 202,
    211n28, 218n41, 219n13
Wolterstorff, Nicholas, 148
women, in creation, 9
Woodley, Randy, 49
Woolman, John, 89
work, 25–28
  as a drug, 28
  in new Jerusalem, 27
  and rest, 35–41, 52
  as self-fulfillment, 30
  as toilsome after entrance of sin, 29
workaholism, 34, 36, 132
worship, 173–87
Wright, N. T., 184
Wurmbrand, Richard, 196
Wytsma, Ken, 218n33

yes-people, 44–46
Yordy, Laura Ruth, 115
youth pastors, and the Sabbath, 72

Zinn, Howard, 4